LATIN AMERICAN
IMMIGRATION ETHICS

LATIN AMERICAN IMMIGRATION ETHICS

Edited by
Amy Reed-Sandoval and
Luis Rubén Díaz Cepeda

THE UNIVERSITY OF
ARIZONA PRESS

TUCSON

The University of Arizona Press
www.uapress.arizona.edu

We respectfully acknowledge the University of Arizona is on the land and territories of Indigenous peoples. Today, Arizona is home to twenty-two federally recognized tribes, with Tucson being home to the O'odham and the Yaqui. Committed to diversity and inclusion, the University strives to build sustainable relationships with sovereign Native Nations and Indigenous communities through education offerings, partnerships, and community service.

ISBN-13: 978-0-8165-4273-4 (hardcover)
ISBN-13: 978-0-8165-4272-7 (paperback)

Cover design by Carrie House, HOUSEdesign LLC
Typeset by Sara Thaxton in 10/14 Warnock Pro (text), Termina, and Trade Gothic Next (display)

Publication of this book is made possible in part by support from the Dean's Office of the College of Liberal Arts at the University of Nevada, Las Vegas, and by the proceeds of a permanent endowment created with the assistance of a Challenge Grant from the National Endowment for the Humanities, a federal agency.

Library of Congress Cataloging-in-Publication Data
Names: Reed-Sandoval, Amy, editor. | Díaz Cepeda, Luis Rubén, 1976– editor.
Title: Latin American immigration ethics / edited by Amy Reed-Sandoval and Luis Rubén Díaz
   Cepeda.
Description: Tucson : University of Arizona Press, 2021. | Includes bibliographical references and
   index.
Identifiers: LCCN 2021014314 | ISBN 9780816542734 (hardcover) | ISBN 9780816542727
   (paperback)
Subjects: LCSH: Emigration and immigration—Philosophy. | Philosophy, Latin American.
Classification: LCC JV6035 .L37 2021 | DDC 170.98—dc23
LC record available at https://lccn.loc.gov/2021014314

Printed in the United States of America
♾ This paper meets the requirements of ANSI/NISO Z39.48-1992 (Permanence of Paper).

CONTENTS

LATIN AMERICAN
IMMIGRATION ETHICS

Introduction

Why "Latin American Immigration Ethics"?

AMY REED-SANDOVAL AND
LUIS RUBÉN DÍAZ CEPEDA

Following an extended period of near silence on the subject, many social and political philosophers are now treating immigration as a central theme of their discipline. In fact, there is now sufficient philosophical literature on immigration to enable us to detect clear trajectories in terms of its broad theorization. What began as a highly abstract debate over whether states do, in fact, have a prima facie right to exclude prospective migrants under at least some conditions evolved into scholarship on increasingly "applied" and "practical" questions such as refugee rights and justifications for family reunification schemes in immigrant admissions programs.[1] Presently, and as part of this notable progression, immigration philosophy is in the midst of an identity "turn" in which philosophers—particularly those working within the traditions of feminist philosophy, Latinx philosophy, and the critical philosophy of race—theorize particular borders and barriers and particular migrant bodies that are visibly sexed/gendered and racialized.[2] This stands in contrast to the more abstract borders and migrants featured in the original open borders debate. Such identity-based approaches tend to operate in the realm of "nonideal theory," considering states as they are—namely, as entities that are often noncompliant with the requirements of justice—and providing conceptual analysis and solutions on that basis.

This recent proliferation of nonideal immigration philosophy is certainly welcome. However, it remains limited in at least three important ways. First, produced as it is in the United States and Europe, it has almost exclusively considered the moral implications of migrations from the (comparatively poorer) Global South to the (comparatively richer) Global North. While this emphasis is, in many respects, highly warranted and appropriate, it nevertheless neglects crucial ethical questions arising in South-South migrations. Second, and related, this philosophical literature is often Eurocentric, employing disproportionately the philosophical frameworks of European thinkers and their descendants in attempts to understand the nature of immigration justice. While European and Anglo-American philosophical frameworks have been employed to make important contributions to immigration ethics, the *overall* Eurocentrism of this literature limits the scope of the philosophical conversations at hand. It also reinforces, albeit unintentionally, sociopolitical hierarchies that position the Global North above the Global South. Third, given that this identity turn in immigration philosophy is relatively recent—at least in the context of philosophical debates about global justice—a number of ethical challenges connected to race, gender, and migration remain unexplored in academic philosophy. This is particularly noteworthy in terms of ethical challenges stemming from migrant pregnancies and migrant children, which are among the most disputed immigration issues in the Americas today.

Latin American Immigration Ethics aims to respond to these three limitations and, in so doing, build upon previous efforts to develop nonideal approaches to immigration justice. This volume brings together new and original works of prominent Latin American, Latinx, and feminist immigration philosophers who are writing about, and often within, the Latin American context. Without eschewing relevant conceptual resources derived from European and Anglo-American philosophies, the chapters of this book also emphasize Latin American and Latinx philosophies, decolonial and feminist theories, and Indigenous philosophies of Latin America in the pursuit of a distinctive immigration ethics. All chapters focus on particular moral challenges of immigration that either arise within Latin America itself or emerge when Latin Americans and Latina/o/xs migrate to and reside within the United States. Additionally, several of the chapters focus on South-South migration, while the pieces on the specifically Latina/o/x experiences in the United States address the aforementioned lacuna of philosophical writing on migration, maternity, and childhood.

I. General Overview of the Book

The book is divided into three sections. Section 1, "Methodological Foundations," makes the case for a Latin American and decolonial approach to immigration ethics and justice and offers concrete examples of what such philosophical work can look like. It also provides an overview of immigration philosophy in the Anglo-American tradition, which is contrasted to the approaches developed and articulated in this volume.

In the ensuing sections, contributors both "unearth" and develop a distinctive Latin American immigration ethics by consulting theoretical frameworks developed by philosophers in the Global South and/or frameworks worked out by those who focus on ethical challenges associated with immigration in, to, and from Latin America. We organize these sections regionally and geographically, starting with South America, in order to "decenter" from the philosophical gaze migrations to the Global North from the Global South (particularly from Latin America to the United States—though, as you will see, we also focus on such migration "streams" toward the end of the volume).

Section 2, "South America," focuses on moral challenges of immigration that arise in Bolivia, Brazil, Chile, Colombia, Paraguay, Peru, and Venezuela, such as internal and cross-border migrations of Indigenous peoples in the Amazon, tensions arising in overlapping immigration and emigration practices in Colombia and Venezuela, the relationship between racist attitudes toward non-European migrants and bio-citizenship in Chile, the movements of landless (Sem Terra) people in Brazil, and Caribbean (particularly Haitian) migrations to Brazil.

Section 3, "Mexico and Central America," explores from a moral point of view some of the challenges that Central American and Mexican migrants experience while attempting to migrate to the United States, such as the much disputed "safe third country program" that forces Central American migrants to remain in Mexico while applying for asylum in the United States. This section also explores conceptual linkages between the walls and barriers that separate Mexico and the United States and those at the center of the Israeli-Palestinian conflict, as well as the wall the Moroccan kingdom built to annex the Saharawi territories and assimilate the occupied population. Finally, in "bottom up" philosophical fashion, this section explores the philosophical significance of popular songs of protest written by Mexican migrants, positioning such creative works on a par with the more celebrated literature and philosophy of so-called exiles.

Lastly, section 4, "Latin Americans and Latina/o/xs in the United States," addresses controversies over birthright citizenship in the United States, as well as the linguistic oppression endured by migrant children and others who must translate for parents or other relatives.

While these chapters share the common theme of expanding the scope of academic conversations about immigration justice, several chapters also argue for specifics policy proposals and solutions. These include protecting birthright citizenship in the United States, creating socioeconomic conditions that make it possible for Central Americans not to have to emigrate in the first place, eliminating the "safe third country" program in the United States and Mexico, demilitarizing the Mexico-U.S. border, and creating new group rights to free movement for Indigenous transmigrants of the Americas. In addition, as readers will see, contributors to this volume employ a wide range of theoretical frameworks in their analyses, including decolonial theory, Latin American liberation philosophy, Latin American and Latinx feminisms, Indigenous philosophies of Latin America, Jewish philosophy (and the ways in which Jewish ethics have been engaged in Latin American thought), Latin American philosophies of exile, Chicana/o/x and Latinx theory, and more. Readers unfamiliar with these systems of thought can learn about them through engaging the chapters contained herein.

We will provide a more detailed, chapter-by-chapter overview at the end of this introduction. Before doing so, let us clarify some of the terminology that will be employed throughout this book.

II. Style and Terminology

A. What Is "Latin American Philosophy"?

> The possibility of and need for a Latin American philosophy is a metaphilosophical question, one that puts the very forms of crystallization of philosophy in jeopardy not just in Latin America, but also in the Western world.
> —Eduardo Mendieta, *Latin American Philosophy: Currents, Issues, and Debates*

As many Latin American and Latinx philosophers have pointed out, the originality, authenticity, and very existence of Latin American philosophy is often disputed.[3] For instance, Peruvian philosophers José Carlos Mariátegui and Augusto Salazar Bondy separately expressed concern that the influence of European philosophy on Latin American philosophy served to turn Latin American philosophers into mere echo chambers of the former.[4] More recently, this concern was reiterated by Mexican philosopher Guillermo Hurtado, who argued against the constant "importation" to Latin America of the latest philosophical models, which so often places "many Latin American philosophers in a teacher/pupil relationship with respect to foreign philosophers."[5] Meanwhile, Carlos Pereda has argued that, within Latin American philosophy, it "is considered that the Headquarters of Thought are elsewhere."[6]

But the list of challenges to Latin American philosophy is even longer than these concerns. For instance, the Gallegos siblings have raised the "Form and Purpose" question, namely: "Is the purpose of philosophical writing different from the purpose of other kinds of writing, such as poetry and literature?"[7] Depending on how one responds to this challenge, a vast number of works composed in Latin America—such as Sor Juana Inés de la Cruz's beloved writings on gender, epistemology, and more, or José Martí's poetic work on the nature of democracy—may not "count" as philosophical. Susana Nuccetelli raises a connected question, asking, *Who counts as philosopher*? That is, do we only "count" people with recognized academic training in philosophy? Or, alternatively, should we include those who offer philosophical insights without any such formal training?

A third challenge comes in the form of the "universality question," regarding the scope of philosophy. If the goal of philosophy is to find universal truths, one might argue, then it makes no sense to talk about "philosophies," regional or otherwise. A final difficulty in defining Latin American philosophy pertains to timeframe. More specifically, one might ask whether pre-Columbian or "preconquest" thinking should be counted as part of the "Latin American" and "Latino" traditions. Relatedly, one might argue that ancient texts are insufficiently "philosophical" given their frequent employment of religious explanations of the world.

A large body of philosophical work has addressed, in varying ways, the challenges of defining Latin American philosophy, and it is beyond the scope of this introduction (and this volume) to engage these issues in their entirety. Instead, in what remains of this section, we briefly defend a conception of Latin American philosophy that, in our view, responds to all the challenges delineated previously.

First, following Jorge Gracia and Manuel Vargas's overview of "Latin American Philosophy" for the *Stanford Encyclopedia of Philosophy (SEP)*, we understand Latin American philosophy to be "philosophy produced in Latin America or philosophy produced by persons of Latin American ancestry who reside outside of Latin America."[8] However, our proposed conception of Latin American philosophy allows for those who are not of Latin American ancestry and/or writing within Latin America to produce Latin American philosophy, provided that their work features substantive engagement with the work of both Latin American thinkers and issues of concern to the Latin American and Latinx communities.

In this vein, we follow the precedent set by Manual Vargas, who in his *SEP* entry "Latinx Philosophy" defines the latter as "philosophical work substantively concerned with Latinxs, including the moral, social, epistemic, and linguistic significance of Latinxs and their experiences."[9] Our definition also echoes that of Susan Nuccetelli, who argues that Latin American philosophy involves both original arguments and topics that are "at least in part determined by the relation its proponents bear to cultural, social, or historical factors in Latin America."[10] However, our classification is also more expansive than Nuccetelli's, as it allows work produced by Latin Americans that may not fall neatly under the rubric of "applied philosophy" to "count" as Latin American philosophy.

This expansive definition responds to the challenges discussed above. First, our definition does not exclude poetry, song lyrics, and ethnographic interviews from the scope of Latin American philosophy (indeed, various chapters in this volume engage such "nontraditional works"; see, for instance, the contributions by Rabinovich, Pereda, and Reed-Sandoval). Second, we submit that practitioners of Latin American philosophy need not have formal training in Latin American philosophy, or academic philosophy more broadly understood. Third, our definition does not require Latin American philosophy (or philosophy itself) to be framed in terms of a search for universal truths. In fact, we recognize that a great deal of Latin American philosophy is focused on the Latin American sociopolitical context, and that this work may or may not feature insights and arguments of universal relevance. Finally, because we do not require practitioners of Latin American philosophy to be of Latin American descent, our definition also allows for pre-Columbian/preconquest philosophies of the Americas to be included in this diverse canon.

In sum, we define Latin American philosophy as including both philosophy produced by Latin Americans and their descendants and/or philosophy that features substantive engagement with issues of concern to the Latin American and Latinx communities. Note, once again, that Latin American philosophy need not resemble traditional academic philosophy in order to "count" for our purposes: poetry, music, op-eds, and other writings are part of this tradition. Indeed, readers will find that contributions to this volume feature a diversity of writing styles characteristic of a wide variety of intellectual and creative influences on the Latin American philosophical tradition. The inclusiveness of our definition, then, allows us to answer various challenges that inevitably come up in adequately defining Latin American philosophy — while also, we hope, encouraging a creative proliferation of such work.

B. *Latinos, Latinxs, Latin@s,* or *Latines?*

A similarly fraught terminological question is that of how to refer to people of Latin American descent who live outside of Latin America, particularly in the United States. Previously, the term "Latino" was used to refer to this group, following the conventions of Spanish grammar. However, the widespread usage of this designation has been criticized (though not without controversy) on the grounds that it uses the term for men of Latin American descent (i.e., Latinos) and applies it to all Latin Americans. Once again, this is a difficulty that stems from Spanish grammar itself — not necessarily from the sexist intentions of any given speaker. For a time, the term "Latin@" was employed to promote gender inclusivity, following a tendency in Mexico and other regions to use the "@" instead of the "o" in certain discursive contexts. More recently, the explicitly nonbinary term "Latinx" has become popular in the United States, though it is not widely used in Latin America, at least in part because it is difficult for many non-native English speakers to pronounce. Currently, an "es" is being used to promote gender inclusivity in certain parts of America — that is, turning words like "Latinos" into "*Latines*." This may be easier for non-native English speakers to pronounce, but the tendency is not yet well-known in places like the United States.

We do not, in this book, adopt any particular term for general use. Rather, we allow contributors to employ the terminology with which they are most comfortable. We acknowledge that terms of social identity, and language itself, are constantly being remapped and renegotiated by communities of speakers. And we believe that it is particularly important to allow for a plurality of terms, particularly given that this volume features the works of many writers who are from, and who are writing from within, *both* Latin America and the United States.

III. Chapter Overview

Section 1: Methodological Foundations

Chapter 1: Latin American Immigration Ethics: A Roadmap

In this chapter, Amy Reed-Sandoval and Luis Rubén Díaz Cepeda explore Latin American migration history and the ways in which Latin American philosophers have engaged the latter to sketch the contours of a distinctive Latin American immigration ethics. More specifically, they focus on Latin American philosophies of exile, Latinx and Latina feminist philosophies of migration, and Enrique Dussel's argument for *more* open borders under a conception of transmodernism in an increasingly integrated Latin America. By way of bottom-up philosophical analysis, they argue that Latin American immigration ethics often has two key characteristics: (1) it engages distinctive Latin American migration histories; and (2) it uses Latin American philosophies to theorize such history.

Chapter 2: Decolonizing Immigration Justice

In this chapter, José Jorge Mendoza argues that radical approaches to immigration justice need to deal more directly with the normative challenges of colonialism, in part through engaging Latin American decolonial theory. In recent years, radical philosophers have tried to carve out a space for themselves within the debates about immigration justice. So far, they have been successful in exposing the shortcomings in liberal approaches to immigration justice, showing that they fail to get beyond traditional and overly idealized conceptions of civic belonging (e.g., citizenship) and political community (e.g., nation-states). In agreement with the radical philosophers, Mendoza argues that liberals have failed to seriously address (and often ignore) important issues, such as the construction of "illegal" and "anchor baby" subjectivities and the violence and disciplinary nature of immigration enforcement mechanisms. In short, radical philosophers have done an excellent job, even if only in the academy, of articulating the need for a different approach to immigration justice. The problem, however, is that radical approaches have so far been too Eurocentric in their methodology. They rely exclusively on the work of European political theorists, while at the same time ignoring important works by non-European philosophers. Mendoza argues that this omission only helps perpetuate the kind of social domination that a radical approach should seek to undermine.

Chapter 3: Oaxacan Transborder Communities and
the Political Philosophy of Immigration
In this chapter, Amy Reed-Sandoval aims to illustrate a Latin American/decolonial approach to immigration ethics by engaging the Zapotec Indigenous philosophical concepts of *tequio, Guelaguetza,* and *cooperación* to theorize Zapotec/Oaxacan Indigenous transmigration in Mexico and the United States. First, she explains what these concepts mean, and how they have been put into practice and reshaped by Indigenous Oaxacans who engage in transmigration to and from the United States, thereby forming "transborder communities." Second, she argues that Zapotec transmigration—in which *tequio, Guelaguetza,* and *cooperación* play a central role—pose challenges to the philosopher Will Kymlicka's widely known views on collective rights for this phenomenon. In particular, she argues that it calls into question his categorical distinction between "national minorities" and "voluntary migrants." She argues that Oaxacan Indigenous transmigrants are *both* national minorities and voluntary migrants, and that they are therefore owed a freedom of movement right that will enable them to preserve their societal cultures in their transborder communities of Oaxaca, Mexico, and the United States.

Section 2: South America

Chapter 4: Decolonial Liberation and Migration Ethics in the Brazilian Context
This chapter, by Amos Nascimento and Margaret Griesse, uses the framework of Latin American liberation ethics and decoloniality theories to reveal the underlying ideologies guiding different phases of immigration in Brazil and to analyze the philosophical relevance of the Brazilian context for discussions on global migration. The chapter is divided into three parts. First, the authors discuss the theoretical contributions of Enrique Dussel, Aníbal Quijano, and Walter Mignolo. While these authors rarely refer to immigrants, their work nevertheless contributes to the development of a

liberation ethics firmly planted in the history of Latin America, which recognizes the influences of coloniality and the social classification of race, class, and gender. They critique the European project of modernity, which requires a non-European "other" to be enslaved and exploited. They also show how the general intersubjective experience in Latin America still relies on Eurocentric models, which causes a distortion within the national multiracial and multicultural context.

Secondly, based on this history and philosophical analysis, Nascimento and Griesse examine the historical phases of immigration in Brazil. They begin with Portuguese colonization and the philosophical justifications for the latter as a counterpart to the Spanish, British, and French colonial ideologies. They then discuss the independence phase of nation building, which was based on a Eurocentric construct of modernity and relied on forced migration (slavery), an ideology of syncretism, policies of whitening, and the consequent "myth of racial democracy." They consider how the number of immigrants to Brazil decreased following World War II while the colonialist project continued, generating a phenomenon of internal migration of *nordestinos* (northeastern) and the Sem Terra (landless) movement that also sparked the formation of new labor movements and other forms of resistance.

Finally, they address recent migration issues in light of globalization processes. They conclude that considering migration issues in Brazil based on Latin American liberation ethics could provide a more comprehensive analysis of issues that are often neglected by the Anglo-American focus on national borders, state-centric approaches, and approaches steeped in political liberalism.

Chapter 5: Remember When It Was You: Exploring the Relevance of History for What Constitutes Immigration Justice for Displaced Venezuelans in Colombia
In 2016 the government of Colombia signed a peace accord with the Revolutionary Armed Forces of Colombia (FARC), officially ending a civil war that had lasted over fifty years. During that half century of violence, Colombia became a country of emigration. According to the Administrative Department of National Statistics of Colombia (DANE), roughly 557,000 Colombians migrated to Venezuela, the United States, Ecuador, Panama, Canada, Peru, Chile, and Bolivia between 1963 and 1973. The Migration Policy Institute reports that as of 2014, an estimated 1.2 million individuals claiming Colombian heritage resided in the United States. Indeed, in 2015 Colombian immigrants represented the largest group of South Americans in the

United States, accounting for roughly 25 percent of all South Americans, with a population of 699,000. Most important for this chapter by Allison B. Wolf, though, is the fact that during the decades of violence, over one million Colombians emigrated to Venezuela, most of whom have since returned.

While traditionally Colombia has been seen as the country of emigration, with recent turmoil in Venezuela, the tables have turned. Shortages of medicine and food, an economy in free fall, and political wrangling have led to an outflow of Venezuelan migrants, seeking refuge primarily throughout Latin America. According to the Migration Policy Institute and the Organization of American States, as of January 2019, over three million Venezuelans had left their country, most over the preceding three years. And there is no end in sight. Given the countries' historical and geographical ties, it is not surprising that the top destination for these migrants is Colombia, with over 1.1 million recent Venezuelans now residing there.

This chapter puts a normative lens on this situation, through the perspective of Jewish ethics, some aspects of which have been particularly influential in Latin American philosophy. In particular, it explores questions of immigration justice arising from the specific circumstances between Colombia and Venezuela as they relate to the current refugee crisis in the region. The principal focus of the analysis is to apply a feminist approximation of immigration justice to interrogate the question: What should be the relationship between the history of emigration and immigration policy?

Chapter 6: Rule by the Bodies: Biological Citizenship and
Politics of Life in Times of Migration in Chile
In this chapter, Raúl Armando Villarroel Soto articulates some philosophical grounds that allow for a better understanding of the phenomenon of migration in Chile in recent years, more specifically how it has revealed the existence of certain apparently racist traits in the behavior of many Chilean citizens in reaction to the increasing arrival of foreigners on national soil. Such presumably xenophobic or racist behavioral expressions can be understood, he argues, by drawing on what French philosopher Michel Foucault described in his term *biopolitics*. In his theory, Foucault explains the means by which attempts are made within the biopower economy to justify death, in which designating an entire race or population inferior permits some to think that the disappearance of those who are deemed "other"—that is, strangers, outsiders, immigrants—would strengthen us biologically.

Crucially, the problem arises from the fact that, according to French theorist Didier Fassin, *politics is exercised over and through the bodies*; in the particular case analyzed here, this phenomenon takes place especially in the bodies of immigrants, on whom the expressions of racism or discrimination fall, based on the biological differences allegedly existing between nationals and foreigners.

Section 3: Mexico and Central America

Chapter 7: Ethics of Liberation: Listening to Central American
Migrants' Response to Forced Migration
The migration of Central Americans to the United States is not a new phenomenon. In fact, mass migration has occurred since at least the 1970s, and its origins can be traced to a mixture of local corruption and imposed capitalism, which has caused economic vulnerability, civil war, and genocide in the region. Forced migration has been, at least in part, caused by the colonial structures and the enactment and legitimization of neoliberal economic policies that only look to increase their profit without any esteem for people's lives. This disregard for life is unequivocally directed specially toward the racialized and sexed/gendered bodies of Indigenous people and dark-skinned *mestizos*.

Migrants suffer the consequences of colonial structures as reflected in internal colonialism, where demeaning social and economic structures place them in a disadvantaged position, as instantiated in discriminatory social practices. Some tokens of these discriminatory practices are xenophobia and aporophobia. Clearly, these practices are immoral and detrimental, and thus need to be challenged. In this chapter, Luis Rubén Díaz Cepeda reveals that migrants themselves are already doing so by creating solidarity networks, demonstrating their high levels of agency and resilience. These solidarity networks are amplified by pro-migrant social activists and organization who assist migrants with shelter, lobbying, and defense services.

In support of this argument, Cepeda first explores sociological explanations of poverty in Latin America, especially Pablo González Casanova's theory of sociology of exploitation, and more concretely its concept of the social relation of exploitation. He then shows how exploitation is instantiated in the migration flows from Central America to Mexico and the United States. In the third, normative, section, Cepeda argues based on Dussel's ethics of liberation that meeting the ethical duty to answer to the Other is a clear and useful answer to discriminatory practices. The chapter concludes by illustrating how migrants help one another and how this effort is supported by social organizations.

Chapter 8: *The Justice of the Other: Mexicans, Palestinians, and Sahawaris on the Same Side of Different Walls*

Thirty years after the emblematic fall of the Berlin Wall, and contrary to expectations, walls that impair free circulation of peoples have multiplied. Today, at least seventy such walls are standing in different places across the globe. In this chapter, Silvana Rabinovich focuses on three of them: the wall stopping Mexicans and Latin Americans from entering the United States, the one that the state of Israel built to prevent the return of Palestinians to their homes and lands, and the one the Moroccan kingdom built to annex the Saharawi territories and assimilate the population under occupation.

Rabinovich approaches these three walls—all symbols of colonial policy—from the perspective of Emmanuel Levinas's heteronomous ethics. She interprets heteronomy not as a subjugation to dominance but rather as the duty to let oneself be taught by the justice *of* the other. Unlike altruism, which intends to apply its own idea of justice to others who do not obtain it in the form of justice *for* the other, heteronomy implies a change of perspective. Striving to listen to the justice *of* the other means recognizing that what we consider acquired rights are in fact privileges from a decolonial point of view.

As a key to the heteronomous ethics, Rabinovich analyzes the role that vulnerability plays in the discourse that justifies the construction of illegitimate walls as well as in the construction of the figures of immigrants and refugees. She then considers the idea of the right of return, invoked both by Palestinians and Saharawis, and reflects on its meaning in the case of Mexico. Lastly, she reviews the meanings of exile in relation to the aforementioned walls.

Chapter 9: *A Purgative Against Despair: Singing with Mexican Emigrants*

Vast crowds of subjugated people, both in their homelands and throughout their displacements, have always sung. In this chapter, Carlos Pereda explores the following questions in relation to the songs of Mexican migrants, and particularly those of so-called illegal aliens: Where do Mexico's poor migrants sing? In what kind of places, and what characterizes those songs?

What do such migrants suggest or manifest with their songs? And what is the content of those songs? Finally, why should we care about those songs—if, as we may presume, they are not just complaints or confessions of despair?

In order to address these questions, Pereda analyzes the content of some *corridos* sung by such popular "northern music" bands such as the Tigres del Norte. Corridos can disclose various interactions between migrants and (a) an external-external Other (their future bosses in the United States), (b) an external-internal Other (those back in the homeland who forced them to emigrate), (c) an internal-external Other (the loved ones who were left behind), and (d) an internal-internal Other (the person itself in dialogue with itself).

Section 4: Latin Americans and Latina/o/xs in the United States

Chapter 10: The Interpreter's Dilemma: On the Moral
Burden of Consensual Heteronomy

The 2016 Census Bureau's American Community Survey found that nearly twenty-eight million people in the United States have limited proficiency in speaking English. Many of these individuals rely on family members to interpret both culture and language in a range of situations. This chapter, by Lori Gallegos, makes the case that the widespread lack of Spanish-language accessibility services in the United States produces linguistic oppression, not only for immigrants but also for the family members and loved ones who engage in language brokering. Gallegos focuses on the challenge to personal autonomy faced by those who interpret for loved ones, which she calls the *interpreter's dilemma*. The dilemma arises when those who interpret for family members face the decision of whether to act in accordance with their personal desires or whether (out of love or loyalty) to acquiesce to their dependent loved one's request to act in a way that the interpreter does not endorse. The difficulty of this dilemma is exacerbated by a racist and/or xenophobic social context, which gives rise to special obligations to amplify the agency of the dependent family member.

The interpreter's dilemma generates a moral burden that can be best appreciated in light of a conception of autonomy as relational, the pragmatics of language, and emotional agency. Gallegos makes the case that this moral burden is an *unjust*, rather than a merely circumstantial burden. An examination of this moral burden reveals one way that the marginalization of non-English speakers ripples throughout the Latinx community.

Chapter 11: Jus Sanguinis vs. Jus Soli: On the Grounds of Justice
Are there normative, rather than contingent and historical, reasons for why we should prefer, and defend, jus soli over jus sanguinis as a ground for membership in a political community? Or put differently, within a democratic polity, guided by the rule of law and an enlightened constitution, how should citizenship be allocated? In this chapter, Eduardo Mendieta argues that birthright citizenship is the utmost form of the rejection of jus sanguinis, the deracialization of both membership and citizenship.

In making this argument, the chapter is framed around two axes: a historical one and a normative one. Along the historical axis, Mendieta discusses the U.S. historical factors that led to the "Reconstructionist" Fourteenth Amendment. In normative terms, he begins with Kant's discussions relating to what he calls Kant's geographical justification for the right of hospitality and the ground for rights in general. But, looking at notes that Kant made for his *Metaphysics of Morals*, he expands on Kant's discussion of the relationship between territory and membership. He also turns to Michael Walzer's discussion of membership in his book *Spheres of Justice* and his more recent discussions of the right to membership.

Notes

1. See, for instance, Michael Walter, *Spheres of Justice* (New York: Basic Books, 1984) and Joseph Carens, "Aliens and Citizens: The Case for Open Borders," *Review of Politics* 49, no. 2 (Spring 1987): 251–73.

2. Just a few examples: Linda Martín Alcoff, *Visible Identities: Race, Gender, and the Self* (New York: Oxford University Press, 2005); Carlos A. Sanchez, "On Documents and Subjectivity: The Formation and De-Formation of the Immigrant Identity," *Radical Philosophy Review* 14 no. 2 (2011): 197–205; Grant Silva, "On the Militarization of Borders and the Judicial Right to Exclude," *Public Affairs Quarterly* 29, no. 2 (April 2015): 217–34; Shelley Wilcox, "American Neo-Nativism and Gendered Immigrant Exclusions," in *Feminist Interventions in Ethics and Politics*, ed. Barbara Andrew, Jean Keller, and Lisa Schwartzman (Lanham, Md.: Rowman and Littlefield, 2005), 213–32. For a more comprehensive review, see, in particular, chapters 1 and 2 of this volume.

3. Lori Gallegos de Castillo and Francisco Gallegos, "Metaphilosophy: Defining Latin American and Latinx Philosophy. A Collaborative Introduction," in *Latin*

American and Latinx Philosophy, ed. Robert Eli Sanchez Jr. (New York: Routledge, 2020), 242–64.

4. José Carlos Mariátegui, *¿Existe un pensamiento Hispanoamericano?* (Mexico City: Universidad Nacional Autónoma de México, 1976); Augusto Salazar Bondy, *¿Existe una filosofía de Nuestra America?*, 11th ed. (Mexico City: Siglo Veintiuno Editores, 1968).

5. Guillermo Hurtado, "Two Models of Latin American Philosophy," *Journal of Speculative Philosophy* 20, no. 3 (2006): 205.

6. Carlos Pereda, "Latin American Philosophy: Some Vices," *Journal of Speculative Philosophy* 20, no. 3 (2006): 194.

7. Gallegos de Castillo and Gallegos, "Metaphilosophy," 249.

8. *Stanford Encyclopedia of Philosophy* (2018), s.v. "Latin American Philosophy," by Jorge Gracia and Manuel Vargas, https://plato.stanford.edu/entries/latin-american-philosophy/.

9. *Stanford Encyclopedia of Philosophy* (2018), s.v. "Latinx Philosophy," by Manuel Vargas, https://plato.stanford.edu/entries/latinx/.

10. Susana Nuccetelli, "Latin American Philosophy," in *A Companion to Latin American Philosophy*, ed. Susana Nuccetelli, Ofelia Schutte, and Otavio Bueno (Oxford: Wiley-Blackwell, 2013), 344.

PART I

Methodological Foundations

CHAPTER 1

Latin American Immigration Ethics

A Roadmap

AMY REED-SANDOVAL AND
LUIS RUBÉN DÍAZ CEPEDA

Introduction

"Mainstream" philosophy of immigration has generally been written without reference to Latin American history or philosophy, despite the fact Latin Americans (and particularly Mexicans and Central Americans) are widely regarded as "quintessential" migrants in places like the United States. This is not to discredit such scholarship, developed as it has in the Anglo-American and European traditions. Certainly, this body of work has generated useful conceptual resources with which to question, among other things, the very legitimacy of immigration restrictions. Still, in neglecting not only ethically relevant aspects of Latin American migrations throughout their history but also Latin American philosophies *about* these processes, mainstream immigration philosophy delivers an incomplete vision of immigration justice. We submit that what ought to be a collective, global effort to achieve immigration justice must engage Latin American immigration ethics.

One might suspect that this is impossible because there do not seem to be any distinctively "Latin American immigration ethics" to engage. Indeed, it may appear that migration theory is the domain of philosophers in recognized "receiving countries." Contrary to such a view, in this chapter we propose that a distinctive Latin American immigration ethics does exist, even if it has not yet been articulated as such. Latin American immigration ethics, we argue, (often) has two characteristics. First, it focuses on lived, contextualized migratory experiences of Latin Americans within and outside of the geographical region of Latin America. This can be contrasted to a highly abstract approach to immigration ethics that seeks out universally applicable moral norms to guide us to immigration justice everywhere (sometimes called the "open borders debate," which we discuss later).[1] Second, Latin American immigration ethics offers conceptual frameworks for achieving immigration justice that call upon the ideas of Latin American philosophers. Following our discussion in the introduction to this volume, we conceive the term "Latin American philosopher" broadly, such that it includes not only academic philosophers but also artists, public intellectuals, and migrants themselves generating philosophical ideas in a Latin American context. Note that we do not present either characteristic as a necessary condition for a piece of work to "count" as Latin American immigration ethics. Our aim is to offer a roadmap rather than construct new scholarly borders. We hope that this chapter, as well as the others in this volume, will encourage a proliferation of philosophical and empirical work on immigration through a Latin American philosophical lens.

This chapter is organized as follows: First, we provide a sketch of immigrations/migrations in Latin American history, from the colonization of the Americas to the present. Second, we explore three key examples of how Latin American philosophers have engaged this history. These include (1) Latin American philosophical work on exile; (2) Latinx philosophy (including Latina feminist philosophy) about Latin American and Latinx perspectives on living in, and migrating to, the United States; and (3) the notion of *transmodernidad*, developed in the context of Enrique Dussel's liberation philosophy, which provides philosophical guidance for a system of more open borders in an increasingly integrated Latin America.

Our conclusion briefly discusses how Latin American immigration ethics delivers important philosophical insights and proposals for achieving immigration justice. Finally, we list several areas in which Latin American immigration ethics could benefit from further philosophical work and development.

I. Immigrations/Migrations in Latin American History

Normative and empirical migration scholarship has focused predominantly on South-North migration. However, understanding Latin American migration ethics requires us to reorient our focus toward South-South and North-South (or Center-Periphery) migrations.[2] The term "South-South" migration designates the migratory movements in which both the sending and receiving countries are situated in the Global South. In Latin America, such movements may occur when migrants do not have the intention of reaching the Global North, opting instead to enter and remain in a neighboring Latin American country. South-South migrations also occur when migrants attempt to reach a Global North country but are prevented from doing so due to factors such as health issues and restrictive immigration enforcement mechanisms encountered along the way. North-South migrations occur when migrants leave Global North countries—which tend to be former colonial powers—and relocate to the Global South. Such migrations, as we shall now explore, have transpired since the colonization of Latin America.

Indeed, understanding Latin American immigration history requires us to travel back to the fifteenth century, to the roots of the current cultural and political structure.[3] At the beginning of the colonial period, thousands of Europeans, overwhelmingly from Spain and Portugal, migrated to the Americas. Enslaved Africans were forcibly transported to the Western Hemisphere and forced to work in the "New World's" burgeoning mines. Illnesses borne by Europeans decimated a large percentage of the Native population, leaving Latin America with extensive uninhabited territories that would continue attracting European migrants in the following centuries. Meanwhile, Indigenous women were often forced into new, oppressive gender roles by Spanish colonizers.[4] Indeed, as Raúl Villarroel explores in this volume, violent colonization and enslavement should be regarded as core aspects of Latin American migratory history.

North-South migrations to Latin America did not end when Latin American countries achieved formal independence from Spain and Portugal in the late eighteenth and early nineteenth centuries. In fact, migration from southern Europe to Latin America continued over the second half of the nineteenth century and the beginning of the twentieth.[5] Latin American political elites encouraged this translocation of an estimated eleven million people, on the grounds that European migration would "improve the race" in Latin America. (The basis of this attitude is expressed in Domingo Sarmiento's book *Facundo o civilización y barbarie*, in which he argues that "blacks and Indians were behind in the march of civilization" and wonders "if it had not been a mistake, during the colonial era, [to] incorporate indigenous people into the life of the Spanish.")[6] As Norambuena claims, in countries like Chile, this idea of "racial improvement" generated an "ideology of migra-tion" that facilitated the creation of attractive conditions for Europeans to settle there.[7] Argentina and Uruguay also offered this type of deference to European migrants (particularly Italians). Additionally, from 1939 to 1942, Mexico received between twenty and twenty-five thousand Spanish refugees and exiles who migrated in order to escape from Francisco Franco's dictator-ship—a process that became known as the *Exilio Español* (we shall return to exile in the Latin American context in the next section). Some of these exiles, such as José Gaos and Adolfo Sánchez Vázquez, found fertile soil in the growing intellectual sphere in Mexico and contributed significantly to the development of academic philosophy in that country.[8]

The decline of this particular wave of European immigration coincided with the development of Latin American urban centers. Starting in the 1930s, there was a vast internal migration from the countryside to large cities throughout the region.[9] At first, this movement transpired within the limits of national boundaries. Later, it morphed into an interregional migration stream originating in the borderlands of Latin America, "where ethnic identities or pre-established ties . . . connected populations beyond the political demarca-tion of the territories."[10] Soon enough, foreigners (from within Latin America) were relocating from Latin American borderlands to regional urban centers. Miguel Villa and Jorge Martínez point out that a scarce availability of informa-tion and the difficulty to standardize national databases (i.e., census informa-tion) make it challenging to establish the exact numbers of Latin Americans migrating from one "local" country to another during this period.[11] However, it is possible to identify at least some general patterns.

By the mid-nineteenth century, Argentina, Costa Rica, and Venezuela were receiving a significant number of migrants from neighboring coun-tries such as Colombia, Paraguay, Nicaragua, Bolivia, and Chile.[12] For the most part, this involved peasants and working-class individuals—for exam-ple, most migrants from Bolivia, Paraguay, and Chile worked in the agricul-tural industry in Argentina. Later, in the 1970s, the Venezuelan oil industry attracted many migrants from Colombia.[13] Given that these workers were considered necessary for the development of the recipient economies, their immigration was not considered controversial until the later part of that decade.[14] Rather, they were generally accepted in Venezuela and were able to regularize their immigration status with ease (for further exploration of this topic, see Allison B. Wolf's contribution to this volume).

New migration trends occurred in the 1980s, as political conflicts and resulting violence in El Salvador, Nicaragua, and Guatemala compelled large numbers of people to flee those countries. While most Central Americans fled to the United States, many also sought refuge in Mexico and Costa Rica. Responding to this influx, Costa Rica agreed to "legalize" these migrants.[15] In the midst of these conflicts in Central America, the economic situation in Latin America deteriorated to the point that 1980s were dubbed the region's "lost decade."

The economic crisis of the "lost decade" came about as follows: During the 1970s, within the context of the Cold War, countries were debating the kind of economic model they should follow. Argentina and Mexico opted for a government-driven process of industrialization, wherein they imported technology in an attempt to upgrade their industries. Meanwhile, as industrialized countries increased their loan-rate interest, Latin American countries were forced to devalue their currency. The heightened interest rates and depreciated currency caused external debt to increase to the point at which it became impossible to pay. This "unbearable debt" was then instrumentalized by the International Monetary Fund to promote an agenda of liberalizing Latin American economies, including a dismantling of the region's welfare state. These factors, in turn, pushed a larger number of people to leave for the United States and Western Europe, where they were often not well received. Many of those unable or unwilling to go to North America or Europe migrated to other countries within Latin America, which they often found easily accessible.

Thus far in this section, we have aimed to center Latin America's deep histories of South-South and North-South/Center-Periphery migrations. However, we must also acknowledge the historical and sociopolitical importance of South-North Latin American migration, particularly to the United States. Note first, however, that Latin Americans and Latina/o/xs in the United States did not always "end up" there through migration. In 1848, through the Treaty of Guadalupe Hidalgo ending the Mexican-American War, the U.S. government violently seized nearly half of Mexico's territory, leaving countless Mexicans with an ambiguous immigration status on their own lands.

A range of subsequent immigration laws, policies, and enforcement practices served to reify the status of Mexicans and other Latin Americans as an oppressed social group in the United States. For instance, the Johnson-Reed Act, or the Immigration Act of 1924, compelled the U.S. government to focus on controlling the Mexico-U.S. border as a major component of its immigration policy. According to Mae Ngai, the Johnson-Reed act made Mexicans paradigmatic "illegal" subjects.[16] Later, during the Great Depression, immigration enforcement officials repatriated over a million ethnic Mexicans—including U.S. citizens who had never been to Mexico—to that country. Shortly thereafter, the Bracero Program invited Mexican workers back into the United States under highly exploitative conditions.

Today, the social "illegalization" of Latin Americans and Latina/o/xs in the United States persists, even as their labor continues to be regarded as "essential" during the COVID-19 pandemic. Meanwhile, the increased militarization of the Mexico-U.S. border, exacerbated by the controversial Prevention Through Deterrence Policy, has led to countless migrant deaths. Female and transgender migrants have been harmed considerably by U.S. immigration enforcement mechanisms, which leave them vulnerable to rape and assault during the increasingly arduous journey toward and across a heavily militarized border. Children who attempt to migrate from Latin America to the United States are also highly vulnerable; in 2018 the administration of Donald Trump began forcibly separating them from their parents in immigration detention centers (for an exploration of other ethical challenges faced by Latin American and Latina/o/x children living in the United States, see Lori Gallegos de Castillo's contribution to this volume).

Finally, and to conclude this section, we propose that understanding migration in a Latin American context requires us to think in terms of an *integrated Latin America*, both real and imagined. Simón Bolívar originally conceived of "the idea of a Pan-American identity: that is to say, a sense of a shared and restricted life experience lived on a commonly-possessed territory and within a set of trans-temporal and trans-individual cultural patterns."[17] One could argue that Bolívar's dream has, in important respects, been kept alive through several prominent attempts to develop a united Latin America. The Caribbean Community (CARICOM), the Andean Community of Nations, and South Common Market (Mercado Común del Sur, MERCOSUR) reflect this ideal. These bodies facilitate the migration and residence of citizens of member countries within the framework of an emerging common market and community space. For instance, in the case of MERCOSUR, these efforts "include major agreements on free movement and equal rights for member state nationals, residency norms and ongoing negotiations to put in place a statute on regional citizenship."[18]

It is important to note that the idea of an integrated Latin American generally follows the Zapatista principle of building a "world where many worlds fit." An *inclusive* Latin America acknowledges its debt to Indigenous people and recognizes them as a valid and useful source of knowledge. Reaching an integrated Latin America in those terms would have fortunate geopolitical and theoretical consequences. Geopolitically, it is likely that countries sharing resources and finding solutions to common problems would improve the social and economic conditions of their inhabitants. A stronger Latin America would also be better positioned to challenge the hegemonic colonial discourse that sets the region in a position of inferiority. This improved position could also improve the quality of life on Latina/o/xs living in the Global North, as they would not be forced to live as migrants if they do not want to and, if they did choose to migrate, would likely endure less discrimination after doing so from a position of strength.

In theoretical terms, an integrated Latin America would reveal the relevance of other ways of living and knowing such as *buen vivir* (from the Aymara expression *sumac kamaña*, which can be translated as "living in fullness and harmony with the Pachamama"). This perspective of having a "full life" refers not to an accumulation of material possessions but to a life in communion with nature and our fellow human beings. Note that when we say "fellow human beings" we do not refer to an abstraction but to the concrete materiality of the flesh and blood of other people—especially of those who suffer the greatest inequities and whom Enrique Dussel calls the victims of the system. We propose that developing a community-oriented epistemology in an integrated Latin America will help us to reconceptualize immigration justice in terms of what Dussel terms a preferential option for the poor. We explore these ideas in relation to Dussel's arguments supporting more open borders in Latin America later in this chapter.

II. Latin American Philosophies of Migration

As we explore in this section, Latin American and Latina/o/x philosophers have responded to the migratory histories delineated above in novel ways, offering conceptual resources of relevance to normative, empirical, and policy-oriented discussions of migration justice.

A. Latin American Philosophies of Exile

One distinctive contribution of Latin American philosophy to the philosophy of migration comes in the form of reflections on exile. The fact that Latin American philosophers have focused on exile in particular (as a migratory experience) can be partially attributed to the widespread importance of banishment as an exclusionary mechanism—indeed, its status as a "major constitutive feature of Latin American politics"[19]—dating back to the colonization of the Americas, when, in a well-established process known as *destierro*, perceived deviants from Spain and Portugal were forcibly sent to the Americas. Conversely, during this time, "disturbers of the peace" from Latin America were frequently exiled back to those colonial "centers." Given the importance of exile in Latin American immigration ethics, let us say a bit more here about the practice in Latin American history.

Exile was frequently employed as a relatively "easy" solution to political dissent during and after the Latin American wars of independence of the early nineteenth century. Note that throughout most of the region's history, banishment, as opposed to slavery and/or execution, was only offered to relatively privileged, white elites, who were frequently able to join communities of *exiliados*, or *desterrados*, in their new countries. For example, whereas the Inca/Indigenous monarch Túpac Amaru, of what is now Vilcabamba, Peru, was executed by Spanish colonizers after a failed attempt to defend the sovereignty of the Neo-Inca State, centuries later, the upper-class Simón Bolívar died in exile in Europe after leading wars of independence in six Latin American countries.

In more recent history, exile in, and from, Latin America has lost some (but not all) of its elitist connotations. As we noted earlier, following World War II and the Spanish Civil War, European exiles, who were not always upper class, built new homes and communities in Latin America—particularly in Mexico, Argentina, and Chile. Fidel Castro and other Cuban dissidents went into exile in Mexico (where Castro met Che Guevara), where they planned for what became the Cuban Revolution. As a result of a series of coups and subsequent military repression in South America in the 1960s and 1970s, thousands of exiles from Brazil, Chile, Argentina, and Uruguay sought refuge in other Latin American countries, including Nicaragua after the Sandinista Revolution. While this history raises important questions about the distinctions between exiles, refugees, and migrants, Sznajder and Roniger offer a sufficiently broad definition to argue that exile, qua political mechanism in Latin America, has become more "inclusive" in terms of its application:

> Exile is a multifaceted phenomenon that can be analyzed from a sociolog-
> ical, psychological, historical, cultural, anthropological, economic, literary,
> artistic, and geographic point of view. It relates not only to expulsion from a
> country but also to reception by host countries, to a dynamics of longing for
> return, and eventually to the return itself. It involves processes of transna-
> tional, regional, and global acculturation and translocation of political, social,
> administrative, and cultural models from abroad to the home society.[20]

For present purposes, let us assume this broad definition of exile and turn to some of the conceptual tools that Latin American philosophers have pro-vided in order analyze and understand it. In what remains of this section, we explore two philosophers who have done a considerable amount of work on the topic: Uruguayan Mexican philosopher Carlos Pereda and Argentinian Mexican philosopher Silvana Rabinovich.

More specifically, Pereda has offered a book-length treatment of exile that philosophically engages the "metatestimonies" on their experiences offered by exiled poets and philosophers in Latin America. He argues that metatestimonies—unlike the contents of, say, ethnographic interviews—are explicitly offered up for critical analysis.[21] According to Pereda, exile should be understood both in terms of a series of phases and as an experience that brings about a unique philosophical perspective.

In the first phase, the exiled person feels a profound, wrenching sense of loss that shatters their very sense of self. Subsequently, the exiled person enters the phase of "resistance," which begins as anger toward one's political opponents but eventually becomes creative and productive, enabling them to rebuild a coherent personal identity. Later still, exile becomes a threshold at which the exiled person builds new ways of experiencing, understanding, and living in the host country. Pereda pays considerable attention to the work of María Zambrano, the Spanish philosopher of the Generation of '36, who lived in several countries as an exile after her opposition to Franco during the Spanish Civil War. For Pereda, Zambrano exemplifies how exile produces "ruptures" that bring out fresh philosophical and political perspectives (i.e., in Zambrano's discussion of "reason" in terms of a willingness to forge new beginnings).

Notably, Pereda does not merely *describe* exile. He also makes normative statements about the importance of experiencing exile as profound loss, and then recovery, and then creative threshold: "We must not objectify a bottomless plunge into melancholy, for anyone who is incapable of taking a step backward and adopting a third person point of view in order to understand their place of suffering will forever remain a prisoner in their orgies of hyperbole."[22] So we might add a third element to Pereda's description of exile: threshold-as-*requirement*. Importantly, Pereda's theory does not merely place a normative burden on migrants/exiles themselves. He compels the reader to imagine, and even try to think from, the migrant's/exile's own point of view. We are compelled, furthermore, to regard that point of view as a source of wisdom and innovation in relation to life in a new world.

Meanwhile, Silvana Rabinovich offers an analysis of exile that, somewhat similarly, traces both the oppression and creative potential inherent in exile. However, her work serves to complicate certain standard assumptions about exile, for she introduces the notion of *exilio domiciliario*—or "exile at home"— to analyze the experiences of various politically oppressed groups, including Native Americans, Palestinians in refugee camps, and the Sawari people living under European colonialism. Rabinovich notes that groups that are "exiled at home" are expected (and often violently compelled) to integrate into dominant sociopolitical culture while renouncing their distinctiveness. While the various groups assessed by Rabinovich in her bottom-up philosophical analysis certainly experience exile in different ways, they all experience "exile at home" through "losing the land beneath their feet."

Rabinovich then attends to the creative, epistemic, and political dimensions of exile. She suggests, for instance, that the "marginality" of exile calls into question the principles of the capitalist nation-state.[23] Exile is also utopian, she argues, compelling us to rethink the possible and impossible (especially in the realm of the political). Finally, like Pereda, Rabinovich offers an account of exile with normative dimensions. She maintains that individual exiled persons ought to embrace utopian reimaginings while resisting integration into the positivist ethos of their host countries. Recently, Rabinovich applied her account of exile to the COVID-19 pandemic, arguing that experiences of quarantine and social isolation can help nonexiled people empathize with the experiences of "exiles at home" who have had the land beneath their feet taken from them.[24]

The respective works on exile by Rabinovich and Pereda exemplify how Latin American philosophers have developed unique conceptual resources in response to the region's particular immigration/migration history, in which exile has played an important role. It is worth noting that Anglo-American and European immigration philosophies have not, as a general rule, theorized exile, focusing instead on the experiences of immigrants (documented and undocumented) and refugees.[25] This brief survey of Pereda's and Rabinovich's respective works also demonstrates a key theme of Latin American migration ethics, which will emerge in the ensuing sections: an emphasis on theory *from the migrant's point of view*.

B. Latinx Immigration Philosophy

Let us now turn to Latinx philosophies of migration—that is, philosophies of migration that focus mainly on the migratory experiences of Latin Americans and Latina/o/xs in the United States. As we shall see, Latinx immigration philosophers have paid particular attention to Latina/o/x encounters with immigration-related restrictions, enforcement mechanisms, and stereotypes. In addition, José Jorge Mendoza explains that "Latinx philosophers are not only already providing challenges to standard open-borders debates, but also challenging the very nature of the ethics of immigration" (for a discussion of the relationship between Latinx immigration philosophy and decolonial theory, see Mendoza's contribution to this volume).[26] Following Mendoza's example, we explore in this section not only Latinx philosophical work on contextualized Latina/o/x immigration experiences but also how Latinx immigration philosophers have challenged and even sidelined the "open borders debate" of Anglo-American political philosophy of immigration. In so doing, Latinx immigration philosophers offer new resources for pursuing immigration ethics.

To begin to understand the distinctive contributions of Latinx philosophers to the ethics of migration, let us first turn to Gloria Anzaldúa's seminal work *Borderlands/La Frontera: The New Mestiza*. In *Borderlands*, Anzaldúa explores how the immigration restrictions targeting U.S. Latina/o/xs, particularly in the Mexico-U.S. borderlands region, contribute to Mexican American and Chicana/o/x identity and oppression.[27] She famously called the Mexico-U.S. border an "*una herida abierta* [an open wound] where the

Third World grates against the first and bleeds."[28] In doing so, Anzaldúa has conveyed the intimate nature of immigration restrictions for many Latina/ox/s. Indeed, she describes her own upbringing at the border as a form of "intimate terrorism" that contributed to the formation of her Chicana identity. Anzaldúa tells the story of Pedro, a Mexican American adolescent farmworker who was apprehended and deported to Mexico—where he had never lived—despite his U.S. citizenship. As Anzaldúa explains, immigration enforcement mechanisms serve to "mark" racialized, working-class bodies as "illegal" regardless of citizenship status. In many respects, Anzaldúa's work set the stage for more recent Latinx immigration philosophy by establishing that immigration restrictions, including borders, are much more than the subject matter of largely abstract philosophical debates. They are, in fact, inextricably connected to many aspects of Chicana/o/x and Latina/o/x identity, subjectivity, experience, and oppression.

Latinx immigration philosophy has continued this Anzaldúan tradition of theorizing on the basis of Latin Americans' lived experiences of immigration restrictions. Grant Silva, for instance, writes that "borders are . . . bolstered by such things as racial, ethnic, or religious difference, even when such differences are the product of national imaginaries. When borders assume these contexts, they become more than just lines in the sand; they become 'color lines.'"[29] Such arguments urge us to think critically about what borders actually *are*, as well as their relationship to social identity formation. Thinking both from and "beyond" the U.S.-Mexico border, Ernesto Rosen Velásquez argues that the competing claims of "economic progress versus the threat of Latin Americans in the north . . . have resulted in a checkered history of massive deportations, bracero programs, periods of amnesty, massacres, riots, and daily harassment of immigrants and others who may look like laborers."[30] Velásquez's analysis focuses on how "visible Latina/o/x identity" intersects with class in ways that can render one particularly vulnerable to immigrant enforcement mechanisms.[31] Other Latinx immigration philosophers have assessed the relationship between immigration restrictions targeting Latin Americans and Latina/o/xs and the very *personhood* of those targeted. As Carlos Alberto Sanchez argues, "certain legislative moves both *thingify* and push undocumented migrants outside the space of the human."[32]

In addition to this body of scholarship on the relationship between immigration restrictions and Latin American and Latina/o/x identity and oppression, Latinx philosophers have also made important contributions to the philosophical "open borders debate" of analytic/Anglo-American political philosophy. By way of review, this scholarly conversation has explored in abstract and largely "ideal" fashion the question of whether states may justly exclude any prospective immigrants whatsoever. On the one side stands the so-called conventional view that sovereign states are entitled to such exclusionary acts;[33] philosophers who support it frequently couch their arguments in terms of the protection of societal culture, freedom of association, and the belief that immigration restrictions do not necessarily violate the moral equality of the excluded (for further discussion on the imperative to "protect society cultures" in relation to Indigenous migration, see Amy Reed-Sandoval's contribution to this volume). So-called open borders theorists, on the other hand, frequently argue against immigration restrictions by appealing to the values like autonomy, social equality, and the pursuit of a meaningful life for immigrants and other border-crossers. Some also emphasize the value of free markets, stressing the right of employers to hire whomever they wish—including foreigners—for a particular job.

It is to this debate that Latinx philosophers have made unique interventions that deserve recognition here.[34] For instance, Jorge M. Valadez and José-Antonio Orosco have debated how we should understand states *themselves* in the context of normative discussions of immigration. Valadez argues that even though modern states have, generally speaking, achieved their power through wrongful means, they may possess a form of conditional legitimacy, as part of which they may operate justly in the present despite their unjust past.[35] Orosco, meanwhile, argues that states not only perform certain administrative functions but also protect societal cultures. On such a view of states, certain segments of the public may see immigrants as threatening societal cultures. Immigration justice therefore demands that states like the United States develop openness to, and appreciation of, the unique contributions that immigrants bring.[36] As these examples show, Latinx philosophers have made important contributions to the open borders debate, often by way of centering the experiences of immigrants themselves.

Latina feminist philosophy is generally read and discussed separately from philosophical work, Latinx or otherwise, on immigration justice. However, it is important to note that this tradition draws attention to a range of migration ethics challenges experienced by Latin Americans, Latina/o/xs, and other marginalized immigrant groups—as illustrated in Natalie Cisneros's study of the widespread phenomenon so-called anchor baby stereotyping and the ways in which the latter reveals how the bodies of immigrant women of color are frequently regarded as "always, already perverse."[37] Furthermore, Latina feminist writers have also articulated how the crossing and recrossing of borders—physical, epistemic, and metaphorical—produce for many Latinas an experience of "in-betweenness," which Mariana Ortega describes in terms of *"multiplicitous selfhood*, of selves characterized by *being-between-worlds, being-in-worlds*, and *becoming-with*."[38]

In "Playfulness, World-Traveling, and Loving Perception," María Lugones offers an influential account of the sort of "in-betweenness" discussed by Ortega, exploring how "women of color in the U.S. practice 'world'-traveling," mostly out of necessity.[39] Like Ortega, Lugones argues that these practices of "world"-traveling—which come, in part, from negotiating hostile aspects of the society one currently inhabits as a woman of color and marked "other"—generate not only burdens but also a unique epistemic standpoint from which to view, assess, and come to understand the world. On the one hand, Lugones refers to literal travels and border crossings, as she discusses her experiences growing up in Argentina and moving to the United States. On the other hand, the sorts of "borders" and "worlds" she explores include racial, cultural, and other boundaries with which women of color must contend. As Lugones writes, "the reason why I think traveling to someone's 'world' is a way of identifying with them is because by traveling to their world we can understand *what it is to be them and what it is to be ourselves in their eyes*."[40]

Thus far, we have seen that Latina feminist philosophers have theorized the unique epistemic standpoint that Latinas (and other women of color) in the United States often develop as they navigate material and figurative borders and the state of *being-between-worlds*. In addition to this, these thinkers have also developed strategies for contending with such border crossings. Ortega, for instance, explores *hometactics*, which she describes as "practices that allow for a sense of familiarity with and a particular sense of 'belonging to' a place, space, or group while avoiding the restrictive, exclusive elements that a notion of belonging might carry with it."[41] Hometactics involve everyday strategies, self-mappings, and the uncovering of what multiplicitous selves are already doing in order to navigate an existential state of in-betweenness.[42] Another strategy of Latina feminists, identified by Stephanie Rivera Berruz, is that of "translation and translocation," through which Latina and Latin American feminists "consider the importance and context of migrations of ideas in a globalized world."[43] Rivera Berruz explores how

Latina feminists often cultivate a hemispheric approach to feminist theorizing. Additionally, Latina feminists have articulated strategies for engaging in collective, mutually supportive scholarship that challenge systems of marginalization in the discipline of philosophy, such as the Roundtable on Latina Feminism.[44]

In sum, we have seen that Latinx philosophy, including Latina feminist philosophy, has made considerable contributions to theorizing the ethics of migration. This body of scholarship both focuses on the unique, contextualized experiences of Latin American and Latina/o/x migrations (in this case, in the United States) and generates new conceptual frameworks for pursuing immigration ethics. Furthermore, like Latin American philosophies of exile, Latinx immigration philosophy often theorizes (or aims to theorize) from a migrant's point of view.[45] Latinx philosophers engage, challenge, and even sidestep the open borders debate, offering important new frameworks, such as hometactics (Ortega), thingification (Sanchez), and translation and translocation (Rivera Berruz). All the while, Latinx philosophers of immigration tend to uphold an "Anzaldúan tradition" of assessing the intimate relationship between immigration restrictions and Latina/o/x identity itself.

C. Liberation Philosophy and Immigration

In this section, we consider an alternative approach to immigration ethics developed in the Global South: an inclusive immigration system based on the ethical duty to respond to the Other. In so doing, we should first note the exclusionary nature of a colonial discourse that promotes the idea of nation-states founded on notions of one unique identity. Within such a discourse, "local cultures are left for dead or expected to die before long, because their condition is one of unquestionable inferiority according to the colonizer's gaze and has no future of its own."[46] When implemented, this ideology is used to generate barriers to both external and internal migration. Borders are closed to prevent non-natives from entering a nation, while exclusionary social practices draw an internal borderline between those who "belong" to the dominant culture and Others who do not. In opposition to such Othering and xenophobia, Enrique Dussel's philosophy of liberation argues for an inclusive system inspired by the lessons learned from the global "periphery." Here, we outline the contours of an ethics of immigration grounded in the ethical principles of Dussel's philosophy.

First, some background. The philosophy of liberation "defines itself as a counter-philosophical discourse, whether it be as a critique of colonialism, imperialism, globalization, racism, and sexism, which is articulated from out of the experience of exploitation, destitution, alienation and reification, in the name of the projects of liberation, autonomy and authenticity."[47] In a strict sense, it emerged in Argentina in the 1960s and then spread to the rest of Latin America in 1975 during the "Philosophy Encounter" in Morelia, Mexico, where Enrique Dussel and Arturo Andrés Roig presented two groundbreaking papers. It should be noted that from the outset, the philosophy of liberation has featured diverse scholarly approaches.[48] However, on a global scale, Dussel is mostly responsible for bringing about its development and fruition. Hence, it is to his philosophy that we will be referring to in this section—specifically to his concept of transmodernity in relation to the ethics of immigration.

In *Ethics of Liberation*, Dussel develops the following three ethical imperatives: the material, formal, and feasibility principles. The material principle refers to "the obligation to produce, reproduce and develop the concrete human life of each ethical subject in community."[49] Here, Dussel argues that to *have human life* is one of the fundamentals of ethics, for without life no ethics would be needed. Indeed, no ethical system can feasibly advocate for the elimination of life, as that would be self-destroying. A second key element of this principle pertains to the ethical subject in the community. Its importance resides in the idea that a person is a member of the community insofar as the actions of that community affect him or her, *regardless of whether they legally belong to it.*

The formal principle serves as the procedural mediation of the material ethical principle, and, as Dussel explains, "it is a universal standard to 'apply' the content (with practical truth or as a mediation for the production, reproduction and development of human life of each ethical subject) of the normative statement."[50] This is to say that since community members are alive, they need to agree on the norms that are necessary to protect human life through symmetrical participation. This "intersubjective consensus" gives validity to the norms upon which they agree.

Finally, the feasibility principle "determines the scope of what can be done [. . .] within the horizon of (a) of what is ethically permitted [and] (b) to what must necessarily be operated."[51] In other words, an ethical community must always strive toward higher ethical behavior, while simultaneously acknowledging that certain norms cannot be met. For example, a flawless legal system is impossible to attain as humans are imperfect beings, but an ethical community still can use this ideal to lead its actions.

It should be pointed out that these principles are not ordered hierarchically. They are unified, and for an act to be ethical, it must meet all three. The lives of the members of the ethical community must be protected by the norms they have agreed on within the limits of feasibility. If community members are alive but have no say in the decisions that affect them, their lives lack in dignity. Furthermore, it is likely that in time, their material conditions will deteriorate to the point where their very lives are threatened. Also, when making decisions, community members must consider the feasibility of their project; failing to do so may amount to endangering people's lives. It is also important to recognize that feasibility changes over time; what may seem impossible now may be attainable in other times and circumstances. Lastly, these principles reach their full potential when the critical dimension is added. This is to say that we should apply them with the well-being of all in mind but give preference to the victims of the system (particularly the most vulnerable among them). Indeed, victims are usually both hidden by the system and existing outside of it. However, as Aníbal Quijano points out, they are, in fact, constitutive of the system.[52]

With this background in mind, let us now turn to Dussel's project of transmodernity, which we apply to the ethics of immigration. Based on the system of ethics we just delineated, Dussel's transmodernist project confirms the need for "the essential components of modernity's own excluded cultures in order to develop a new civilization for the twenty-first century."[53] Unlike modernity and its false neutrality, and postmodernity and its neutralizing relativism, Dussel proposes a system in which the *locus enuntiationis* (place of enunciation) is not only acknowledged but also plays a vital role. This is because to talk, or think, from the perspective of conquered people is not equivalent to speaking from a position of privilege. Once these differences are recognized and the voice of the Other is heard, we are ready to have a meaningful dialogue in favor of life, especially human life. In Linda Alcoff's words, "Modernity must be transcended by a retelling of its history, which will reincorporate the other who it has abolished to the periphery and downgraded epistemologically and politically."[54] This proposal is still being developed, but it is clear that a future transmodern culture will "have a rich diversity and will be the fruit of a genuine intercultural dialogue, which must clearly take into account existing asymmetries."[55]

While Dussel's philosophy of liberation has not directly reflected on immigration (for more on this, see Amos Nascimento's and Margaret Griesse's co-authored contribution to this volume), it is clear that his theoretical categories could be of great use for a Latin American immigration ethics. For instance, the ethical duty to respond to the Other, and to try to think from the Other's perspective, compels us to learn how respond to the needs of the migrants in an open, inclusive manner. This inclusion does not mean to immerse migrants completely in the predominant culture of the receiving country but, rather, to respect and value their diversity. For Dussel, it is that very diversity that leads to growth and the revealing of truth. The transmodern project—which seems to support, in many respects, an open borders position, does not advocate for the complete elimination of borders. Rather, it calls for an ethical immigration system that is open to Otherness. Such an immigration system would protect the lives of immigrants through norms agreed upon by the ethical community—which, once again, includes immigrants—within the limits of what is feasible.

Recent developments in Bolivian politics offer us an important example of a Dusselian approach to immigration ethics. During the presidential terms of Evo Morales, Bolivia was conceived of as a plurinational state, meaning that unlike the colonial notion of "one people, one nation" that tends to obliterate pre-Columbian civilizations, Bolivia's constitution acknowledges their existence and recognizes them as equal nations within the Bolivian state. This can be understood in terms of an openness to the Other, as Bolivia (as well as other nations such as Ecuador under Rafael Correa's administration) took clear steps to create an inclusive Latin America where nature, Indigenous people, and mestizos would interact in a way that promotes life, especially the lives of the usually excluded.[56] This openness to the Other, in turn, extends to other countries, as they establish relationships based on solidarity and collaboration, which facilitates the achievement of *buen vivir*. This spirit of collaboration against poverty and exclusion was shared by the signatory countries of the Bolivarian Alliance for the Peoples of Our America—People's Trade Treaty (*Alianza Bolivariana para los Pueblos de Nuestra América—Tratado de Comercio de los Pueblos*, ALBA—TCP) signed in 2004 by so-called progressive governments. In a transmodern spirit, this treaty is based on principles of collaboration and mutual assistance aimed at eradicating economic and social inequities in search of the common good. Clearly, this idea is opposed to economic liberalism's conception of human beings as competitors and nation-states as divided by an us-them logic, in which nations are obligated to protect their borders from strangers. A widespread tradition of accepting political exiles in Latin America, as explored in this chapter, is also evidence of a Dusselian, transmodernist approach to immigration ethics based on openness to the needs and experiences of Others on the global periphery.

III. Conclusion

Our aim in this chapter has been to show that there is, indeed, a distinctive Latin American immigration ethics that philosophers, empirical scholars, and policy makers working on immigration issues can learn from and engage. Latin American and Latinx scholars have produced important works on the normative dimensions of exile, the unique experiences of oppression and resistance of Latin American migrants and their descendants in the United States, and the idea of "transmodernity," which, we have argued, can be used to support a new system of immigration ethics. We have proposed that Latin American immigration ethics often responds to the particular histories of immigration/migration within and outside of Latin America, and to the ideas and conceptual frameworks generated by Latin American philosophers. Engaging this work can shift the course of our academic and policy-oriented discussions about migration by drawing attention to patterns and streams of migration that have gone underexplored, as well as the relevant strategies and proposals of Latin American scholars and migrants themselves.

Notes

1. For a helpful overview of this literature, see Sarah Fine, "The Ethics of Immigration: Self-Determination and the Right to Exclude," *Philosophy Compass* 8, no. 3 (March 2013): 254–68.
2. In his conception of Center and Periphery countries, Raúl Prebish argues that while countries of the Center have fully retained the benefits of the technical progress of their industry, countries of the Periphery have transferred a part of the fruit their own technical progress to the Center; this has caused increasing economic and technological inequalities between the two poles. See "El Desarrollo económico de América Latina y algunos de sus principales problemas," in

La teoría social Latinoamericana: Textos escogidos, ed. Rui Mauro Marini, vol. 1 (Mexico City: UNAM, 1994), 238.

3. Enrique Dussel, *1492: El encubrimiento del Otro* (La Paz: Plural editores, Facultad de Humanidades y Ciencias de la educación–UMSA, 1994).
4. See Stephanie Wood, *Transcending Conquest: Nahua Views of Spanish Colonial Mexico* (Norman: University of Oklahoma Press, 2003) and María Lugones, "Heterosexualism and the Colonial/Modern Gender System," *Hypatia* 22, no. 1 (Winter 2007): 186–219.
5. Adela Pellegrino, "La migración internacional en América Latina y el Caribe: Tendencias y perfiles de los migrantes," *Serie Población y Desarrollo* 35 (March 2003): 11.
6. Enrique de Gandia, "Sarmiento y su teoria de 'Civilizacion y Barbarie,'" *Journal of Inter-American Studies* 4, no. 1 (January 1962): 70. [que los negros y los indios eran elementos de atraso en la marcha de la civilización y se preguntaba si no había sido un error, durante la colonia, incorporar los indígenas a la vida de los españoles.]
7. Carmen Norambuena, "La inmigración en el pensamiento de la intelectualidad Chilena 1810–1910," *Contribuciones Científicas y Tecnológicas* 109 (1995): 73–83.
8. Carlos Beorlegui, *Historia del pensamiento filosófico Latinoamericano: Una búsqueda incesante de la identidad*, 3rd ed. (Bilbao: Universidad de Deusto, 2010).
9. Pellegrino, "Migración internacional," 11.
10. Pellegrino, 15.
11. Jorge Martínez and Daniela Vono, "Geografía migratoria intrarregional de América Latina y el Craibe al comienzo del siglo XXI," *Revista de Geografía Norte Grande* 34 (2005): 39–52.
12. Martínez and Vono, "Geografía," 47.
13. Stephen Castles, Hein de Hass, and Mark J. Miller, *The Age of Migration: International Population Movements in the Modern World* (New York: Guilford Press, 2014), 129.
14. Reinhard Lohrmann, "Irregular Migration: A Rising Issue in Developing Countries," *International Migration* 25, no. 3 (September 1987): 258.
15. Alicia Maguid, "The Importance of Systematizing Migration Information for Making Policy: Recent Initiatives and Possibilities for Latin America and the Caribbean," *OIM Sobre Migración Latinoamericana* 11, no. 3 (1993): 5–67.
16. See Mae Ngai, *Impossible Subjects: Illegal Aliens and the Making of Modern America* (Princeton, N.J.: Princeton University Press, 2004), 26.
17. Sara Castro-Klarén, "Framing Pan-Americanism: Simón Bolívar's Findings," *CR: The New Centennial Review* 3, no. 1 (Spring 2003): 32.
18. Ana Margheritis, "Mercosur's Post-Neoliberal Approach to Migration: From Workers' Mobility to Regional Citizenship," in *A Liberal Tide? Immigration and Asylum Law and Policy in Latin America*, ed. David James Cantor, Luisa Feline

Freier, and Jean-Pierre Gauci (London: School of Advanced Study, University of London, 2015), 57.

19. Mario Sznajder and Luis Roniger, "Political Exile in Latin America," *Latin American Perspectives* 34, no. 4 (July 2007): 7.

20. Sznajder and Roniger, "Political Exile," 25n2.

21. Here, we follow the analysis of Pereda's arguments offered in Amy Reed-Sandoval, "Immigrant or Exiled? Reconceiving the Displazada/os of Latin American and Latino Philosophy," *APA Newsletter on Hispanic/Latino Issues in Philosophy*, 15, no. 2 (Spring 2016): 11–14.

22. Carlos Pereda, *Lessons in Exile*, trans. Sean Manning (Leiden: Brill Rodopi, 2019), 40. See also Carlos Pereda, *Los aprendizajes del exilio* (Mexico City: Siglo XXI Editores, 2008).

23. Silvana Rabinovich, "'Exilio domiciliario': Avatares de un destierro diferente," *Athenea Digital* 15, no. 4 (December 2015): 339. See also Silvana Rabinovich, "Al Ándalus en el exilio: Andanzas de morriscos y maranos," in *Mímesis e invisibilización social: Interdividualidad colectiva en América Latina*, ed. Carlos Mendoza Álvarez, José Luís Jobim, and Mariana Méndez-Gallardo (Mexico City: Universidad Iberoamericana, 2017).

24. Silvana Rabinovich, "De exilios y pandemia: Cavilaciones heterónomas," presented May 29, 2020 (online), to the Instituto de Investigationes Filosóficas, Universidad Autónoma de México. Accessible at https://www.youtube.com/watch?v=OcV2E4uU-WE.

25. An exception to this can be found in the work of Hannah Arendt.

26. José Jorge Mendoza, "Latinx Philosophy and the Ethics of Migration," in *Latin American and Latinx Philosophy: A Collaborative Introduction*, ed. Robert Eli Sanchez Jr. (New York: Routledge, 2020), 199.

27. Anzaldúa's work has been critiqued by some feminist scholars working in Mexico on the grounds that it neglects the experiences of immigration enforcement south of the border and particularly in Mexico. See, for instance, Debra A. Castillo, *Border Women: Writing from La Frontera* (Minneapolis: University of Minnesota Press, 2002).

28. Gloria Anzaldúa, *Borderlands/La Frontera: The New Mestiza* (San Francisco,: Aunt Lute Books, 1987), 3.

29. Grant Silva, "On the Militarization of Borders and the Juridical Right to Exclude," *Public Affairs Quarterly* 29, no. 2 (April 2015): 223.

30. Ernesto Rosen Velásquez, "States of Violence and the Right to Exclude," *Journal of Poverty* 21, no. 4 (2017): 311. For additional analysis of ways in which immigration enforcement has undermined U.S. Latina/o/xs in particular, see Eduardo Mendieta, "The U.S. Border and the Political Ontology of 'Assassination Nation': Thanatological Dispositifs," *Journal of Speculative Philosophy* 31, no. 1 (2017): 82–100, and José Jorge Mendoza, "Doing Away with Juan Crow: Two Standards for Just Immigration Reform," *APA Newsletter on Hispanic/Latino Issues in Philosophy* 15 no. 1 (Fall 2015): 14–20.

31. We borrow the term "visible Latina/o/x identity" from Linda Martín Alcoff. See also Amy Reed-Sandoval, *Socially Undocumented: Identity and Immigration Justice* (New York: Oxford University Press, 2020).

32. Carlos Alberto Sanchez, "'Illegal' Immigrants: Law, Fantasy, and Guts," *Philosophy in the Contemporary World* 21, no. 1 (Spring 2014): 4.

33. Joseph Carens, *The Ethics of Immigration* (New York: Oxford University Press, 2013), 11.

34. Here, we follow closely José Jorge Mendoza's overview of Latinx contributions to the open borders debate, in "Latinx Philosophy and the Ethics of Immigration," in *Latin American and Latinx Philosophy: A Collaborative Introduction*, ed. Robert Eli Sanchez (New York, Routledge, 2019), 198–219.

35. See Jorge Valadez, "Immigration, Self-Determination, and Global Justice: Towards a Holistic Normative Theory of Migration," *Journal of International Political Theory* 8, nos. 1/2 (April 2012): 135–46.

36. See José-Antonio Orosco, *Toppling the Melting Pot: Immigration and Multiculturalism in American Pragmatism* (Bloomington: Indiana University Press, 2016).

37. Natalie Cisneros, "'Alien' Sexuality: Race, Maternity, and Citizenship," *Hypatia*, 28, no. 2 (Spring 2013): 209–306.

38. Mariana Ortega, *In-Between: Latina Feminist Phenomenology, Multiplicity, and the Self* (Albany: SUNY Press, 2006), 3.

39. María Lugones, "Playfulness, 'World'-Travelling, and Loving Perception," *Hypatia* 2, no. 2 (Summer 1987): 3.

40. Lugones, "Playfulness," 17.

41. Ortega, *In-Between*, 194.

42. Ortega, 202.

43. Stephanie Rivera Berruz, "Latin American and Latinx Feminisms," in Sanchez Jr., *Latin American and Latinx Philosophy*, 175.

44. Cynthia M. Paccacercua et al., "In the Flesh and Word: Latina Feminist Philosophers' Collective Labor," *Hypatia* 31, no. 2 (Spring 2016): 437–46.

45. Note, however, that not all U.S. Latina/o/xs are, in fact, migrants. Still, the work of Latinx philosophy is relevant, as they are often treated as such in the United States and elsewhere.

46. Javier Sanjinés, "The Nation: An Imagined Community?" in *Globalization and the Decolonial Option*, ed. Walter Mignolo and Arturo Escobar (London: Routledge, 2010), 153.

47. S.v. "Philosophy of Liberation," in *Stanford Encyclopedia of Philosophy*, by Eduardo Mendieta, January 28, 2016, https://plato.stanford.edu/entries/liberation/.

48. For more on this topic, see Horacio Cerutti Guldberg, *Filosofía de la liberación Latinoamericana*, 2nd ed. (Mexico City: Fondo de Cultura Económica, 1992).

49. Enrique Dussel, *Ética de la liberación en la edad de la globalización y de la exclusión* (Madrid: Trota, 1998). [el principio de la obligación de producir, reproducir y desarrollar la vida humana concreta de cada sujeto ético en comunidad. Este principio tiene pretensión de universalidad.]

50. Dussel, *Ética*, 215. [es la mediaci'ón formal o procedimental del principio ético material. Se trata de una norma universal para «aplicar» el contenido (con verdad practica) como mediación para la producción, reproducción y desarrollo de la vida humana de cada sujeto ético del enunciado normativo.]

51. Dussel, 268. [determina al ámbito de lo que puede-hacerse dentro del horizonte a) de lo que esta éticamente permitido-hacerse, b) hasta lo que necesariamente debe-operarse.]

52. Aníbal Quijano, *Aníbal Quijano: Ensayos en torno a la colonialidad del poder* (n.p.: Ediciones del Siglo, 2019); also see Walter Mignolo, *The Darker Side of Western Modernity* (Durham, N.C.: Duke University Press, 2011).

53. Enrique Dussel, "World-System and 'Trans'-Modernity," trans. Alessandro Fornazzari, *Nepantla: Views from South* 3, no. 2 (2002): 224.

54. Linda Martín Alcoff, "Enrique Dussel's Transmodernism," *TRANSMODERNITY: Journal of Peripheral Cultural Production of the Luso-Hispanic World* 1, no. 3 (2012): 63.

55. Enrique Dussel, "Transmodernidad e interculturalidad: Interpretación desde la filosofía de la liberación," *Erasmus: Revista para el Diálogo Intercultural* 5, nos. 1–2 (2003): 65. [tendrá una pluriversidad rica y será fruto de un auténtico diálogo intercultural, que debe tomar claramente en cuenta las asimetrías existentes.]

56. The creation and development of Bolivia's and Ecuador's constitutions was a highly complicated process, not exempt from difficulties and contradictions. For more on this topic, see Boaventura de Sousa Santos, *Refundación del estado en América Latina: Perspectivas desde una epistemología del Sur* (Mexico City: Siglo XXI Editores, 2010).

CHAPTER 2

Decolonizing Immigration Justice

JOSÉ JORGE MENDOZA

Introduction

In perhaps one of the strangest ironies of history, many of today's settler colonial states have come to regard immigration as a problem. As a reminder, these are states (e.g., the United States, Canada, Australia, and Israel) in which most citizens trace their lineage to immigrant ancestors rather than to an Indigenous community. For decades, there has been much heated debate about how best to stem undocumented immigration and reform immigration policies. The proposals that appear to have the highest chances of success, even in today's exceedingly nativist climate, are those that in some way offer an eclectic mix of stricter enforcement, increased distribution of visas (especially for skilled workers), and a pathway toward legalization for undocumented immigrants who can be said to be either blameless or contrite about their irregular status. Individually, each of these components represents one of the three dominant approaches to immigration justice: reactionary, free market, and liberal egalitarian.

Often missing in public debates about immigration policy is the radical perspective. By radical I do not mean "extreme;" rather, I use the term in the classic sense, which means to get at the root of the problem instead of only attending to its symptoms. In recent years, the radical methodology has been able to carve out a space for itself within academic and activist circles by directly confronting the reactionary approach and exposing the theoretical shortcomings of both the free-market and liberal-egalitarian positions. However, as essential as the radical perspective is to achieving immigration justice, its current manifestations display some serious Eurocentric shortcomings.

With this in mind, this chapter sets out to accomplish three tasks. First, it provides a general survey of the three dominant approaches to immigration justice and exposes the deficiencies inherent to them that make a radical approach necessary. Second, it gives an overview of the radical position and highlights three of its strengths. Third, the chapter points out the ways in which the radical approach has failed to foreground relationships of coloniality. These, following Ramón Grosfoguel, are "an entanglement . . . of multiple and heterogeneous global hierarchies ('heterarchies') of sexual, political, epistemic, economic, spiritual, linguistic and racial forms of domination and exploitation where the racial/ethnic hierarchy of the European/non-European divide transversally reconfigures all of the other global power structures."[1] The failure to take coloniality into account has made most radical approaches to immigration justice too Eurocentric to live up to their liberatory potential. I therefore end the chapter by suggesting some pathways toward a decolonial approach to immigration justice.

I. The Three Dominant Approaches to Immigration Justice

A. Enforcement First: A Reactionary Approach

Perhaps no slogan better encapsulates the feeling and attitude of today's anti-immigrant movement than "enforcement first." Supporters of the reactionary approach have come to believe that too much (and some would say *any*) immigration is detrimental to the nation and should be limited, if not altogether brought to a halt.[2] On this view, undocumented migrants are the primary perpetrators of immigration injustice. Proponents of this view suggest that, by their own actions, immigrants have shown that they do not respect the laws of the nation they are asking to join. When faced with such a situation, especially in a post-9/11 world, it is not unreasonable for states to do what they can to enforce their laws and protect their people. Whatever harm befalls immigrants as a result of such enforcement cannot properly be said to be the fault of the state but will be something immigrants have done to themselves. As Oxford professor David Miller has argued, enforcement measures—such as "prevention-through-deterrence"—might initially appear extreme based on their consequences (e.g., thousands of dead migrants in the Sonoran Desert or the Mediterranean Sea). But as Miller is quick to point out, these tactics are preventative (i.e., defensive) and not coercive (i.e., offensive) and as such are not necessarily immoral or unjust.[3]

Based on such an account of immigration justice, a state would be responsible for the "immigration problem" to the extent that it is unwilling or unable to enforce its immigration policy.[4] Hence, immigration justice cannot begin by requiring states to reform their current immigration policy but must start with states first demonstrating that they can enforce the laws already on the books; concurrently, noncitizen migrants must display a willingness to obey these laws. The solution to the immigration problem from this point of view is therefore as simple as its slogan: enforcement first.

It does not require a whole lot of effort to find fault with this approach. For starters, receiving countries like the United States have been vigorously enforcing immigration law for decades and doing so in an exponentially expanding fashion. The problem with the "enforcement first" strategy, as pointed out by many migration scholars, is that it reaches a point of diminishing returns rather quickly. For example, in 1993—the year before the prevention through deterrence strategy went into effect in the United States—the budget for U.S. border enforcement was close to 1.5 billion dollars, and there were around four thousand immigration agents in total.[5] In 2020 the requested budget for border enforcement was over 28 billion dollars, and the number of immigration agents had topped twenty thousand.[6] This is close to a 2000 percent increase in funding and a fivefold increase in personnel. At the same time, before this dramatic ramp-up in enforcement, the estimated number of undocumented immigrants living in the United States was believed to be about 3.5 million. In 2020—so twenty-seven years into the "enforcement first" policy—the same population was estimated to be between ten and twelve million, a 300–400 percent increase.[7] By any measure one takes, be it humanitarian, economic, or effectiveness, the "enforcement first" strategy has proven itself to be an absolute failure.

This suggests that, to the extent that there is an immigration problem, states cannot and should not simply try to enforce their way out of it. To be fair, there is a tiny kernel of truth to the "enforcement first" position. Immigration justice should not bracket or ignore the issue of enforcement. However, we need to be concerned morally with the methods states use to forcibly keep out or remove individuals, separate children from their parents, or imprison civilians for no other reason than the fact that someone was born on the wrong side of an arbitrary line or to the wrong set of parents. This is why the opening line to Joseph Carens's now-classic essay on open borders is so compelling (and so often cited). Carens poignantly reminds his readers that "borders have guards and the guards have guns."[8] He concludes that borders should be open, giving three arguments in support of that conclusion. These can be boiled down to the other two approaches to immigration justice, one of which is a combination of the libertarian and utilitarian arguments put forth in Carens's essay. This approach to immigration justice holds that markets, not governments, ought to determine immigration flows. The other position is essentially a call for extending the Rawlsian argument, specifically its difference principle, to the global level and allowing a concern for equality and fairness to guide our immigration policy. In the next two subsections, we look at these alternatives to the reactionary approach.

B. Market-Based Borders: A Free-Market Approach

In places like the United States, not all political conservatives are primarily motivated to preserve tradition. Instead, some of them are more interested in promoting a free-market ideology premised on two core liberal and specifically libertarian commitments:

1. The primacy of liberty for the individual (especially respect for their private property).
2. The belief that open and free markets are the best (and fairest) way to distribute the goods of the world.

With respect to the issue of immigration, these commitments tend to put free-market conservatives at odds with reactionary conservatives, as the former see restrictions on immigration as fundamentally opposed to their core ideals. In denying freedom of movement, immigration restrictions unjustly infringe on the liberty of individuals. They also unfairly protect co-nationals from open competition in the global labor market, thereby distorting the ability of the market to distribute the goods of the world as effectively and efficiently (i.e., as fairly) as possible.

Free-market conservatives are also quick to point out that migrant flows are largely determined by economic forces, not a lack of enforcement. For this reason, it is not the intransigence of immigrants that is to blame for the current "immigration problem" but the obstinate determination of states to enforce bad, or perhaps even any, immigration exclusions. On this view, immigration policy should be left for the market to decide and not the government.[9]

Theoretically, there might be a lot to like about this position. The problem, however, is that real life is always messier than abstract economic models. We do not live in a historical vacuum, and our world is deeply sedimented with layers upon layers of unjust historical relationships that continue to affect the present. Market-based policies are not immune to these realities and for this reason have tended (even if unintentionally) to create or perpetuate conditions that push people out of their homes and pull them across international boundaries. This suggests that a free-market approach may be more the source of the immigration problem rather than a response to it.

For example, using the North American Free Trade Agreement (NAFTA) as a case study, David Bacon has done a masterful job of showing how free-market policies have caused more displacement than accommodated voluntary movement.[10] In his follow-up work, Bacon has suggested that perhaps the best way to respect the liberty of individuals and to more fairly distribute the goods of the world would be to foster conditions where people not only have a right to leave but also, more importantly, gain the right to stay home.[11]

C. Equitable Borders: A Liberal-Egalitarian Approach

Much of the recent philosophical literature on the ethics of migration has been dominated by what we might call liberal egalitarianism. This approach tends to conclude that borders should be more open than they currently are, but not necessarily for the sake of economic gains or as a result of a fundamental distrust of government. Liberal egalitarians arrive at their "equitable borders" position by arguing that there are specific kinds of noncitizens who have a moral claim to admission. Unlike the free-market approach, the liberal-egalitarian position starts by recognizing that the issue of immigration puts two core liberal commitments into conflict: the right to democratic self-determination of political communities versus the equal consideration (i.e., dignity) owed to all individuals. We can call this the political tension of liberalism, which according to Michael Blake exposes a kind of theoretical blind spot that can leave one with the impression that "the conventional methodology of liberalism [might be] quite inappropriate for use when the question is not one affecting the rights of members, but the composition of membership itself."[12] The liberal-egalitarian approach to immigration justice is therefore unique in that it looks at immigration not as just another applied issue but as potentially exposing the moral limits of political liberalism. In other words, this approach is perhaps as much about evaluating and developing a just immigration policy as it is about repairing or supplementing liberalism.

The literature in this vein is vast and can roughly be divided between those who take an ideal theory perspective and those who take a nonideal position.[13] Philosophers in favor of the former believe that a noncitizen's moral claim to admission is triggered when their human rights are being either violated or cannot properly be respected in their country of origin. When this occurs, not only do noncitizens have a right to exit (which nearly everyone is always assumed to have) but this also generates duties for other countries to admit them.[14] For theorists such as Michael Blake and David Miller, this approach makes an issue like immigration, which initially might have appeared to a poor fit with political liberalism, more palatable to the tradition. Following the liberalism of John Rawls, they believe that the question of immigration justice is ultimately one about fairness, such that "it searches for norms of fairness to set the terms on which immigrant groups and host societies interact without regard to the particular circumstances of any individual immigrant or category of immigrants."[15]

There are other liberal egalitarians, however, who think that one cannot properly address the question of immigration justice without taking into consideration the particular circumstances under which immigration is taking place. These theorists tend to take a nonideal approach. For example, Shelley Wilcox has pointed out that in reality, few international borders are totally open or totally closed, and the demand for entry into affluent societies by those who have a just claim to be admitted is often greater than the number of spots available. When framed in this way, the question to consider is not which immigrants deserve admission but which of the deserving immigrants ought to receive priority when not all can be admitted.[16]

As a way of resolving this issue, Wilcox suggests that the discretion states have over immigration decisions should be circumscribed by what she calls the Global Harm Principle (GHP). This principle states that "societies should not harm foreigners; and societies that violate this duty must: (1) stop harming these foreigners immediately; and (2) compensate their victims for the harm they have already caused them."[17] The strength of this principle, according to Wilcox, is that it is not parasitic either on the freedom-of-movement or property rights arguments that, as we saw above, have been deployed by proponents of the free-market approach. Instead, it is a claim for redress—for harm that is being or has been done—that morally prioritizes noncitizens for admission.

In *Immigration Justice*, Peter Higgins makes a similar argument focusing on the nonideal nature of the immigration issue. The difference, however, is that Higgins does not just focus on the harm that restrictions have on would-be-immigrants; instead, he also takes into consideration the potential harm immigration admissions can have on nonmigrating residents of sending countries. In particular, Higgins is concerned with issues such as "brain drain," or the flight of human capital from the Global South to the Global North via admissions policies that encourage or recruit professionals to migrate. He writes, "The emigration of skilled, college educated, middle-class professionals in large numbers from relatively poor countries harms those who remain in several ways, but, in the most general sense, it does so by undermining prospects for human development . . . [and these harms] would surely be magnified in the absence of restrictions on immigration."[18] Indeed, the loss of professionals would (and does) disproportionally harm those who are already the most unjustly disadvantaged and least well off globally. Thus, while Higgins supports limiting a state's ability to exclude noncitizens, he argues that there should be limits on the discretion states have to *admit* any noncitizen they wish. For example, an immigration policy that grants admission to wealthy and skilled foreigners but denies it to poor and unskilled foreigners could potentially allow for more immigration, but this policy would be less just than one that admits fewer immigrants but focuses on the needs of the globally poor and unskilled.[19]

As a way of summarizing this approach, we should note that none of these are necessarily open borders positions, even though they would entail significantly more open borders than currently exist. They are also arguments that arise from, work within, and attempt to rehabilitate political liberalism. Unlike free-market conservatives (who in their own way are also part of the liberal family), the liberal-egalitarian approach has the advantage of recognizing that we start from a world that is inherently unjust. Because of, or in light of, these injustices, liberal egalitarians propose that we should design immigration policies such that they either work to rectify or at least do not further exacerbate or create new immigration-based injustices.

II. No Borders: A Radical Approach

Unlike the liberal-egalitarian approach, a radical approach to immigration justice neither confines itself within nor seeks to repair or supplement political liberalism. In fact, this position largely assumes political liberalism to be a kind of ruling-class ideology that deploys humanistic language to evade or even justify existing forms of oppression. Instead, the radical approach seeks to put forth an alternative political vision and makes use of issues such as immigration to draw attention to the limits and failures of political liberalism. In this section, I outline three ways in which radicals have criticized the liberal-egalitarian approach and have tried to offer an alternative vision of immigration justice.

A. Failures of the "Conventional View"

The first criticism leveled by radicals against the liberal-egalitarian approach is its overreliance on the "conventional view," a theoretical starting point that assumes, largely for the sake of argument, that states have a presumptive right to control immigration. This assumption, however, works under a strict set of conditions. First, the political community in question is understood to be a "legitimate" state. In other words, it is an autonomous and democratically self-determined nation-state that respects and is compliant with human rights norms. Second, it tends to deal with immigration as an exceptional case, performed voluntarily by discrete individuals (i.e., nonrefugees).

The strength of adopting such a view, as Joseph Carens has pointed out, is that it makes it difficult to assail whatever rights for immigrants are derived under such unfavorable starting conditions and concessions.[20] The problem, however, is that real-world states do not come close to meeting philosophers' strict standard for legitimacy. For example, most existing states—and especially those that currently see themselves as experiencing an "immigration problem"—were initially established through violence and conquest, not through a process resembling public reason. Tactics such as gerrymandering and voter suppression continue to plague most democracies, to the point that it is sometimes a stretch to say that governments truly reflect the will of their people. Along with these issues, it is also the case that most states have dismal human rights records. So even if adopting the conventional view can sometimes prove helpful for strategic reasons, it is unclear how well those conclusions will translate when the entities in question are less-than-legitimate states and when actual justifications for exclusion are based more on security concerns than on a polity's legitimacy.

A related problem is that the conventional view works within the framework of methodological nationalism. As Alex Sager has noted, "Methodological nationalists imagine the world as a set of homogenous societies bounded by impermeable national borders. Mobility within state territories is mostly unremarked, whereas mobility across international borders is seen as pathological."[21] According to Sager, the conventional view adopts four general characteristics of methodological nationalism that make its recommendations suspect. The first assumes that people are generally sedentary, which is not necessarily the case. Drawing from the work of Thomas Nail, Sager believes that a more accurate view of the world is to see it as composed of regimes of motion. As Nail puts it, this would be a view in which "societies are always in motion: directing people and objects, reproducing their social conditions (periodicity), and striving to expand their territorial, political, juridical, and economic power through diverse forms of expulsion."[22] When we start to think of the world in this way, we see that it actually better reflects our reality, in which hundreds of millions of people move across international boundaries every year and millions more migrate (and commute) within national boundaries.

A second methodological nationalist assumption is the idea that sovereignty is unified and exists (or only matters) at the state level. This view of sovereignty has been dominant in Western political philosophy since at least the work of Thomas Hobbes, but it can also be found in more contemporary political philosophy. While there are some contemporary theorists, such as Thomas Pogge, who have suggested that we put more emphasis on the various levels of sovereignty that exist both above and below the nation-state, the conventional view continues to assume that the level of sovereignty that matters for questions of immigration is the one that takes place at the nation-state level. This ignores both the power of international treaties and the ability of local cities to erect sanctuary programs and offer migrants protection.

A third methodological nationalist assumption is the idea that the borders of a state are fixed and immutable. There are two problems with this postulation. The first is that borders are constantly being remade and contested. Just as an example, in the nineteenth century alone, the territorial borders of the United States underwent five separate and significant alterations. These resulted from the Louisiana Purchase of 1803, the purchase of Florida from Spain in 1819, the extraction of territory from Mexico as a prize of war in 1848, the purchase of Alaska from Russia in 1867, and the annexation of Puerto Rico and Hawai'i in 1898. Consistent with the idea of seeing the world as composed of regimes of motion, territorial borders should also be best thought of as constantly in flux, always in contention, and never permanently fixed.

But even during times when territorial borders appear to be stable, they nonetheless expand internally and externally. For example, the U.S. Border Patrol can and does extend its operations up to one hundred miles into the U.S. interior, which is an area where nearly two-thirds of Americans live. Externally, the United States now helps to patrol the border between Mexico and Guatemala, as well as Guatemala's border with Honduras and El Salvador. As Gen. John Kelly once put it, "border security cannot be attempted as an endless series of 'goal line stands' on the one-foot line at the ports of entry or along the thousands of miles of border between this country and Mexico . . . I believe the defense of the Southwest border starts 1,500 miles to the south, with Peru."[23]

The fourth methodological nationalist assumption is the idea that political membership involves exclusive membership in one state and to a society that is culturally and ethnically homogenous. As Sager points out, "This [assumption] ignores dual citizenship, transnational families and communities, sub-state political communities (which in some cases enjoy substantial autonomy), long-term permanent residents without citizenship, temporary residents, as well as people who for a variety of reasons lack the legal status to remain on the territory."[24] It also presupposes that assimilation into the dominant national culture is or should be the desired outcome for any and all cultural and ethnic minorities. This view of membership can and does lead to a kind of civic ostracism that Ronald Sundstrom and David Kim have described as "a subjective belief or affect . . . that some other person or group cannot be a part of that nation. These strangers cannot be authentic participants of the . . . traditions of the nation they inhabit; they do not derive from soil of the nation's land or the blood of its people."[25]

In summary, liberal egalitarians tend to accept the conventional view holding that states have a presumptive right to control immigration. This opinion, however, is premised on conditions that cannot be met in the real world. It assumes that states are the primary sources of sovereignty and are sufficiently legitimate. It further supposes that the borders of states are fixed and that the people living within them are homogenous and by default sedentary. The radical approach rejects each of these assumptions and instead begins with the idea that nation-states are a historical aberration. They therefore propose an alternative starting point, one that sees the world as composed of regimes of motion.

B. Overlooking the Social Tension

A second concern raised by radicals is the tendency of liberal egalitarians to focus too much on the political tension and thereby miss, avoid, or be complicit in what they term the "social tension," which arises when immigration is considered a threat to social cohesion or trust (e.g., national identity) and the response to this perceived threat (e.g., harsher immigration enforcement) turns out to produce as much, if not more, social tension or mistrust. To get at the heart of this tension and expose the white supremacy, sexism, classism, and ableism that undergird it, radical philosophers argue that we need to engage with and deconstruct repugnant terminology such as "illegal" and "anchor baby." Yet, most liberal egalitarians are uncomfortable doing this and assume that, since these forms of oppression and discrimination are already too far beyond the pale of justice, this kind of work does not need to be carried out.

For this reason, when liberal-egalitarian philosophers discuss the issue of undocumented immigration, they seek to avoid what they, not incorrectly, consider to be loaded terms and instead adopt more neutral language such as "irregular" or "unauthorized" migrants. Consistent with a strategy that employs the conventional view, liberal egalitarians concede at the start that any "migrants who deliberately enter or stay in a territory without authorization are (at least prima facie) committing a wrong against the state."[26] From here, most liberal-egalitarian philosophers eventually conclude that, despite this disadvantageous starting point, most undocumented immigrants actually deserve to have their status regularized. This is usually because the undocumented immigrants in question have shown themselves to be law abiding and have either established sufficient roots or lived in the country for a significant length of time.[27]

For proponents of immigrants' rights, there is much to like about this strategy. First and foremost, whatever rights for undocumented immigrants are obtained under such unfavorable starting conditions will be on strong footing. But radical philosophers point out that addressing the question of regularization does not exhaust the issues that surround undocumented immigration. Beyond questions of political inclusion, there is also the social dynamic of designating certain people as "illegal" or "anchor babies," which tends to get overlooked when more neutral terms are substituted in their place.[28] These pernicious terms are only the tip of an insidious iceberg, and by shaving off the tip (i.e., not engaging with terms like "illegal"), nothing is done to address the greater danger lurking beneath. It is therefore important to analyze these terms and expose how, even while appearing to refer only to laws or policies, they convey animus and foster (if not justify) discriminatory attitudes and treatment toward members of already oppressed groups.

The social tension latent within such repugnant terminology finds its best articulation in the social trust argument, which can be articulated in two ways. The first argues that social trust is (or should be) based on a shared race or ethnicity. According to this racist iteration of the argument, immigration dilutes or destabilizes social trust by introducing different races or ethnicities into the political community, which, as we saw in the discussion of methodological nationalism, is assumed to be homogenous. In the late nineteenth and early twentieth century, this version of the social trust argument was often deployed to justify notoriously discriminatory U.S. immigration policies, such as the 1882 Chinese Exclusion Act and the "national origin" quota introduced in 1924.

A second, and superficially neutral, way in which this argument can be articulated is to suggest that social trust is based on shared institutions (e.g., welfare services, social programs, and public education) and a mutual desire for security (e.g., antiterrorism and drug enforcement). According to this second version, a political community must have discretionary control over immigration, not for overtly racist reasons but because immigration threatens these shared institutions and poses a security risk either by undermining the faith people have in institutions, straining institutions beyond their capacity, or by introducing a criminal or terrorist element. Today, U.S. immigration policy officially eschews the earlier racist version of the social trust argument, but since the 1990s, and especially after 9/11, it has often appealed to the second type.

Liberal egalitarians have either taken the social trust argument as a given or have avoided it altogether for its lack of sophistication. Radicals, on the other hand, directly engage it and do so more often than engaging with polit-ical arguments over immigration. They point out that the distinction made between the good and bad version of this position is not as sharp as some of its proponents might want to believe and that repugnant terminology (i.e., the use of terms like "illegal" and "anchor baby") holds the key to showing the continuity between the two. For example, in *Biopolitics of Race*, Sok-than Yeng uses Michel Foucault's notion of "state racism" to show how social groups become "racialized" when they are excluded by a state's immigration policy as unhealthy or otherwise a threat to the life of the nation.

In this account, "postracial" states no longer need to deploy explicitly rac-ist immigration policies to exclude nonwhite immigrants. Instead, policies of exclusion need only appeal to laudable goals, such as the safety and health of the nation, which all states are assumed to be permitted to pursue. These goals, however, serve as cover for the continued exclusion of racial groups the state deems undesirable. The use of repugnant terminology holds the key to unraveling this bait and switch. These terms make no explicit reference to race, ethnicity, national origin, sex, sexual orientation, or even ability, so their deployment appears to be nondiscriminatory. Yet it functions as both a code for people of color and as a way of defining the categories of threatening (i.e., unhealthy) social groups. This, in turn, shows how the apparently race-neutral version of the social trust argument continues to operate as a kind of racial contract argument.[29]

Similarly, Nicholas De Genova, relying on Agamben's notions of bare life and state of exception, has argued that terms like "illegal" and "anchor baby" are deployed to make certain groups more vulnerable and easier to exploit. As with the notion of bare life, which is initially attached only to oppressed minorities, these "exceptional" statuses eventually come to encompass most of society. This exposes the self-defeating nature of the social trust argument. As harsher immigration controls are deployed in response to a perceived threat to social trust, they engender deeper and more pernicious forms of social mistrust as these controls continue to expand and become more diffused within society.[30]

Thomas Nail, inspired by the work of Gilles Deleuze and Félix Guattari, proposes that the way to resolve the paradox of the social trust argument is to adopt a new understanding of membership. Nail argues that we should take the figure of the nomad as the central concept for belonging, calling this position "solidarity without status." He summarizes this view by stating, "Instead of defining political participation and belonging by one's categorical status (place of birth, financial assets, color of one's skin), we should instead define it by how and to what degree one already participates in political life where one is."[31] He suggests that we should "consider the figure of the nomad to be a flexible enough figure such that anyone could find themselves in such an inclusive struggle. Anyone regardless of status, identity, or division can act in nomadic solidarity with anyone else. They do not need to share the same goals, backgrounds, territories, or states; they only need to be able to affirm and believe that their struggles are the same struggle."[32]

In summary, for radicals it is not enough to show that some undocumented immigrants are deserving of having their immigration status regularized. They argue that the social problems run much deeper. Even apparently neutral forms of exclusion will tend to produce an underclass that will be considered inferior or less than fully human, and under a strictly liberal-egalitarian approach, this oppression will either go unrecognized or, if it is acknowledged, will be considered self-inflicted. Radicals further suggest that this should worry all citizens because in many ways immigrants (and especially undocumented immigrants) function as canaries in the nation-state coal mine: that which can be done to immigrants today will eventually extend to citizens tomorrow. In response, radicals recommend forms of solidarity that extend beyond a sense of national belonging.

C. Misunderstanding the Role of Capitalism

Lastly, the liberal-egalitarian approach tends to leave out or downplay the role of capitalism in manufacturing the "immigration problem." Most liberal accounts seem to assume that the immigrants in question are individuals making idiosyncratic choices, when in fact most of these choices are made under economic duress. Working under the assumptions of methodological nationalism, they also fail to account for the role played by third-party

private entities (e.g., transnational corporations) in the creation and perpet-
uation of the "immigration problem." As already mentioned in the section on
market-based borders, capital's incessant need for cheap and easily exploitable labor is a primary driver of much of today's migration. Add to this the
fact that apprehending and detaining migrants has now become a booming
business, and it quickly becomes clear that we cannot talk about immigration
justice without talking about the role played by capital in making movement
across international borders easier for some entities (e.g., multinational corporations and the global elite), more difficult for others (e.g., workers), but
always profitable.

Earlier we saw that some libertarians, specifically those who endorse a
market-based approach to immigration justice, believe that immigration
restrictions create market inefficiencies and are inconsistent with capitalism. What advocates of this position fail to recognize is the way that actually existing capitalism—and not capitalism as is often posited in abstract
economic models—has developed. Border controls are not neutral but are
in fact designed to give large corporations an immense advantage in their
dealings with both labor and their smaller competitors. In today's world
of increased militarized borders, large corporations (unlike workers) have
little trouble moving and relocating anywhere in the world. They set up
shop wherever they find tax, environmental, or labor laws that they like,
and they can also threaten to leave if governments do not change laws to
better meet their interests. This creates a bizarre situation, which Todd
Miller perfectly illustrates when he writes, "Multinational corporations are
doing exactly what nativist groups accuse undocumented people of doing in
the United States: invading, taking over swaths of territory with little local
consultation, and destroying the well-being of local people. And they are
coming through the wide-open gates of what are otherwise heavily policed
borders."[33]

While this might not be the kind of capitalism that advocates of the market-
based approach refer to when they conjure up their world of open borders, it
is the kind of capitalism that we have today. When we accept and begin from
this reality, we find that border policies have never had the maximization of
global GDP or the economic prosperity of everyone as their stated goal. Borders operate in our world to increase the wealth of a select few, irrespective
of their nationality. They exist to maintain a global caste system, not to ensure
the sanctity of the nation-state system.

To a large degree, most liberal egalitarians agree with this criticism of actually existing capitalism. As we saw above, theorists like Wilcox and Higgins accept that it is capital's incessant need for cheap and easily exploitable labor, as well as for the resources of underdeveloped parts of the world, that is the source of today's bad immigration and free-trade policies. But liberal egalitarians are often loath to take the next step and say that we should therefore get rid of capitalism. Instead, they propose reforms based on liberal-egalitarian conceptions of justice. What this approach fails to consider is not just how capitalism exploits the labor and dispossesses the global poor but also how the apprehending and detaining of migrants has become both profitable and a source for possibly millions of jobs globally.

To just give the reader an idea of the growth in the border-enforcement business, consider that at the end of World War II, there were approximately seven militarized borders around the world. By the time the Berlin Wall (the most famous of militarized borders) fell in 1989, there were fifteen. Today there are seventy-seven, and nearly two-thirds of those were erected after 9/11.[34] Recalling what Joseph Carens had to say about borders, keep in mind that all these borders have guards and that all those guards have very expensive weapons. What liberal egalitarians often do not talk about is the fact that these guards have gainful employment precisely because there is a job for them to do, which is to locate, apprehend, detain, and deport undocumented immigrants. And they perform this job for a significantly higher-than-minimum-wage salary. The continuation of actually existing capitalism is dependent on making sure that these sorts of people stay gainfully employed.

Guards also need weapons and the latest technology if they are to perform their jobs. Procuring these goods creates demand for their production, which in turn gainfully employs a further set of people. These weapons and technology are very expensive and therefore very profitable. This creates a further incentive for the actually existing capitalist system to seek the proliferation of militarized borders, not their reduction, and to try to privatize as much of the immigration enforcement process as possible. One does not need to be cynical or subscribe to conspiracy theories to see that there is a strong economic motivation to never actually resolve the "immigration problem."

In short, this is how actually existing capitalism works. It seeks to create needs that can never be fully satisfied because doing so would mean a drop in consumption and a drop in consumption leads to economic crisis. If this economic system is to continue, border enforcement's growth, as both an

employer and a consumer, cannot stop. This is why companies that produce these products and the politicians (and news outlets) either sponsored
or owned by these companies will make sure that whatever immigration
policy is put into effect will maximize employment of border guards, the
consumption of new technologies, and the building and operation of more
detention centers. Solving the "immigration problem" turns out to be bad for
business. In response, radicals propose the overthrow of capitalism and its
replacement with an economic system that puts the interests of people first.

III. No One Is Illegal on Stolen Land: A Decolonial Approach

While radical accounts are important and helpful—especially in their critique of methodological nationalism, capitalism, sedentary biases, and the
dehumanization that comes with systemic forms of exclusion—they fail to
give a satisfactory account of immigration justice in that they do not foreground the role of coloniality. By failing to do so, radical approaches have
either overlooked or misrepresented the role that Indigenous populations
ought to play in shaping immigration justice; they also tend to downplay the
role that nation-states—and especially nation-building projects—continue
to have and exaggerate the threat that border controls pose for citizens (especially white citizens) of the West or Global North. In this section, I outline
what a decolonial approach is and why I believe most radical approaches
continue to be too Eurocentric to live up to their liberatory potential.

A. The Colonial Difference

A decolonial approach to immigration justice is ultimately a subset of the
radical approach. It shares with it the suspicion, if not outright rejection, of
both political liberalism and the capitalist economic system. It also directly
engages with the delineated social tension by interrogating the pernicious
discourse used in the immigration debate. Most radical approaches, however, have continued to perpetuate an unhealthy relationship with Western thought. A decolonial approach therefore seeks to compensate for this
deficiency by decentering Anglo-American and European perspectives and
putting the relationship of coloniality front and center.

As we saw above, radical approaches attempt to expose and reject the sedentary bias inherent in most articulations of the "immigration problem" by pointing to the long history of human migrations and the nomadic lifestyles of many human societies. One example of this can identified in the work of Thomas Nail, which argues that human history can be expressed in the expulsion and circulation of four principal figures (nomads, barbarians, vagabonds, and proletarians). Reece Jones, in his book *Violent Borders*, takes a similar view of the ubiquitous nature of human mobility, noting, "Although the technologies states use today to control resources, land, and people—drones, heat sensors, smart borders, global positioning systems, remote sensing images, biometric passports—would have been unimaginable for ancient rulers, the underlying problem of people who move would have been all too familiar to them . . . movement [is] consistently a problem, for ancient rulers and modern states alike."[35]

To be fair, these views do acknowledge that the movement of migrants is not always the same, and they do not deny that colonialism has played a key role in shaping current migration patterns. They do, however, assume two things that make these radical views problematic for a decolonial approach. The first assumption is that Indigenous people who have been dispossessed and displaced from their land will fit neatly into patterns of human mobility that have been developed primarily with Europeans in mind. The second is that there would be something like an "immigration problem" even without the advent of colonialism since forces of expulsion and circulation are inherent to the human condition and always a threat to those in power.

A decolonial approach takes issue with both these assumptions because even if the forces of expulsion and circulation are an ontological given, we still need a lens by which we can more clearly explain why the movement of Spanish conquistadors and English Pilgrims to the Americas was not the same (or even similar) to the migration of Central Americans to the United States today. Or as acclaimed journalist Juan Gonzalez has noted about Latin American immigration to the United States, "[Latin American immigrants] were in a different position from Italians or Swedes or Poles. [Their] homeland was invaded and permanently occupied, its wealth exploited, its patriots persecuted and jailed, by the very country to which [they] had migrated. [Their] experience was closer to Algerians in France before independence, or to Irish Catholics in England today."[36]

What a decolonial approach therefore seeks is not a theory of human mobility in general but a theory that foregrounds the colonial relationship in particular when trying to understand and define the "immigration problem." An added benefit of doing so is that it helps resolve the perceived liberal-egalitarian tension between Indigenous groups, whose right to self-determination has been undermined by settler colonialism, and immigrants, who have been displaced by the forces of imperialism. Instead of seeing these groups in tension with each other, as some philosophers have argued,[37] from a decolonial perspective we can see the forces that have displaced and dispossessed both of them as two sides of the same coin. As Amy Reed-Sandoval has persuasively argued, when we think of borders (especially of settler colonial states) as Indigenous spaces, we can see the error in assuming that Indigenous peoples are settled and in tension with non-Indigenous migrants, when the truth is that often these two groups overlap.[38] The fight against colonialism therefore presents us with an opportunity for broad solidarity in the face of perceived tension, and nowhere is this sentiment better articulated than in the following slogan: no one is illegal on stolen land.

Similarly, there is much to admire in Alex Sager's criticism of methodological nationalism, but a decolonial approach reminds us that nation-states, and especially projects of nation-state formation, still play an important role in constructing the "immigration problem." Nation-states, and specifically the creation of their borders, have always been a product of colonialism. Current borders are not thousands of years old; most are, in fact, very recent.[39] These nation-states and borders were also not created to protect the culture and way of life of Indigenous peoples; on the contrary many of these boundaries divide these traditional communities. The borders we encounter today neither mark out natural divisions among peoples nor merely express the interests of capital. They have been drawn up and are enforced by Western powers in a way that best promotes Western hegemony.

The nation-state also continues to play an important role with respect to migrant labor. As Aviva Chomsky correctly points out, "Colonialism sets up a system in which colonized peoples work for those who colonized them. This system is not erased after direct colonialism ends. Rather, it evolves and develops. The colonizer continues to use former colonial subjects as cheap workers, and the unequal economic relationships is also reinforced in this way."[40]

While this system undoubtedly serves the interest of capital, it is the nation-state that sets the terms and conditions under which migrant labor takes place. The nation-state decides, through legislation, which migrant

workers will operate as "illegal" and therefore be subject to hyper exploitation and which will operate as guest workers and therefore operate with
some protections but without the same rights as citizen workers. So, while
citizen (and especially white citizen) workers are still exploited under capitalism, their condition can often be assuaged by the colonial relationship.
Citizen workers might see their social safety net shrink due to the effects
of neoliberalism domestically, but this loss can be artificially supplemented
by cheaper health, child, and elder care supplied by immigrants from the
Global South who are displaced by global neoliberalism. So, while workers,
as workers, labor under the same capitalist system, there is a colonial difference between them that is maintained by the operations of the nation-state,
which in turn makes international solidarity among workers difficult when
the relationship of coloniality is not foregrounded.

This brings us to the insights of Sokthan Yeng and Nicholas De Genova,
which suggest that immigration restrictions are not just a product of prejudice and animus toward nonwhites, nonheterosexual males, and people with
disabilities; rather, these exclusions themselves helped to shape our categories of what counts as white, normal, and healthy (i.e., nondeviant). What a
decolonial approach points out, however, is that much of the normative trac-
tion that accounts like those of Yeng's and De Genova's are able to generate is
based on the idea that eventually anyone could potentially (or will eventually)
fall prey to the state apparatus. Everyone is potentially subject to being made
an exception or to being reduced to bare life. But as I have hinted at above
already with the example of immigrant workers as opposed to (white) citizen
workers, this does not seem to be the case. Membership in the Global North
still provides protection against this kind of marginalization. We see this
every time we cross international borders and find that different passports
bring with them different levels of scrutiny. While for some this scrutiny can
be a form of marginalization, for others it is the precondition for their obtain-
ment of a global elite status such as Global Entry and other forms of trusted
traveler programs. The scrutiny is therefore not arbitrary but, in fact, follows
a kind of colonial logic. We also see this when countries in the Global North
continue to exercise their sovereign power to exclude anyone they do not
wish to admit, including refugees, while denying this same sovereign power
to countries in the Global South when they force them to take in deportees,
even those who might be carrying infectious diseases (e.g., COVID-19).

B. Decolonizing the Ethics of Migration Literature

So far, I have outlined what I take to be some of the colonial blind spots in the radical approach. I suspect that many of these are the result of radicals not consulting the work of non-Western philosophers. For non-Western radical philosophers, the issue of coloniality is always front and center. Colonialism never falls into the background of their normative thinking, and the experiences of the Global North are not prioritized. I propose that philosophers working on immigration justice should therefore not only do more to foreground the relationship of coloniality but also should try to decolonize their theoretical resources.

To begin with, it is a fact that most canonical Western philosophers were not concerned with questions of immigration, so it always requires some (often a lot) of legwork to adjust their frameworks to address questions of immigration justice. Therefore, if we must expend effort to make the ideas of our favorite theorists fit the issue at hand and if the issue at hand primarily affects formerly colonized peoples, why not take this as an opportunity to decolonize both immigration justice and the broader philosophical canon? Why not see if something like William Flores and Renato Rosaldo's notion of "cultural citizenship" provides as good, if not better, ground for solidarity with immigrants than Deleuze and Guattari's "figure of the nomad"? Why not consider Frantz Fanon's notion of the "damnés" in place of Giorgio Agamben's "bare life"? Why not see if a genealogical account like that provided by Walter Mignolo would not make a better fit for understanding the current "immigration problem" than the one proposed by Michel Foucault? Why not approach questions of immigrant identity and oppression through the frameworks offered by Gloria Anzaldúa and María Lugones rather than those offered by Judith Butler and Iris Marion Young?

Part of the answer (and perhaps a dirty little secret) is that much of the radical literature on immigration is not really about immigration justice at all. It is either part of an ongoing dispute between "analytic" and "continental" philosophers or an in-house debate that pits philosophers of the same tradition against each other. For example, it does not take long for radical discussions over immigration justice to devolve into arguments over whether to endorse Agamben or Foucault or Deleuze and Guattari. I call this phenomenon the "immigration as proxy" problem, in that the point of the discussion is not so much to arrive at an account of immigration justice as it is to either criticize the "analytic" method or to sing the praises of one's favorite radical philosopher.

As long as immigration is treated as a proxy for these other battles, it is unlikely that we will arrive at a truly decolonized perspective. Fortunately, we do have some examples of a decolonized approach, which come to us from the work of Latinx philosophers. In the rest of this section, I outline some of the most prominent examples but must caution the reader that this is far from an exhaustive list. The brief summaries below are meant mostly as a sample of what decolonizing immigration justice might begin to look like, not its limits.

The first example is the way theorists such as Natalie Cisneros and Edwina Barvosa have taken up the work of Gloria Anzaldúa. Anzaldúa's *Borderlands/La Frontera* is today a staple in Latin American and Latinx philosophy, and given its subject matter, one would have expected that philosophers working on the issue of immigration would have already consulted her work. Sadly, this has not been the case. But Cisneros, Barvosa, and other Latinx philosophers are working to change this. For example, Cisneros has incorporated Anzaldúa's insights by putting them in conversation with Foucault's notion of biopower. As alluded to earlier in the work of Yeng, biopower for Foucault is a normalizing regime that deems those who fall outside or resist the norms of society as threatening and perverse. While Foucault uses this concept to explain how various groups within society are wrongfully marginalized, he does not really consider the role biopower would play in the formation and deformation of an "illegal" identity.

According to Cisneros, Anzaldúa's autobiographical and genealogical account of how "illegal" identities "are constituted as perverse, abnormal, and threatening [and] thus made vulnerable to physical violence and economic exploitation" provides us with a helpful supplement, if not an outright alternative, to Foucault's notion of biopower.[41] Furthermore, Anzaldúa's work also offers a counterdiscourse, via her notion of mestiza consciousness, which unlike Foucault's notion of biopower allows one, according to Barvosa, to derive a positive and productive notion of subjectivity even, and especially, in its fragmented form.[42]

Another example can be found in the work of José-Antonio Orosco, specifically his use of Cesar Chavez's social and political thought. According to Orosco, Chavez's definition of social membership provides an underexplored argument for why most undocumented immigrants ought to, given their participation in the community and the density of the relationships they have come to form, already be considered formal members of the polity. This use of Chavez not only provides social and political philosophers with a new and original lens by which to think about the nature of citizenship but also helps to highlight the depth, richness, and underutilization of Chavez's thought.[43]

A third example has been my use of Enrique Dussel and his philosophy of liberation, which argues that in order to understand or pinpoint an ethical or political failure of a system or institution, one must first locate its victims. Once they are identified, we have the obligation to address the given failure from the victim's perspective. Adopting this Dusselian starting point, while also seeing the world as composed of regimes of motion, helps to both problematize the conventional view and give us an account of the ethics of migration from the underside of philosophy.[44] Similarly, Amy Reed-Sandoval has begun to deploy the idea of "Desplazada/o," inspired by Carlos Pereda's notion of "exile," to describe the experience of Latin American immigrants and their descendants.[45] Reed-Sandoval has also used the epistemology of Native American philosophers to help us understand and combat the hermeneutic marginalization faced by Latin American Indigenous immigrants.[46]

A final example is Daniel G. Campos's use of María Lugones and Octavio Paz. In *Loving Immigrants in America,* Campos employs Lugones's concepts of "playfulness," "'world'-travelling," and "loving perception" to help make sense of his attempts to make a home for himself in the United States as a Latin American immigrant. Campos's account also highlights the fact that part of the immigrant experience includes a severing of the people and places they have cherished. When this happens, a sense of solitude, as described by Paz in *Labyrinth of Solitude,* begins to seep into one's life. Campos, however, provides a more optimistic reading of Paz, by suggesting practices of communion that can help one dance their way out of this labyrinth.[47]

What I would like to note about all these approaches is that while they do not necessarily ignore Western thought, they are not trapped in it. Understanding the root of the "immigration problem" and trying to provide a solution to it is what is most important, not trying to make a case for any particular thinker or school of thought, especially an already established European one. I therefore suggest that radicals should adopt a modified version of the Bechdel test as a rule of thumb for their approaches to immigration justice. Radicals should check in with themselves and see whether their account has engaged with at least two non-Western theorists, put them in conversation with each other, and done so on topics that are not necessarily about a Western philosopher or their theories. This will not in itself ensure a decolonial approach, but it will make it much more likely.

Conclusion

In this chapter, I have tried to make a case for a decolonial approach to immigration justice. I have done so by looking at the three dominant approaches to immigration justice and exposing the deficiencies in each. I have suggested that a radical approach, through its criticism of methodological nationalism, capitalism, sedentary biases, and the dehumanization that comes with systemic forms of exclusion, can help us overcome those deficiencies. Yet, few radicals have dared to venture beyond the figures and thought we find in the Western philosophical canon. This failure has essentially reproduced a colonial divide in immigration justice that either overlooks or misrepresents the role that Indigenous populations can play in immigration justice, as they have tended to downplay the role of the nation-state or exaggerated the threat that border controls pose for (primarily white) citizens of the Global North.

It has also reaffirmed the perspective of the Global North when addressing the "immigration problem" and the belief that there is nothing of theoretical importance taking place outside of the West. This has, in turn, stifled the creativity of organic intellectuals who address the issue of immigration justice from the perspective of the Global South. In short, even though a radical approach to immigration justice is necessary, most of its current manifestations continue to display an unhealthy form of Eurocentrism. My recommendation here is that we start to decolonize immigration justice by making a concerted effort to work from and build on the frameworks developed by non-Western radical thinkers.

Notes

1. Ramón Grosfoguel, "The Epistemic Decolonial Turn," *Cultural Studies* 21, nos. 2–3 (2007): 217.
2. See Philip Cafaro, *How Many Is Too Many?: The Progressive Argument for Reducing Immigration into the United States* (Chicago: University of Chicago, 2014) and Ann Coulter, *Adios, America: The Left's Plan to Turn Our Country into a Third World Hellhole* (Washington, D.C.: Regnery Publishing, 2015).
3. David Miller, *Strangers in Our Midst* (Cambridge, Mass.: Harvard University Press, 2016), 74.

4. It appears that there is a consensus among all parties involved that there is an immigration problem. The difficulty, as we will see throughout this chapter, is how to actually define the problem. One potential area of general agreement is that there are too many resident immigrants who lack a regularized status and many more precluded migrants who are desperately seeking (and arguably deserve or are entitled to) admission.

5. "Immigration and Naturalization Service," U.S. Department of Justice, accessed June 10, 2021, http://www.justice.gov/archive/jmd/1975_2002/2002/html/page 104-108.htm.

6. White House, "Fact Sheet on Immigration and Border Security," accessed March 2020, https://www.whitehouse.gov/wp-content/uploads/2020/02/FY21 -Fact-Sheet-Immigration-Border-Security.pdf.

7. "Unauthorized Immigrant Population Trends for States, Birth Countries and Regions," Pew Research Center, December 11, 2014, http://www.pewhispanic .org/2014/12/11/unauthorized-trends/#All.

8. Joseph H. Carens, "Aliens and Citizens: The Case for Open Borders," *Review of Politics* 49, no. 2 (Spring 1987): 251.

9. For proponents of this approach, see Chandran Kukathas, "The Case for Open Immigration," in *Contemporary Debates in Applied Ethics*, ed. Andrew I. Cohen and Christopher Heath Wellman (Oxford: Blackwell, 2005), 207–20; Javier S. Hidalgo, *Unjust Borders: Individuals and the Ethics of Immigration* (New York: Routledge, 2018); and Michael Huemer, "Is There a Right to Immigrate?" *Social Theory and Practice* 36, no. 3 (July 2010): 429–61.

10. See David Bacon, *The Children of NAFTA: Labor Wars on the U.S./Mexico Border* (Berkeley: University of California Press, 1997) and idem., *Illegal People: How Globalization Creates Migration and Criminalizes Immigrants* (Boston: Beacon, 2008).

11. See David Bacon, *The Right to Stay Home: How US Policy Drives Mexican Migration* (Boston: Beacon, 2013).

12. Michael Blake, "Immigration," in Cohen and Wellman, *Contemporary Debates in Applied Ethics*, 36.

13. For a more comprehensive overview of this distinction, see Amy Reed-Sandoval, "The New Open Borders Debate," in *The Ethics and Politics of Immigration: Core Issues and Emerging Trends*, ed. Alex Sager (Lanham, Md.: Rowman and Littlefield, 2016), 13–28.

14. See Michael Blake, *Justice, Migration, and Mercy* (New York: Oxford University Press, 2019) and Miller, *Strangers in Our Midst*.

15. David Miller, "Immigrants, Nations, and Citizenship," *Journal of Political Philosophy* 16, no. 4 (December 2008): 373.

16. Shelley Wilcox, "Immigrant Admissions and Global Relations of Harm," *Journal of Social Philosophy* 38, no. 2 (Summer 2007): 275.

17. Wilcox, "Immigrant Admissions," 277.

18. Peter Higgins, *Immigration Justice* (Edinburgh: Edinburgh University Press, 2013), 67.

19. For a more developed version of this argument, see Desiree Lim, "Selecting Immigrants by Skill: A Case of Wrongful Discrimination?" *Social Theory and Practice* 43, no. 2 (April 2017): 369–96.

20. Joseph Carens, *The Ethics of Immigration* (New York: Oxford University Press, 2013).

21. Alex Sager, *Toward a Cosmopolitan Ethics of Mobility: The Migrant's-Eye View of the World* (Cham, Switzerland: Palgrave Macmillan, 2018), 1.

22. Thomas Nail, *The Figure of the Migrant* (Stanford, Calif.: Stanford University Press, 2015), 24.

23. Quoted in Todd Miller, *Empire of Borders* (Brooklyn: Verso, 2019), 7.

24. Sager, *Toward a Cosmopolitan Ethics of Mobility*, 22.

25. Ronald Sundstrom, "Sheltering Xenophobia," *Critical Philosophy of Race* 1, no. 1 (2013): 68–85.

26. Adam Hosein, "Arguments for Regularization," in Sager, *Ethics and Politics of Immigration*, 160–61.

27. See Joseph H. Carens, "The Rights of Irregular Migrants," *Ethics and International Affairs* 22, no. 2 (Summer 2008): 163–86.

28. One notable exception in the liberal-egalitarian literature is Amy Reed-Sandoval's *Socially Undocumented* (New York: Oxford University Press, 2020), but it should be noted that this book is in many ways a criticism of the liberal-egalitarian tradition for not paying sufficient attention to the social tension undergirding undocumented status.

29. Sokthan Yeng, *Biopolitics of Race: State Racism and U.S. Immigration* (Blue Ridge Summit, Pa.: Lexington Books, 2013).

30. Nicholas De Genova, "The Deportation Regime: Sovereignty, Space, and the Freedom of Movement," in *The Deportation Regime: Sovereignty, Space, and the Freedom of Movement*, ed. Nathalie Peutz and Nicholas De Genova (Durham, N.C.: Duke University Press, 2010), 33–65.

31. Thomas Nail, "Violence at the Borders," *Radical Philosophy Review* 15, no. 1 (2012): 253.

32. Nail, "Violence at the Borders."

33. Todd Miller, *Empire of Borders* (Brooklyn: Verso, 2019), 170.

34. Kim Hjelmgaard, "From 7 to 77: There's Been an Explosion in Building Border Walls Since World War II," *USA Today*, May 24, 2018.

35. Reece Jones, *Violent Borders: Refugees and the Right to Move* (London: Verso, 2016).

36. Juan Gonzalez, *Harvest of Empire: A History of Latinos in America* (New York: Penguin Books, 2011), 94.

37. See Angelo J. Corlett and Kimberly Unger, "The Collateral Damage of Opening Floodgates: Problems with Kevin R. Johnson's Arguments for U.S. Immigration Reform," *Philosophy and Society* 24, no. 4 (2013): 299–314.

38. Amy Reed-Sandoval, "Settler-State Borders and the Question of Indigenous Immigrant Identity," *Journal of Applied Philosophy* 37, no. 4 (August 2020): 543–61.

39. For example, the nation-states and borders of the African continent were set out by Western powers at the Berlin Conference of 1884. Something like this is the case for just about all postcolonial states.

40. Aviva Chomsky, *"They Take Our Jobs!" and 20 Other Myths about Immigration* (Boston: Beacon, 2007), 146.

41. Natalie Cisneros, "Mestizaje and 'Alien' Identity: Gloria Anzaldúa on Immigration," *APA Newsletter on Hispanic/Latino Issues in Philosophy* 12, no. 2 (Spring 2013): 6.

42. See Edwina Barvosa, "Applying Latina Feminist Philosophical Approaches to the Self to Reinterpret Anti-Immigrant Politics in America," *APA Newsletter on Hispanic/ Latino Issues in Philosophy* 11, no. 2 (Spring 2012): 16–21.

43. See José-Antonio Orosco, *Cesar Chavez and the Common Sense of Nonviolence* (Albuquerque: University of New Mexico Press, 2008) and idem., *Toppling the Melting Pot: Immigration and Multiculturalism in American Pragmatism* (Bloomington: Indiana University Press, 2016).

44. See José Jorge Mendoza, "The Political Philosophy of Unauthorized Immigration," *APA Newsletter on Hispanic/Latino Issues in Philosophy* 10, no. 2 (Spring 2011): 2–6.

45. See Amy Reed-Sandoval, "'Immigrant' or 'Exiled'? Reconceiving the Desplazada/os of Latin American and Latina/o Philosophy," *APA Newsletter on Hispanic/Latino Issues in Philosophy* 15, no. 2 (Spring 2016): 11–14.

46. Reed-Sandoval, "Settler-State Borders."

47. Daniel G. Campos, *Loving Immigrants in America: An Experiential Philosophy of Personal Interaction* (Blue Ridge Summit, Pa: Lexington Books, 2017).

CHAPTER 3

Oaxacan Transborder Communities and the Political Philosophy of Immigration

AMY REED-SANDOVAL

Introduction

Roberto, a thirtysomething Zapotec man from the Central Valleys of Oaxaca, sits at his kitchen table in Woodburn, Oregon, thoughtfully sipping coffee.[1] He is speaking with sadness about his village in Oaxaca. The community's annual festival has just taken place, and Roberto was unable to attend. As he is an undocumented migrant, a visit to Oaxaca could make it all but impossible for him to return to his life in Oregon. Roberto's four-year-old son, José, sits at his side drawing pictures on sheets of scrap paper. The boy was born in the United States and has never visited Oaxaca.

"I want José to meet his grandmother, aunts, and uncles," says Roberto.[2] "I want him to experience all of our festivals and customs. I want him to speak in Zapotec with his *abuelita*."

A shadow crosses Roberto's face as he mentions his elderly mother. She is sick and weary after seventy years of grueling farmwork and is having trouble moving about and taking care of herself. Roberto wants to bring her medicine, fix up her house, and see that she is properly cared for.

"It's not that I want to move back to Oaxaca forever," explains Roberto, whose living room is decorated with a map of Oaxaca displayed prominently on a wall. "My life and community are here, in Oregon, too. José's mother and school is here; we have [traditional Oaxacan] festivals here; I have family and work here."

Instead, Roberto yearns for the legal right to move freely across the U.S.-Mexico border. He explains that he wants to move back and forth between parts of his community that exist simultaneously in Oaxaca and Oregon. He wants to work the land in both places, engage with his family and friends on both sides of the border, and participate in festivals and traditions that happen not just in Oaxaca but also in Oregon. Only then, says Roberto, will he be a full participant in his community.

Two weeks later, in the Central Valleys, Antonio is enjoying the shade of a big tree in front of his local church and reflecting upon his past life in Oregon. Antonio is nearly seventy years old and has crossed and recrossed the U.S.-Mexico border a total of sixteen times in his life—back when he would follow the harvest seasons along the coast in a perpetual search for work. Like Roberto, Antonio feels that his life and community exist simultaneously in Oaxaca and Oregon. But unlike Roberto, Antonio was able to migrate (and remigrate) with relative ease during the '70s, '80s, and early '90s.

"Things were very different then," he explains.

This period preceded the increased militarization of the border through Operations Gatekeeper and Hold the Line, which suddenly made it extremely difficult for migrants to enter the United States via urban routes along the El Paso-Ciudad Juárez and San Diego-Tijuana corridors. Now, most unauthorized migrants wishing to enter the United States through Mexico must brave the open desert, a situation only exacerbated by even more militarization in the wake of 9/11 and the initiation of U.S.-led "War on Drugs" in Mexico in 2006. Antonio crossed and recrossed the border prior to the increased dominance of violent drug cartels, whose members frequently kidnap and otherwise abuse migrants in the Mexican borderlands. The costs of *coyotes*—people who are hired to "cross" undocumented migrants into the United States through Mexico—have skyrocketed given the increased difficulty and danger associated with border crossings.

"Back then we could cross and recross to work and visit family," says Antonio. "But with all these changes, all this violence, people are trapped on either side [of the US-Mexico border]. I still have family and friends in Oregon. I close my eyes, and I think of my life there: my bed, house, my work—all the streets I used to walk and drive on. Yes, I used to come and go [between

Oregon and Oaxaca], but I can't now. I'm too old; it's too dangerous. I'd probably die if I tried to reenter my life in Oregon."

I. The Philosophical Problem

Roberto and Antonio are members of Oaxacan Indigenous "transborder communities" of Oaxaca, Mexico, and the West Coast of the United States. These populations have been studied extensively in the social sciences but remain unexplored in Anglo-American political philosophy.

Members of such communities are *transmigrants*, or "those persons, who having migrated from one nation-state to another, live their lives across borders, participating simultaneously in relations that embed them in more than one nation-state."[3] Oaxacan transmigrants may cross the same border numerous times without breaking contact with the communities they leave behind on either side. Indeed, they continue to play important roles in both "parts" of their transborder community regardless of the nation in which they happen presently to live.

Transborder communities comprise multistranded webs of social relations that almost continuously link transmigrants to their societies of origin and settlement. Through their membership in these communities, transmigrants are politically and culturally active on both sides of the border. Importantly, transborder communities consist not only of migrants who regularly cross borders but also of nonmigrants, return migrants who have permanently resettled in their countries of origin, and migrants who have settled permanently on foreign soil.[4] Transborder communities do not necessarily flank physical borders. Indeed, key parts of the Oaxacan transborder community exist a great distance away from the U.S.-Mexico border.

The phenomenon of transborder communities sits uneasily with prominent positions on collective rights and multicultural citizenship such as that of Will Kymlicka, which I consider in this chapter. In his defense of minority group rights, Kymlicka introduces a sharp distinction between "national minorities," who are entitled to self-governance, and "voluntary migrants," who are entitled to the polyethnic rights that will enable them to assimilate into the dominant societal culture. As we shall see, Oaxacan transborder communities do not fit neatly into either of these categories, and defending their unique societal culture may require neither self-governance nor assimilation.

These communities also complicate the policy proposal—widely invoked by immigrant rights activists and philosophers of immigration such as Joseph Carens—of granting the right to remain to *long-term* undocumented migrants as a means to achieve justice for them.[5] While this proposal is certainly an important start for the purpose of crafting just immigration policies, it does not account for the unique interests, needs, and migration patterns of (many) Oaxacan transborder community members.

Nevertheless, I argue that there is a reasonable extension of Kymlicka's view that can account for Oaxacan transborder communities. Furthermore, I propose that on such an extended view, members of these communities should be granted increased freedom of movement between the United States and Mexico, such that people like Roberto and Antonio can cross and recross the border and thereby be full participants in their community.

In practical terms, I propose the following: Oaxacan transborder community members should be given a visa that allows them freely to enter the United States for a period of up to six months (more or less). They should be able to use this visa to enter the United States as frequently as they wish. (It is important to note that most Indigenous Oaxacans lack access to tourist visas granting entry to the United States from Mexico, which are, as a general rule, reserved for those Mexicans who happen to be middle and upper class.) Similarly, Oaxacan transborder community members born in the United States should enjoy a similar right to enter Mexico on a tourist visa. In fact, they already do possess such a right; U.S. citizens are almost always granted such visas automatically upon entry to Mexico.

With such a right, Oaxacan transmigrants would not need to pay nearly $4,000 to a *coyote* to cross the border illegally; they would not need to risk death, sexual assault, and other forms of violence at the hands of drug cartels; and they would not need to risk dehydration and starvation in the desert. Thus, while I am not arguing for an economic right per se, such a policy could have important economic consequences for Oaxacan transborder community members.

Note that while I focus upon Oaxacan Indigenous transborder communities in this chapter, I am not suggesting that this is the only group that counts as a transborder community and is thus potentially deserving of the freedom-of-movement right I argue for. Though I do not make claims on behalf of other ethnic and/or national minority groups (Indigenous or non-Indigenous), I derive from the phenomenon of Oaxacan transborder communities a proposed list of criteria that a binational group must meet in order to be considered transborder.

I begin by presenting additional details on Oaxacan transborder communities. Here too, I derive from this discussion a proposed list of criteria that a given binational community must meet in order to count as transborder. Then I consider what Kymlicka's argument for collective and national minority rights has (and does not have) to say about them. Third, I discuss how Oaxacan transborder communities trouble Kymlicka's argument. Fourth, I argue that there is, in fact, a reasonable extension of Kymlicka's view that would allow for freedom-of-movement rights between the United States and Mexico.

I make two important assumptions in this chapter. First, I assume that Kymlicka is correct in arguing that just states must take steps to protect the societal cultures of minority groups within their territories. Second, I suppose, following Joseph Carens, that undocumented migrants are often owed robust rights (like a right to remain) by the state to which they have migrated without authorization—even though the state never "invited" them to enter and remain in the first instance. While this is certainly a controversial claim, it is beyond the burden of this chapter to defend it. My aim here is strictly to explore philosophically the case study of Oaxacan transborder communities with a view to moving forward philosophical conversation on immigration and multiculturalism.

II. Oaxacan Transborder Communities

Let us briefly consider the following features of Oaxacan transborder communities: (1) their geographical scope, (2) examples of "traditional Oaxacan culture" in the United States, (3) examples of "American values" in Oaxaca, and (4) the distinctive transborder Oaxacan culture that is neither "Oaxacan" nor "American" (of the United States). We will then be in a position to see how the Oaxacan transborder community differs from what could be considered, more strictly, a (mere) "ethnic community in a foreign land."

1. The state of Oaxaca has the highest representation of Indigenous peoples in all of Mexico, with over 90 percent of the population self-identifying as Indigenous in 209 Oaxacan municipalities.[6] Across the border, "sides" or "parts" of Oaxacan transborder communities can be found in the United States in towns like Woodburn, Oregon, where 45 percent of local residents are Mexican and a large percentage of the Mexican population is Indigenous Oaxacan. Other U.S. cities and towns featuring Oaxacan transborder communities include Santa Ana and Oxnard, California, where "the numbers of Mexicans are so great . . . that we could speak of them as extensions of Mexico."[7] These communities are connected to, and part of, Oaxacan communities in Mexico, such as San Agustín and Teotitlán, whose citizens have been crossing and recrossing the Mexico-U.S. border to perform labor for up to five generations.

2. There has been extensive anthropological research on Oaxacan Indigenous culture in the United States, particularly along the West Coast. For example, Alicia Barabás explores how foods, language practices, and regional Oaxacan celebrations have been brought to the United States. Herbs, other plants, and foods that are used for traditional medicine in Oaxaca—*tortillas, chiles, barbacoa, mole*, and more—are regularly transported across the border from Mexico to Los Angeles.[8] Jonathan Fox notes that California features five different *Guelaguetza* festivals (Oaxacan celebrations of Indigenous culture and identity) per year. He argues that "these California festivals are the embodiment of 'Oaxacalifornia' as an autonomous, pan-ethnic public sphere that is both uniquely Mexican and differently Mexican."[9]

3. While Oaxacan culture is being "transported" to the United States by Oaxacan transborder community members, Oaxacan transborder communities *in Oaxaca* also experience changes as a result of transnational migration. For instance, in her discussion of the transborder community of Teotitlán del Valle, Oaxaca, anthropologist Lynn Stephen explores how Oaxacan migration to the United States has influenced gender roles in Oaxaca. Female migrants who left Teotitlán to work in the United States or other parts of Mexico began to question traditional views about female sexuality and capacity for political participation. As a result, it has become acceptable for women to practice serial monogamy and to talk with men openly in the street. Since 2000 local political assemblies have been attended by both women and men. Such changes in gender roles have occurred not only as a result of female migrants' experiences outside of Oaxaca but also because

of the experiences of women who were "left behind" when a considerable number of male migrants left Oaxaca to labor in the United States (beginning, most notably, with the Bracero Program of the 1940s).

4. Crucially, Oaxacan transborder communities feature a societal culture that is neither Oaxacan nor American (of the United States); rather, it is unique to the transborder community. In addition to changing gender roles in Oaxaca, these transborder communities feature striking examples of transnational political, cultural, and activist organizations. One prominent organization is the Frente Indígena de Organizaciones Binacionales, or Indigenous Front of Binational Organizations (FIOB), which is located in Oaxaca, Baja California, Fresno, California, and Los Angeles. Its mission is "to contribute [to] the development and self-determination of . . . migrant and non-migrant indigenous communities, as well as struggle for the defense of . . . human rights with justice and gender equality at the binational level." Other important examples include the Oaxacan community of San Agustín (located in Oaxaca), which has a public works committee that is transnational with federated chapters in ten cities in the United States and also in San Agustín itself; the Coalition of Indigenous Communities of Oaxaca (in San Diego); and the Binational Center for Indigenous Oaxacan Development.

This had led to the emergence of what may be called panethnic Indigenous identity throughout Oaxacan transborder communities. In addition, Oaxacan participation in "traditional" community obligations like *tequio* and *cooperación* have evolved as a result of Oaxacan migration in the United States; Oaxacan migrants in the United States, as well as their children, participate in "traditional" Oaxacan culture as a part of a transnational cooperation strategy.[10]

These features of Oaxacan transborder communities inspire an important question. Namely, in what sense does the experience of a Oaxacan transmigrant in the United States—qua Oaxacan transmigrant—differ from that of a member of a *nontransborder* minority ethnic group (in the United States) who happens to spend a significant amount of time interacting with other members of the minority group of which she is a part?

In both cases, the interactions in question can generate deep senses of meaning and identity on the part of the group member. Importantly, however, the Oaxacan transmigrant is a member of a distinctively binational group that is neither strictly Oaxacan nor strictly of the United States. This means that while political and social events occurring in Oaxaca shape her life, she also actively impacts the lives of transborder community members in Oaxaca through her participation in social movements and events in the United States. Politically, she is influenced by and can become engaged in Oaxacan transborder politics, journalism, and activism that are all decidedly binational. And if she chooses to leave the United States and continue her life in Oaxaca (assuming this is an option for her), she can continue to live her life this way; she will have simply relocated to another part of her transborder community.

We can see, then, that the Oaxaca transborder community differs significantly from a mere "ethnic community in a foreign land." It is geographically and culturally binational, and many of its members' political and social identities are deeply shaped by this fact.

As stated at the outset, my policy proposal focuses primarily on Oaxacan Indigenous transborder communities and the particular politics of the U.S.-Mexico border. However, I have also suggested that we can derive from the Oaxacan Indigenous transborder experience a possible set of criteria that a binational group (Indigenous or non-Indigenous) must meet in order to be considered transborder—in a way that renders them eligible for the freedom-of-movement right that I advocate.

Here, then, are my proposed criteria. We have seen that the most important distinction between a *transborder* community and a community that is merely *transnational* or *binational* is that the community itself must possess a societal culture that is *unique to the transborder community*. Once again, Oaxacan Indigenous transborder culture is neither of Oaxaca nor of the United States but rather is generated in the context of a migratory web that features constant movement, back and forth, across it. Thus, what happens in one part of the transborder community affects the other part of the transborder community, and vice versa. That is the first criterion for a transborder community. The other relate to those elements that inspire and sustain this binational web of movement. There must be a critical mass of community members in each of the states where the transborder community is represented, generated by a substantial history of border crossings.

In sum, I propose that for a given binational community to count as transborder, it must (1) exist simultaneously in more than one state, (2) feature a critical mass of community members in both states, (3) possess a societal culture that is *unique to the transnational web itself*, and (4) be sustained by regular movement by community members back and forth along the transnational web.

III. The Political Philosophy of Immigration

I now turn to the following question: what might Kymlicka's view on collective/national minority and immigrant rights have to say about Oaxacan transborder communities (and other communities that meet the previously identified criteria)?

Kymlicka argues that liberalism begins with the notion of freedom—specifically, the freedom to build a life for one's self. Such lives must be led from the inside, in accordance with values upon which one has been able to deliberate. One's societal culture is crucial for this. As Kymlicka describes, "societal culture" provides "its members with meaningful ways of life across the full range of human activities, including social, educational, religious, recreational, and economic life, encompassing both private and public spheres."[11] Liberal governments, which must provide individuals with the rights and resources they need to build a good life, are therefore obligated to support the protection and preservation of societal cultures.

We have seen that Oaxacan transborder communities provide to their members narratives, sources of meaning, and ways of life that are distinctively transborder. This is evidenced in transborder political activism, changes in gender roles, panethnic Indigenous identity that has emerged in the transborder context, cross-border cooperation strategies for participating in "traditional" community political practices, and the ways that cyclical migration patterns have become important parts of Oaxacan household survival strategies.

I submit that the flourishing and survival of Oaxacan transborder societal culture depends upon the movement of members between the various binational "parts" of the community. Given that transborder communities are not territorially concentrated, movement within them is required to maintain the connectedness and exchange of ideas that give rise to the transborder senses of meaning. Such movement gives purpose to the transborder political organizations that have emerged along with new notions of panethnic Indigenous identity. It generates the societal culture that provides Oaxacan transmigrants with "meaningful ways of life across the full range of human activities" in Kymlicka's terms.

Unfortunately, the U.S.-Mexico border is rendering vulnerable the societal culture of Oaxacan transborder communities. As monetary costs of migration, violence at the border, deportations, and the probability of being physically attacked while migrating through Mexico increase drastically, migration to the United States from Oaxaca is decreasing. In addition, more undocumented Oaxacan transmigrants living in the United States are choosing not to travel back to Oaxaca for fear that they will be unable to make the return trip north. All this is rendered clear in the differences between the migration stories of Antonio and Roberto. If this trend continues, it could lead to far less communication between both "parts" of the transborder community as a result of decreased mobility and to an eventual disappearance of this distinctive transborder community culture. Thus, it may seem that Kymlicka's view should require the United States and Mexico to open their borders for Oaxacan transborder community members on both sides.

However, Kymlicka's view cannot, as it stands, require this. This is due to the sharp, categorical distinction he draws between "national minorities" (e.g., First Nations, the Québécois) and "voluntary migrants."[12] He claims that while national minorities are entitled to the self-governance rights that enable them to maintain their distinctive culture, immigrants are only entitled to polyethnic rights that will enable them to *assimilate* into the dominant culture. This is because, he argues, immigrant groups are insufficiently "compact, self-conscious [and] culture maintaining to have the . . . prerequisites for self-governance."[13] Furthermore, Kymlicka claims it is significant that immigrants choose to leave behind their societal cultures; though they "bring their language and historical narratives with them," they effectively "uproot themselves" from the institutionalized practices that gave meaning to their cultural activities.[14]

The experience of Oaxacan transborder communities demonstrates three significant problems with Kymlicka's position. First, it assumes that the only reasonable alternatives are self-governance or assimilation. Second, it supposes that groups need to be territorially concentrated into order to maintain a distinctive societal culture. Third, it presumes that migrants "uproot themselves" from their societal cultures (to a highly significant extent) upon migrating.

As we have seen, Oaxacan transborder communities do not require self-governance, or a separate Oaxacan state, in order to maintain their distinctive culture. Rather, they need to maintain flows of movement between parts of the transborder community. The fact that they neither require nor demand a separate state does not mean, however, that they want or ought to assimilate into "mainstream" U.S. or Mexican culture; instead, the transborder communities maintain distinctive societal cultures while interacting with "mainstream" U.S. and Mexican institutions. Furthermore, this case study demonstrates that groups need *not* be territorially concentrated in order to maintain their distinctive societal culture. Finally, we have seen that Oaxacan transmigrants do not "uproot themselves" from their societal cultures upon migrating; they simply migrate to a new part of their transborder community.

IV. A Proposed Solution

We need not, however, confine Kymlicka's view on the importance of protecting societal cultures to the options of "self-governance" or "assimilation" within the confines of a particular nation-state. Instead, his outlook can plausibly be extended in terms of the following principle: in immigration policy, states must take steps to protect the societal cultures of the migrants in their territory. For those migrants who have assimilated, or who intend to assimilate, into the dominant societal culture of the host society, the appropriate solution may be a right to remain in the new society (as Carens has powerfully argued). On the other hand, for transmigrants such as those of Oaxacan Indigenous transborder communities, protecting societal culture entails a right to freedom of movement between both parts of the binational community. Note that what I am proposing is a binational solution; the United States has an obligation to allow Oaxacan transborder community members from Oaxaca to enter and remain, and Mexico must do the same for their U.S.-born counterparts.

It is also important that I distinguish my proposal from two alternative programs that grant only limited freedom of movement into the United States to a subset of the Mexican population. I am not proposing a guest worker program, which gives some guest workers a right to perform undervalued labor in a foreign country for a limited period of time without political rights. While a guest worker program could allow (and, historically, has allowed) some Oaxacans to live and work in the United States for a limited period of time, it fails to promote the flourishing of Oaxacan transborder societal culture in several ways.

First, guest worker programs generally only grant opportunities to the relatively young and able-bodied; thus, the majority of Oaxacan transborder community members would be ineligible. Second, these programs generally discourage, rather than encourage, political action and consciousness on the part of guest workers themselves. Third, I am proposing a binational solution through which the U.S. and Mexican governments will both open their borders to Oaxacan transborder community members on both sides, which is very different from the scope of traditional guest worker programs. Fourth, such programs subject guest workers to the perceived economic needs of the host country, a situation that differs fundamentally from a freedom-of-movement right designed to acknowledge and promote the societal culture of a national minority group.

Furthermore, my proposed freedom-of-movement right is also much broader in scope than the Border Crossing Card (BCC) enjoyed by some Mexican nationals. While the BCC does enable some Mexican citizens to enter into the United States, it contains the following limitations: (1) stays are limited to thirty days and (2) travel is limited to twenty-five miles north of the Mexico-U.S. border. The limitations on travel are too restrictive for Oaxacan transborder communities, which are geographically vaster than the BCC allows. The thirty-day stay is also too restrictive, given that Oaxacan transborder community members need time to visit with family, participate in local celebrations, and traverse by car or bus the vast stretch of territory between Oaxaca and the Pacific Northwest (if plane travel is not an option).

Instead, I believe that we can find a precedent for the type of freedom-of-movement right I advocate by looking outside of the United States. José Antonio Lucero has argued that "Indigenous peoples across the Americas pose a challenge to (and are challenged by) the political boundaries of national states" and that "Indigenous identities are constituted by these very border tensions."[15] For instance, in South America, many Indigenous groups—such as the Aymara, Quechua, Aguaruna, and Guarani—span across borders; many members of these groups cross and recross national borders countless times over the course of their lives.

In 1998 Ecuador and Peru adopted, as part of their peace treaty, a policy that recognizes (to a certain extent) the political and moral importance of these systematic Indigenous border crossings: "The peace treaty of 1998 recognizes the importance of indigenous peoples in the border region, and proposes special funding and development projects for native communities.

It also provides for indigenous input and involvement in the development of binational ecological preserves."[16] Furthermore, the Ecuadorian constitution grants to Indigenous peoples the right "to uphold and develop contacts, ties and cooperation with other peoples, especially those that are divided by international borders." These policies and statements demonstrate (again, to a certain extent) a commitment to responding to the unique challenges and rights claims presented by Indigenous transnationalism in the Americas. The United States and Mexico should employ a similar methodology on behalf of Oaxacan transborder communities.

V. Possible Objections

In this section, I consider two possible objections to my argument. First, one might ask, if Oaxacan transborder community members are granted freedom of movement between the United States and Mexico, as I have proposed, would this not open the floodgates to demands by numerous transnational groups to a similar freedom-of-movement right? This could prove to be politically unfeasible.

This is a difficult question, for answering it satisfactorily requires vast knowledge of multifold transnational groups around the world. I suspect that there are a number of transnational groups that would meet the proposed criteria for a transborder community and thus be entitled to a similar freedom-of-movement right. And yet I submit that there are important features of Oaxacan transborder communities that make them rather unique candidates for such freedom of movement:

1. Once again, they possess a societal culture that is unique to the transborder community itself. In other words, this "culture" cannot be protected in either the United States or Mexico; it flourishes as part of a transborder web. This distinguishes Oaxacan transborder communities from many other transnational networks that have not themselves developed unique societal cultures *as a transnational network*.

2. Key features of the U.S.-Mexico relationship have allowed for, and encouraged, almost unparalleled migration across the border. Not only are the United States and Mexico geographical neighbors, which makes for some ease of movement across the border, but the economic activities of both

countries (e.g., trade agreements like NAFTA, guest worker programs, etc.) are intensely intertwined and have been for generations. Indeed, it is widely argued that NAFTA *caused* a significant amount of Oaxacan Indigenous migration to the United States. Thus, in the interest of avoiding an opening of floodgates to an untenable amount of migration to the United States by members of multifold transborder communities, we might limit the granting of this right to cases in which U.S. economic policies are, in part, the *cause* of the transmigration in question.

I readily acknowledge that deciding which transnational groups are entitled to this right will likely entail assessing differences of degree rather than kind among transnational groups. Nevertheless, while it may be difficult to draw a precise line between which groups are or are not entitled to the right in question, this does not mean that no reasonable line can be drawn. I submit that Oaxacan transborder communities are a paradigm case of entitlement to this freedom-of-movement right, which can serve as a point of reference when assessing the situations of other transnational groups.

A second possible objection is as follows. I am proposing that the U.S.-Mexico border be opened for members of Oaxacan Indigenous transborder communities (and, possibly, other binational groups that meet the previously stipulated criteria). I have argued that this is necessary in order for the transborder community to preserve its unique societal culture. This is because, once again, Oaxacan Indigenous transborder culture requires freedom of movement along the different parts of the transborder web, and the violent U.S.-Mexico border impedes this movement.

But one might worry that some Oaxacan transborder community members may use this freedom-of-movement right in a way that does not promote the preservation of Oaxacan transborder societal culture. For instance, a musically talented young Oaxacan might choose to move to New York City to pursue a singing career as opposed to working in the service industry in Los Angeles alongside many of her fellow Oaxacan transborder community members. Would this not fail to promote the flourishing of the transborder community? And, furthermore, would this not give an unfair advantage to Indigenous Oaxacans—not only over Mexican nationals from other states of Mexico but also over would-be migrants across the globe?

There are several responses to this two-part objection. First, I caution the reader not to underestimate the constraining poverty and discrimination that almost all Oaxacan Indigenous transmigrants endure in both Oaxaca and the United States. Most Oaxacan transborder community members find themselves almost inescapably relegated to work in agriculture, domestic labor, and the service industry.

Indigenous peoples of Mexico face discrimination in the realms of the government, the workplace, and often during interpersonal interactions with mestizos. Oaxacan Indigenous persons are frequently referred to in racist terms such as *Oaxaco, Oaxaquitos* (little people from Oaxaca), and *Inditos sucios* (dirty little Indians).[17] Bilingual Indigenous Oaxacans are frequently accused of "not even knowing how to speak Spanish."[18] Indigenous Oaxacans often report having "humiliating experiences" when interacting with mestizo governmental bureaucrats when attempting to obtain marriage licenses and birth certificates.[19]

In his ethnographic report on mestizo migrants working in the border region of northern Mexico, Michael Kearney reported on blatant employment discrimination against Indigenous Mixtec employees working for a Mexican company that also employed mestizos. Mixtec workers were forced to take on the most physically grueling work in comparison to their mestizo counterparts. They lived in crammed employer-provided labor camps, which were particularly striking in comparison to the single-family apartments in high rises provided for mestizo workers. Mixtecs also earned significantly less pay than mestizos for their work. In the town where this was taking place, Mixtecs were regularly denied entry to public buses if mestizos wanted to get on board and there was limited room. While Kearny reported on a single case study, such discrimination against Indigenous peoples in Mexico is rampant.

Importantly, the very same prejudices that serve to marginalize Indigenous peoples in Mexico are often carried over to the United States, where Indigenous migrants continue to be discriminated against and marginalized in comparison to their mestizo counterparts. Speaking of Mexican Indigenous migration to the United States, Jonathan Fox argues that "the point of departure for analyzing collective identity formation here is that *both* in the US *and* in Mexico, indigenous migrants as subordinated *both* as migrants *and* as indigenous people—economically, socially and politically."[20] Lynn Stephen described her visit to a migrant farmworker camp in Woodburn, Oregon, where Mexican migrants are assigned to different houses in accordance with the particular region of Mexico from which they originated. This serves as an effective way of distinguishing Indigenous from non-Indigenous workers. For his part, Michael Kearney has reported on the fact that Oaxacan Indigenous workers in the United States continue to be paid less for their labor than their non-Indigenous counterparts. He has also described how these workers are effectively cut off from broader U.S. society, as their interactions in the workplace are limited to exchanges with mestizo *mayordomos* from Mexico, who have significant control over their working conditions. Thus, the critic should be aware that the hypothetical scenario under consideration would be a rare one indeed.

Second, I grant that Oaxacan transborder community members are, on this view, granted a rather unique freedom-of-movement right for which other Mexican citizens and foreign nationals may not be eligible. But this only seems like an unfair advantage if we restrict ourselves to thinking of the ethics of immigrant admissions in terms of *individual* rights. The philosophical literature on immigrant admissions has tended to conceive of admissions ethics in this restricted way. Alternatively, I am arguing for a *group right* for Oaxacan transborder communities to cross and recross the U.S.-Mexico border. The freedom-of-movement right that I propose for Oaxacan transborder community members only seems like an unfair advantage if we confuse the ethics of immigrant admissions for individual migrants with an immigrant admissions policy that is firmly premised upon the rights that are owed to groups.

Third, it is important to note that the U.S. government does not tend to grant other existing forms of group rights—be they national minority rights or polyethnic rights—on the condition that *all* members of the minority group in question actively promote their societal culture. For instance, few would argue that the U.S. government should strip Native American tribes of their reservations and political autonomy simply because some members of those tribes choose to live off the reservation while declining to participate in tribal politics. The morality and political legitimacy of group rights is simply not contingent on all members of the minority group in question actively promoting the flourishing of their unique societal cultures.

Finally, I submit that *even if* a critical mass of Oaxacan transborder community members chose to, say, study European art history in Chicago or work as electrical engineers in Philadelphia, this need not undermine the flourishing of the transborder community. I have argued that the societal culture of Oaxacan transborder communities is unique to the transborder web itself; it is neither of Oaxaca nor of the United States. If the urbane Oaxacan transborder community members of Chicago and Philadelphia impact life in Oaxaca, and if developments in Oaxaca continue to have an impact on them, they are indeed promoting and participating in their societal culture as part of a transnational web.

Conclusion

In this chapter I have argued that Kymlicka's view on multiculturalism can reasonably be extended to account for Oaxacan transborder communities. Furthermore, I have argued that on such an extended view, members of Oaxacan transborder communities should be granted freedom of movement between the United States and Mexico. That is, the U.S.-Mexico border should be opened for Oaxacan Indigenous transborder community members (and possibly some other transborder groups).

I believe that this argument has the following implications for the political philosophy of immigration. First, it points to a need for more exploration of the highly varied experiences of different migrant groups. We are currently far too limited by our simple categories of "immigrant community" or "national minority." Second, it shows that political philosophers should be more attentive to the phenomenon of transborder or transnational networks, in which communities thrive—both with and without legal authorization—simultaneously in more than one state. Finally, it shows that the voices of migrants themselves, like those of Roberto and Antonio, are not only highly relevant to the political philosophy of immigration but also frequently its source.

Notes

1. A version of this chapter was originally published in *International Journal of Applied Philosophy*. It is reprinted here with permission from the editors.
2. The names and certain identifying details of specific Oaxacan migrants mentioned in this chapter have been changed to protect their identities. These stories were told in the context of personal/informal conversation.
3. Michael Kearney, "Transnational Oaxacan Indigenous Identity: The Case of Mixtecs and Zapotecs," *Identities* 7, no. 2 (2000): 173.
4. Lynn Stephen, *Transborder Lives: Indigenous Oaxacans in Mexico, California, and Oregon* (Durham, N.C.: Duke University Press, 2007), 23.
5. See Joseph Carens, *Immigrants and the Right to Stay* (Cambridge, Mass.: MIT Press, 2010). For another compelling justification of a right to remain for undoc-

umented migrants, see Shelley Wilcox, "Who Pays for Gender Institutionalization?" in *Gender Identities in a Globalized World*, ed. Ana González and Victor J. Seidler (Amherst, N.Y.: Humanity Books, 2008), 53–74.

6. See "Facts About Oaxaca," SiPaz, accessed January 22, 2015, http://www.sipaz.org/en/oaxaca/facts-about-oaxaca.html.

7. Stephen, *Transborder Lives*, 63.

8. See Alicia Barabás, "Los migrantes indígenas de Oaxaca en Estados Unidos: Fronteras, asociaciones y comunidades," in *Migración, fronteras e identidades étnicas transnacionales*, ed. M. L. Velasco Ortiz (Tijuana: Colegio de la Frontera, Norte Tijuana), 171–96.

9. Jonathan Fox, "Reframing Mexican Migration as a Multi-Ethnic Process," *Latino Studies* 4, nos. 1–2 (March 2006): 51.

10. For further discussion, see Jeffrey Cohen, *Cooperation and Community in Oaxaca* (Austin: University of Texas Press, 1996).

11. Will Kymlicka, *Multicultural Citizenship: A Liberal Theory of Minority Rights* (New York: Oxford University Press, 1995), 86.

12. See Iris Marion Young, "A Multicultural Continuum: A Critique of Kymlicka's Ethnic-Nation Dichotomy," *Constellations* 4, no. 1 (April 1997): 48–53.

13. Kymlicka, *Multicultural Citizenship*, 96.

14. Kymlicka, 95–96.

15. José Antonio Lucero, "Indigenous Borderlands: States and Identities in the Amazonian/Andean Borderlands," paper presented at Borders and Borderlands in the Americas Conference, Stanford University, Stanford, California, June 18–19, 2012.

16. Raúl Saba, "The Arizona-Sonora and Ecuador-Peru Borderlands: Common Interests and Shared Goals in Diverse Settings," *Journal of the Southwest* 45, no. 4 (Winter 2003): 633.

17. Stephen, 210.

18. Fox, "Reframing Mexican Migration," 4 and Stephen, 210–11.

19. Stephen, 210.

20. Fox, 41.

PART II

South America

CHAPTER 4

Decolonial Liberation and Migration Ethics in the Brazilian Context

AMOS NASCIMENTO AND
MARGARET GRIESSE

Introduction

This chapter uses the framework of Latin American liberation ethics and decoloniality theory to reveal the underlying ideologies guiding different phases of immigration in Brazil and to analyze the philosophical relevance of the Brazilian context for discussions on global migration. We argue that this approach could contribute to a more comprehensive conception of immigration ethics and address issues that are often neglected by Anglo-American and European theories.

Many contemporary attempts to conceptualize global migration risk reaffirming old expressions of coloniality, as well as engendering cynical attempts to impose authoritarian power and strategies that silence ethical claims to "decolonial liberation." Before we explain the latter normative claim, we would like to identify two challenges.

The first concerns the very concepts we use. While "immigration" has a liberal connotation and is used to describe the movement of individuals *into* a particular nation with the intention of dwelling in a new territory for an undefined time, "migration" refers to a movement *in* and *out* of different locations—within or beyond the borders of nation-states. Studying the concept of "Diaspora" as it applied to the newly founded state of Israel and within Palestine in the 1950s, Shmuel Eisenstadt proposed a simple definition: "We define migration as the physical transition of an individual or a group from one society to another. This transition usually involves abandoning one social setting and entering a different one."[1] With this definition as a starting point, we can further qualify human migratory movements as voluntary, coerced, forced, or prompted by multiple factors. We can also integrate into the concept debates on specific terms, such as refugee, asylum, citizenship, nationality, naturalization, legal status, and so on.[2] Despite attempts by theorists to disaggregate them, the United Nations Organization and the International Organization for Migration consider "migration" as an umbrella term that covers all these constructs.[3] For the purposes of simplicity, we follow their lead here.

A second challenge concerns how migration issues emerge in various contexts and receive different philosophical justifications. Historically, migratory processes were justified in Eurocentric ways by Spanish colonizers, who used Francisco de Vitoria's concept of *jus communicationis*, and by British settlers, who applied John Locke's ideas regarding "possession" and Thomas Malthus's proposals for population control, among other justifications. Today, we can observe a greater philosophical plurality.[4] In North America, mainline reflections are based on John Rawls's political liberalism, Michael Walzer's communitarianism, and Joseph Carens's pioneering work on "immigration ethics" and defense of "open borders."[5] Moreover, Will Kymlicka has proposed "multicultural citizenship" as a tool to integrate minority ethnic and religious immigrant groups into the liberal framework, while Michael Blake envisions the possibility of relaxing strict requirements for closed borders based on a political and theological understanding of "mercy."[6] In Europe, the Critical Theory tradition relies on Immanuel Kant's views on "hospitality" and his definition of a *jus cosmopoliticum* [*Weltbürgerrecht*] as the right "not to be treated with animosity by another because of his arrival on that other person's land."[7] Hannah Arendt took this up in reflections on her own experiences as an immigrant, refugee, and stateless person, while for his part Jürgen Habermas criticized the lack of solidarity in the European Union's immigration policies.[8] More recently, Seyla Benhabib combined these approaches to propose "porous borders" and defend the rights of "strangers" to affirm their dignity through discursive practices such as "democratic iterations" and cosmopolitanism.[9]

Absent from these philosophical discussions in the Global North is the systematic consideration of experiences and reflections in the Global South: Africa and the Middle East, Asia Pacific, and Latin America and the Caribbean. The question arises as to why these regions have been neglected, despite their centrality to modern global migration. In Africa, Mokoko Sebola proposes Ubuntu philosophy as a guide for migration policies on the continent; meanwhile, Yen Le Spiritu discusses how the Filipino migration can be interpreted according to postcolonial studies and critical race theory.[10] In this spirit, we will focus our discussion on migration ethics in Latin America and the specific case of Brazil.

Our task is threefold: to present our understanding of Latin American decolonial ethics; to reinterpret specific immigration policies in Brazilian history through a decolonial lens; and finally, to apply these concepts to contemporary issues in migration ethics, which reveal intersections with race, gender, and class exploitation. As we focus on these intersections, we propose the concepts of postcolonial syncretism, mobility, and interlocation as tools to understand key dynamics of migratory processes. We conclude that a philosophical analysis of the Brazilian context is relevant for Latin American and global discussions on migration ethics.

I. Latin America, Liberation Ethics, and Decoloniality Theory

Liberation ethics and decoloniality theory are built upon a long historical tension between the oppressive reality of the conjunction of colonization, colonialism, and coloniality prompted by the *Conquista* of the Americas and the struggles of oppressed peoples, who insist on the normative validity of their claim to *liberation*. By criticizing the oppression generated by early modern economic globalization and questioning the alienation produced by Eurocentric values, liberation ethics and decoloniality theory focus on the "otherness" of the racialized, sexualized, and impoverished individuals and groups who are continuously "crossing borders" within Latin America and around the globe. How does all this apply to an ethics of migration in Brazil? This question has ontological, epistemic, and normative dimensions. To elucidate them, we will first clarify what we mean by Latin America, liberation, and decoloniality.

A. Latin America

"Latin America" is a contested and under-researched idea.[11] Walter Mignolo sees it as the expression of a double colonial "otherness," one that implies a difference in relation to Anglo-America and negates the interests of oppressed people based on class, racial, and gender categories upheld by traditional institutions ruled by local Latin American elites. For Mignolo, "the 'idea' of Latin America is the sad one of the elites celebrating their dreams of becoming modern while they slide deeper into the logic of coloniality."[12] He identifies the problematic legacy of celebrating a hybrid "Latinity" [*Latinidad*] based on a "global ethno-racial pentagon," but also sees positive possibilities in revealing alternative "political projects originating among the silenced population," which substitute decolonial intentions for colonial intentions.[13]

Due to the ambiguity of "Latin America," we start with an ethical imperative: the obligation to define our *locus enuntiationis* and interrogate economic, racialized, and gendered "otherness."[14] This point of departure is distinct from individualistic Anglo-American liberalism and the reactionary corporativist colonialism of elites below the Rio Grande. To avoid the limits of these positions and their views on migration, we adopt the critical standpoint of liberation ethics and decoloniality theory, following the contributions of Enrique Dussel, Aníbal Quijano, Walter Mignolo, Linda Martín Alcoff, and María Lugones.

B. Liberation Ethics

Liberation ethics emerged from debates involving Enrique Dussel, Horacio Cerrutti, and José Scanonne in Argentina, as well as the contribution of Leopoldo Zea in Mexico, Salazar Bondy in Peru, Hugo Assmann in Brazil, and other philosophers in Latin America. Here, we focus primarily on the ideas of Dussel, as he developed a historical sensitivity to the reality of oppression. More specifically, he followed Karl Marx's critique of economic liberalism, adopted the ontological dimension of Emmanuel Levinas's ethics and its emphasis on the encounter with the "exteriority" and "alterity" of human beings, and established a dialogue with liberation theology and Paulo Freire's pedagogy for liberation.[15] Initially, these elements came together in Dussel's concept of a "community of life," which functioned as an antidote to liberal individualistic ethics. Later, in dialogue with liberation theology, Dussel adopted and expanded the moral maxim of a "preferential option for the poor."[16]

Relying on all these references, Dussel developed his liberation ethics as an answer to the ongoing impact of the Conquista, finding a correlation among Hernán Cortéz's affirmation of an *ego conquiro*, René Descartes's *ego cogito*, and the solipsistic epistemology of the *ego cognosco*.[17] This led to his emphasis on a symmetric face-to-face interaction with a collective people (*pueblo*) exploited by oppressive colonial systems, and to his affirmation of critical voices audible throughout history—be that of prophets, priests, workers, or leaders, who hear the interpellation of the poor and are prompted to act in an emancipatory way. Examples include Bartolomé de Las Casas's defense of the rights of Indigenous peoples in 1545, Felipe Guamán Poma de Ayala's testimony condemning European domination in 1616, and the concrete actions of liberation movements in the 1960s.[18] However, these examples are not simply descriptions of events but are rather normative discourses that reflect on the encounter with the ontological exteriority of the "other" and recognize the validity of their ethical claims to liberation.

Dussel articulates these points in *Ethics of Liberation*, in which he goes from the geopolitical study of world-systems to a critical discussion of contemporary philosophers and finally to the affirmation of a "liberation principle" based on the "communitarian intersubjectivity of new social-historical subjects."[19] In the process, he criticizes the colonial project of establishing the "center" of the capitalist world-system in Europe while relegating the Americas as the "periphery"; he opposes Eurocentrism as an exploitive system that generates a "community of victims"; and he identifies these victims as the collective agent prompting the very *process of searching for liberation*.[20] How might this be related to migration? Dussel shows that people cross borders because of an economic system and are oppressed again in their new location because the economic system is global and not limited by artificial national boundaries. His philosophy thus offers an important entry point for an ethics of migration.

C. Decoloniality Theory

Aníbal Quijano was originally involved in debates on dependency theory, but his most important contribution is a social analysis of coloniality and its dismantling through decoloniality. He starts by defining globalization as the culmination of a domination process based on a powerful "social classification of the world's population around the idea of *raza*" and shows how this concept became a tool of colonization to subjugate *Indios*, *Negros*, and *Mestizos* under the "whiteness" [*blanquitud*] of Europe.[21] The control of commodities produced by unpaid labor enabled Europe to become the center of global capitalism and create a new intersubjectivity based on ethnocentrism. By globalizing racist myths, Eurocentric political leaders were able to establish themselves as moderns and spread their hegemonic power into a colonial "matrix of power."[22]

This last point establishes a connection with the discussion about migration. For Quijano, Eurocentrism subsumed Aztecs, Mayas, Aymara, Incas, Chibcha, and others into the category of Indios and forcefully generalized Ashanti, Yoruba, Zulus, Congos, Bacongos, and others as Negros. These different groups were subjected to forced migration and subordinated to an encompassing geopolitical category of "America" in general and "Latin America" in particular. Against this background, Quijano proposes the concept of "coloniality of power" to explain how new waves of migrants identified themselves with the dominant whites (*Blancos*) in Europe, without perceiving that their struggles and interests were more aligned with the plight of other exploited ethnic groups.[23] Moving forward in the historical perspective, Quijano concludes that "the coloniality of power still exercises its dominance, in the greater part of Latin America, against democracy, citizenship, the nation, and the modern nation-state."[24] He does not develop a systematic analysis of migration but does offer new impulses for discussions about its connection to racism, colonialism, and modernity, as well as intersections with feminism.

Mignolo builds on Quijano's views and provides some terminological nuances. While "decolonization" refers to a strategy of political independence espoused by political elites in Africa, Asia, and Latin America, "decoloniality" is an epistemic concept defining a new critical way of questioning persistent colonial categories. For Mignolo, the "logic of coloniality" is always intertwined with "geopolitics of knowledge."[25] He shows how global territorial designs of the Spanish and Portuguese in the sixteenth century were complemented by the universalist ambitions of the Christian mission to evangelize pagans, the goal of the European "uni-versity" to civilize barbarians, and the creation of geopolitical markers such as the "idea" of Latin America. Building on Gloria Anzaldúa's critical view of "Borderlands,"[26] Mignolo highlights voices that cross borders, transgress geopolitical orders, and challenge the imperial, colonial, and global designs, generating what he defines as "diversality." In a series of publications, he presents the nexus between modernity, coloniality, and decoloniality in ways that can be applied to an ethics of migration.[27] At the same time, in *On Decoloniality: Concepts, Analysis,*

Praxis, coauthored with Catherine Walsh, he summarizes his views on the "decolonial option" as an ethical imperative that updates liberation theology's "preferential option for the poor" and liberation ethics' obligation to confront the negation of the victim by oppressive systems: "Decoloniality is an option called to intervene in (a) the system of disciplinary management of knowledge (all the disciplines in the social sciences, humanities, and natural sciences, as well as professional schools); (b) the system of beliefs (religions); and (c) the systems of ideas (liberalism, conservatism, and socialism)."[28] This is defined, in an interesting synthesis, as "decolonial liberation."[29] However, the normative claim and the intersections with race and gender remain underelaborated.

Linda Martín Alcoff adopts Mignolo's views on border thinking and coloniality of power but criticizes him for underemphasizing the colonized identities.[30] For instance, in "Anti-Latino Racism," Alcoff describes various forms of violence against Latino immigrants to the United States and reviews the various implications of Latinidad. She corrects for Mignolo's disregard for identity politics and reveals the techniques of Anglo-American racism—from *invisibilization* and *colorism* to the disparaging of ethnic and race identities—which can be contrasted with a corresponding proliferation of Latino identity categories as attempts to escape from racist annihilation. Important for our discussion is her conclusion that antiracist strategies need to acknowledge the connection between racism and anti-immigration sentiments; these strategies also need to acknowledge the pluralism of various kinds of borders imposed by colonial power—geographical, cultural, linguistic, racial, and gendered.[31] A complementary dimension of Alcoff's contribution to this discussion is her work on feminist epistemologies and social identity, in which she insists that knowledge is always situated, embodied, and engendered, a point that leads to her proposal for "Decolonizing Feminist Philosophy."[32]

However, it is María Lugones who makes a very explicit plea for "decolonial feminism," focusing on the power of coloniality to impose gender and sexuality categories that cut across politics, economics, ecology, and other areas.[33] Building on Quijano's concept of "coloniality of power" and Nelson Maldonado-Torres's "coloniality of being," she conceives a "coloniality of language" and proposes to decolonize gender by making the language of women of color the point of departure. Taking the example of women in Bolivian communities, she concludes that while colonial *languaging* denies the gender identities that do not fit into the colonial binary *man/woman*, decolonial feminism seeks to affirm what is different or has been suppressed.

By expanding on Mignolo's definition of the "colonial difference," she shows that decolonial feminism implies the ethical task of resisting the "epistemological habit of erasing" those who are different.[34] Moving beyond liberalism, Lugones concludes, "One does not resist the coloniality of gender alone . . . Communities rather than individuals enable the doing."[35]

Taken together, these positions provide a rich vocabulary for a Latin American ethics of migration. Coloniality operates according to a "*Leitmotif* of class, race, and gender identities" and provokes a forced migration under the aegis of a "colonial matrix of power." Decoloniality motivates an option for "decolonial liberation" and questions discourses and systems that oppress, dismiss, and erase a localized, identifiable, and embodied "other." This ethics of migration based on decolonial liberation guides our discussion of the Brazilian context.[36]

II. Syncretism, Multiculturalism, and Neocolonialism in Brazilian Migration Policies

With the concepts discussed thus far, we can demarcate various developments within Brazilian history and reread them from a decolonial perspective. First, we define the extractivist and agrarian practices of Portuguese settlers as "colonization," the oppressive systems guiding migration as "colonialism," and the logical premises and tacit knowledge underpinning this system as "coloniality." More specifically, colonization can be defined as a biological process of occupying a certain habitat; colonialism is socially institutionalized in religious, legal, academic, military, and economic systems; and coloniality covertly incorporates a package of philosophical rationalizations for dominance. Second, we develop an analysis of Brazilian migration policies in light of our research on the postcolonial ideology of syncretism, the failed attempt at an anticolonial multiculturalism, and the neocolonial character of the national security state.[37]

A. Colonization, Colonialism, and Coloniality

Colonization in Brazil was an extractivist process initiated in 1500 by the Portuguese Crown in its territories, in which undesirables or degraded (*degredados*) persons were forcibly migrated from Portuguese territories and placed as settlers in strategic locations in order to claim possession of natural resources. Simultaneously, the Portuguese took measures to establish a central authority by attempting to move, control, annihilate, or assimilate the Indigenous population in the Brazilian colony, often with the support of religious orders such as the Jesuits, who both defended and attacked an ambiguous natural law conception of voluntary slavery.[38] The increasing large-scale plantation of sugar, cotton, coffee, and cacao, together with gold mining, required labor-intensive extraction, planting, harvesting, and building in the colonies. This required the importation of large numbers of enslaved Africans, generating a complex global "forced migration."[39]

The destruction of historical documents has made it difficult to reconstruct a precise account of the Indigenous peoples, the number and ethnic origin of the enslaved Africans, and the identities of original settlers in Brazil. The Trans-Atlantic Slave Trade Database estimates that "three times as many enslaved Africans crossed the Atlantic as Europeans" until 1820 and that approximately six million people were brought as slaves to Brazil.[40] The vast majority appears to have come from West Africa near the Guinea Gulf, known then as the Slave Coast, and the area of the Bantus consisting in the regions of Angola, Mozambique, and the Congo.[41] By 1820 well over half of the population in Brazil was made up of Indigenous and mixed race, freed, and enslaved people. Interestingly, this is the same proportion shown in the 2010 Brazilian census.[42]

Colonialism is the ideological structure that integrated these various aspects of colonialization into established systems: the plantation, church, market, military, and court, among others. Each system required unique relations of power, codes, and structures, which were applied differently. In the plantations of the agrarian northeast, some authors described relaxed and "paternalistic" relations between plantation owners and enslaved people; in the Dutch colonies in northern Brazil, Jewish interactions with slaves led Baruch de Spinoza to write about a "Black scabby Brazilian";[43] in commercial or urban centers in the South, African women were sent to sell and barter for items in the markets; and within the ecclesiastic system, African brotherhoods and sisterhoods were created. These structures with their varieties of relationships functioned to control the enslaved people, catechize them, prevent rebellion, and otherwise filter their contact with the free world.[44]

Images, words, attitudes, and internalized prejudices along racial lines were integrated into "coloniality's" matrix of power, which had profound epistemic and geopolitical implications. As Quijano argues, this power functioned as an invisible premise to morally justify the conquest by dehumanizing Indigenous people through the reduction of their diversity to that of a singular Indio, represented as "savage" and "cannibal." Similarly, this power significantly altered the demographic, economic, and cultural development of the African continent, by reducing complex cultures and civilizations to the stereotype of a primitive, backward, and undeveloped race in order to justify the "civilizing" effects of European domination upon Negros. The power of language in expressions such as "piece of ebony" [*peça de ébano*] or "boy" [*moleque*] both reduced enslaved Africans to a commercial product and marked them as mentally and physically inferior.[45] Likewise, patriarchal organizations determined the gendered positioning of colonized women according to their reproductive functions in order to control their bodies.[46]

However, there were also movements for resistance and liberation. As early as 1549, the Jesuit Manuel da Nóbrega criticized the treatment of Indigenous peoples—comparably to Las Casas in Mexico—and the Jesuits' autonomous missions protected Indigenous peoples, albeit with paternalistic methods. Due to the competing power relations among the Portuguese, the Spanish, and the Papal authority, as well as to the protection Jesuits extended to Indigenous groups, the religious order was expelled from the colonies in 1759 on the grounds that they were forming a "state within a State."[47] Similarly, enslaved Africans escaped from plantations and established maroon communities [*quilombos*], the most famous of which was the Palmares Quilombo in the Pernambuco region, led by Zumbi. Also a "state within a State," this quilombo was formed in 1604 and grew to a population of thirty thousand, resisting decades of attacks by the Dutch and the Portuguese, until it was destroyed and Zumbi killed on November 20, 1695.[48] Later, African Muslims—who were often literate, known to do well as "profit slaves" [*escravos de ganho*], and employed out as trade smiths—became famous as leaders of many revolts in urban settings.[49] Thus, while the diversity of the Indigenous and enslaved peoples was occluded by attempts to dehumanize them, possibilities for liberation also emerged. Recent research demonstrates the resiliency of these communities and their power to change the narrative from one of total victimhood to a more nuanced history of oppression, agency, resistance, and liberation.

In 1808 the Portuguese Crown "migrated" to Brazil to escape Napoleon Bonaparte's invasion of Portugal, which generated a complex "interlocation" of colonization, colonialism, and coloniality: the systems of power, once located in the European center, were installed in the colony.[50] King D. João VI's decree of May 6, 1818, sought to promote civilization through science and culture, which required people skilled in industrial, clerical, educational, and artistic work. This demanded new migration policies allowing for the "importation" of Portuguese, Swiss, French, and German immigrants, leading to a new immigration phase in Brazilian history.[51]

So it was that the Portuguese implemented the military, juridical, ecclesiastic, and economic systems and institutions we define as colonialism and the epistemic and somewhat invisible justification provided by coloniality. Analyzing this period, Dussel insists with Russell Thornton that the annihilation of Indigenous peoples and the mass deaths of Africans due to the Atlantic slave trade correspond to the two first "Holocausts" of modernity. Yet few people connect these events to the Jewish Holocaust. Dussel underscores the importance of decentralizing Europe in our reading of world history and understanding the Conquista as a precondition to recognizing the victims of modern mass migration and genocide. This critique of coloniality also reveals liberation movements that have been obscured and disregarded.[52]

B. Decolonization, Anticolonial Nation Building, and the Problems of Postcolonial Syncretism

Decolonization, anticolonial, and postcolonial forces led to Brazilian political independence in 1822. Yet the resulting Brazilian Empire launched the next migratory phase guided by the discourse of a civilizing process that continued to affirm coloniality. In fact, the ideological colonial premise of a racial hierarchy supported a migratory wave of white Europeans and their integration based on the idea of "syncretism."[53] The new regime directed immigration policies to construct a Brazilian identity based on the very miscegenation, hybridity, "Latinity," and *mestizaje* that Mignolo criticizes in Latin American elites. In the case of Brazil, a postcolonial syncretism implemented within the political, military, scientific, cultural, and religious systems forced the assimilation of differences into a single nationalist model based on "whiteness."

Political syncretism is the ideology of connecting a new postcolonial racial identity with territorial sovereignty. Thus, the government promoted the occupation of "demographically empty" areas in border regions with

Argentina, Paraguay, and Uruguay to claim territorial integrity and implement "whitening." Law 601, issued on June 18, 1850, defined how unoccupied lands could be used for colonization by the "importing of European settlers," a racial characterization that overshadowed any criminal or moral qualities, since many German and Irish migrants were mercenaries recruited and dispatched to protect the Southern frontier.[54]

This securitization process implied a *military syncretism*. The new nation situated the Indigenous people as both a problem to be resolved and a tool for securing the borders. Brazil won the war with Paraguay (1865–1870), in part, through strategic alliances with the Indigenous populations, who were "mobilized" in a double sense through the military and by dislocation from their lands.[55] Also included in the military securitization were enslaved Africans whose owners offered them as soldiers with a promise of freedom.[56] Thus, the state claimed unity of purpose when it was convenient but easily disregarded the Indigenous and Black identities as inferior and less civilized when whiteness or territory were at stake.

Scientific syncretism emerged at the end of the nineteenth century, as biological determinism came to undergird a flawed "ethics of migration" that saw immigration as a tool for racial improvement. On the one hand, in 1867, Tavares Bastos offered the following reflections: "Emigration ceased to be, like the exodus of the Hebrews, forced exile and became the most effective instrument for civilization on the planet."[57] On the other, French ambassador to Brazil, Arthur de Gobineau, wrote in *An Essay on the Inequality of the Human Races* that miscegenation is the reason for the eventual downfall of civilizations. His distaste for "inbreeding" influenced his assessment of Brazil in 1869: "Not a single Brazilian has pure blood because the pattern of marriages among whites, Indians and Negroes is so widespread that the nuances of color are infinite, causing a degeneration of the most depressing type among the lower as well as the upper classes."[58] Harmonizing these ideas, the philosopher Sílvio Romero recognized that the creation of the *mestiço* in Brazil was an undisputed fact. While he upheld White superiority, he also argued that the Brazilian population must be "helped" by the Black and Indigenous races to withstand the tropical conditions.[59] He then wrote, "After having rendered the necessary help, the white type will continue to predominate by natural selection until it emerges pure and beautiful as in the old word. That will come when it has totally acclimated on this continent. Two factors will greatly contribute to this process: on the one hand the abolition of the slave trade and the continuous disappearance of the Indians, and on the other hand European immigration!"[60]

Thus, scientific racism advanced coloniality under the Brazilian Empire in the early 1880s, when the Central Society for Immigration combined Darwinist theories of biological enhancement with the idea of moral progress and civilization. Likewise, the philosophy of positivism inspired the abolition of slavery in 1888 and the proclamation of the Republic in 1889 through key values enshrined in the new Brazilian flag: "Order and Progress." Influenced by the positivist emphasis on science, the government implemented policies of social engineering and integrated the assimilation of differences into a new "scientific ideal."[61]

Cultural syncretism was the next step of the nation-building process, codified by Gilberto Freyre in the idea of a "racial democracy."[62] The discourse shifted to the idea of "melting of cultures" as one of the most enduring forms of assimilation, one that went hand in hand with immigration policies in the transition from agrarian colonization to industrialization at the turn of the twentieth century. This development required another wave of European immigrants who would undergo what was called a "Brazilianization" process. The African identity would manifest itself through cultural elements in music, dance, and cuisine, while the Indigenous identity was idealized in literature and music as a distant "primitive" reference to nature—as in the case of *O Guarani*, a famous romance by José de Alencar, set as an opera by Carlos Gomes.[63] However, such romanticism had no practical application to the lives of Indigenous people and the freed Africans, who retreated to the "hinterlands." The emerging Brazilian republic instituted a policy of "directed immigration" aimed at attracting white and Catholic Europeans to "civilize" the Brazilian nation.[64] Cultural syncretism, later expanded into religious syncretism, led to the Brazilian state's affirmation of what Mário de Andrade caricatured as the "myth of the three races" in 1924: the peaceful synthesis of Indigenous, African, and European identities.[65]

The analyses of Quijano and Dussel are clearly applicable here. While race was the prominent category guiding syncretism, the class divisions apparent in the Brazilian constitution of 1824 established a threshold of wealth for voting few immigrants could pass, thus curtailing their political involvement and limiting them to second-class citizenship. Moreover, the positioning of gender within this matrix confirms Alcoff's and Lugones's points: Indigenous women were labeled as natural and seductive or perverse and sinful;[66] women of African descent suffered forced labor, sexual abuse, and torture, while some managed a degree of commercial success;[67] and while some European women became the "mistresses" [*patroas*] of the plantations, many were among the destitute, single mothers living on the streets.[68] At the same time, the syncretic mixed-race woman was identified as the sensual ideal. Again, by combining the leitmotif of class, race, and gender with the colonial matrix of power, Brazil shrouded differences by projecting itself as a singular synthesis of the Americas, Africa, and Europe.

Combining decolonial liberation and our critique of syncretism also exposes the global implications of migration. As European nations promoted emigration of destitute populations in accord with Malthus's population control theories, the Americas provided key destinations. Between 1850 and 1950, approximately five million immigrants entered Brazil from Italy, Portugal, Spain, Germany, Japan, Syria, Turkey, Russia, Poland, and other eastern European nations.[69] In line with Quijano's analysis, although Africans were disparaged as inferior, white Europeans were not necessarily welcomed as new members into a "human community" but rather recruited as "instruments of labor." In an economy geared toward the exportation of tropical commodities, which benefited only a small elite, there was no interest in developing an internal market. Therefore, immigrants joined a fluctuating group of workers, living in extremely precarious conditions.[70] Thus, we see that the framework of decoloniality can reveal not only the geopolitical designs promoting territorial expansion, border securitization, and connection to global capitalism but also the internal syncretic strategies utilized by the state to deal with local populations and immigrants according to class, race, and gender relations.

C. Failed Multiculturalism and the Neocolonial Character of the National Security State

Thus far, we have applied decoloniality to highlight the power of colonialism within various systems and institutions while indicating how postcolonial syncretism simultaneously integrated and discriminated against migrants according to class, racial, and gendered interests. Why was there no mass revolt and unrest against these structures? Counterintuitively, most immigrants to Brazil absorbed the ideology of racial hierarchies and differentiated themselves from the Indigenous and African Brazilian population. At the beginning of the twentieth century, new waves of immigrants created the possibility of a mul-

ticultural society, but instead of welcoming their diversity, governmental policies absorbed them into "whiteness." In what follows, we highlight the various
national, ethnic, and cultural identities that were assimilated into a "Brazilian"
matrix from the period of independence through the turn of the century.

The phenomenon of immigration from the United States stands out as
unique in the history of Brazilian immigration. Advertising of opportunities
for settlers in Brazil arrived in the hands of former Confederates dealing with
the devastation of the Civil War and the frustration with Reconstruction.
Approximately ten thousand Southerners emigrated to other countries after
1865. Most Confederate settlements in Brazil were unsuccessful, and many
émigrés returned to the United States or were assimilated into the general
Brazilian population; however, a notable exception was the Santa Barbara
settlement in São Paulo state. This community eventually offered a foothold
for Protestant missionaries from the United States, who later built schools
and churches considered progressive by the newly formed republic.[71]

Germans and Italians had been part of the first wave of European immigrant groups to Brazil in the 1820s, and new waves brought more immigrants
from these countries after the 1880s. However, they initially confronted
deplorable working conditions; forced to work in semislave circumstances,
many quickly returned home. Paradoxically, while Brazil instigated policies
to encourage immigration, the agrarian class maintained its colonial mind-
set and continued to treat immigrants as subservient labor. Alternatively,
private associations were successful in encouraging Germans and Italians
to settle in southern Brazil after 1890, forming autonomous communities in
rural and urban areas. The economic crisis in Italy motivated larger numbers
of Italians to emigrate, to the point that they made up about a third of all
immigrant entries to Brazil.[72]

Successive waves of immigrants from Portugal and Spain followed. From
1890 to 1929, over a million Portuguese migrated to Brazil, the majority setting up small commercial shops.[73] They often settled in cities, intermarried
with African Brazilians, and were subjected to attacks due to their economic
mobility and questionable loyalty to whiteness. Spanish immigrants were
another significant group in the early twentieth century. Having been poor
farmers in Spain, they worked on Brazilian plantations, where they suffered
the same abuse as other immigrants, although some were able to buy land
in São Paulo's coffee region and establish their own productive plantations.[74]

Other migrants arrived from the Middle East. Jews who had been forced
to convert as "New Christians" in Portugal after 1497 migrated to Brazil in

the early 1600s. With the outbreak of the Spanish Moroccan War (1859–1860), several hundred Jewish Moroccan families emigrated. Later, young men migrated to the Amazon region to work in the rubber boom or as small merchants; by 1891 they also began to form Jewish agricultural colonies. After 1924 the Jewish Colonization Association helped nearly sixty thousand Eastern European Jewish immigrants to find work in commerce and manufacturing during the two world wars. Arab immigrants from Syria and Lebanon moved to Brazil on their own and became part of the merchant class. While records are contradictory, estimates are that approximately 180,000 Middle Easterners came to Brazil in the early 1920s. Due to their questionable "whiteness," Jews and Arabs negotiated their Brazilian identity by confronting the caricatures or jokes that mocked their culture and suggesting that the Portuguese who came to Brazil had originally been of Arab or Jewish descent.[75]

The next wave was represented by the Japanese. The Brazilian state, having failed in its attempt to import Chinese workers in the 1820s, was concerned with the socialist and anarchist views of European immigrants and dissatisfied with the Jews and Arabs. Therefore, Brazilian elites looked to Japan, which was promoting itself as an Asian "white" empire and attempting to address its own overpopulation by providing incentives for emigration. With the arrival of Japanese immigrants in 1908, some Brazilian intellectuals speculated that Japanese "blood" would help Brazil attain higher industrial production levels, while others espoused racist fears of the "Yellow Peril." Similar to the experiences of previous immigrants, the low wages and harsh working conditions compelled the Japanese to organize colonies or to set up small commercial shops. Despite these constraints, nearly 190,000 Japanese immigrants arrived in Brazil from 1908 to 1941. Continued interest in biological-race theory led to the hypothesis that the Amazonian Indigenous people were a lost Japanese tribe. This in term led to the argument that the Japanese were themselves a mixed race of Whites, Indigenous people (Mongols), and Black Indonesians, which testified to the positive results of miscegenation.[76] After World War II, Japanese economic development surged, and emigration abated. Later, descendants of Japanese immigrants to Brazil would return to Japan as *Nisei* and *Dekasegi*, in search of work.

What do these migratory patterns reveal? First, Brazil lost an opportunity to embrace multicultural policies by invalidating cultural diversity through the promotion of syncretism. Second, Brazil based its immigration policy on a faulty ethical argument that North American, European, Middle Eastern, and Asian immigrants would have a "moralizing effect" on the country. These two points are incompatible with the normative ethical framework of decolonial liberation, because they maintain an underlying asymmetry in racial, gender, and class relations.

Due to the world wars, the number of European immigrants diminished, but new policies continued to promote forced assimilation, albeit within a "nationalization campaign" based on the "imperatives of national security."[77] The Constitutional Assembly of 1934 adopted the Quota Law, which established annual limits on immigration to Brazil, while the Immigration and Colonization Council (1937–1945) emphasized the surveillance of immigrants from Axis power countries and oversaw a new stage of the "Brazilianization" process, securing the primacy of the Portuguese language in rural schools and imposing Brazilian customs and festivities within small immigrant communities.[78] The council also investigated the internal migration of workers from the northeast to the growing industrial centers in the south of Brazil, based on the fear that radicalized peasants would influence labor movements in the urban centers.

The postwar government of Brazil also emphasized "national development." By the 1950s, the dominant agrarian class used the developmentalist and modernization discourses to compel the state to support their economic consolidation efforts. The Land Law of 1964 and the Pro-Ethanol Program of 1975 promoted modernization, concentration of capital, and mechanization of agriculture, a process that expelled immigrant colonies from their land and purged rural workers of their labor rights. This resulted in an internal migration of the rural poor to the urban centers.[79]

An interpretation of these processes reveals strategies to maintain coloniality and new efforts to resist it. For example, peasant movements, union workers, intellectuals, religious activists, and student leaders were eager to decolonize the power of the agrarian class through agrarian reform. However, when these voices claimed "decolonial liberation," they were met with a military coup d'état in 1964, the first of several military coups in South America. Guided by Cold War ideology and fearing that the Cuban revolution would cause subsequent revolutions throughout Latin America, the United States assisted in the establishment of the Superior School of War in Brazil and Operation Condor, a secret inter-American network of intelligence and counterinsurgency operations mandated to find and persecute citizens fleeing the military regimes of Brazil, Argentina, Chile, Uruguay, and Paraguay.[80] Within this context, the military regime defined internal migratory movements as "threats" and accused about five thousand individuals of being communist infiltrators, subversives, or "enemies of the state." A period of illegal imprisonments, tortures, executions, and extraditions led to a new migratory movement, this time of Brazilians leaving the country.[81]

After twenty years, however, the political process of "Opening" (*Abertura*) enabled a negotiated peaceful transition to democracy in 1986. One of the conditions for this process was the declaration of "broad, general, and unrestricted amnesty," which pardoned not only political prisoners and exiles but also those involved in torture and other crimes during the military dictatorship. With democracy, new actors emerged in the public sphere, bringing a validation of their identities and enshrining their rights claims in the new Constitution of 1988. In this process, a new multicultural plurality of identities emerged, bringing challenges against the ideology of syncretism and the "myth of racial democracy." This led to another moment in Brazilian history and new perspectives on migration.

III. Democratization, Human Rights, and the Dynamics of Migratory Interlocation

We now turn to current migration issues generated by coloniality often disregarded by other philosophical perspectives. Based on a decolonial ethics of migration, which prompts us to ask who the excluded are, we will reflect on two dimensions: first, people in constant mobility, including the homeless, tourists, the Indigenous, and other displaced peoples who are crossing internal borders; and secondly, the current waves of immigrants coming to Brazil from Latin American and Caribbean countries such as Haiti, Bolivia, and Venezuela.

A. Migratory Interlocation: Mobility, Homelessness, Social Movements, and Tourism

Contemporary perspectives on migration, mobility, and border crossing within Brazil enable us to expand the scope of migration ethics. As defined previously, migration includes the movement of people from one setting to another, within and beyond nation-states. This movement reveals what we call "inter-location," the process of transitioning from one locality to another by creating new meanings that justify border crossing and the settling in a new space.[82] Based on this concept, we observe how groups previously oppressed by colo-niality reemerge in social movements that rely on democracy, citizenship, and human rights discourses to reframe the meaning of migration and claim rights for those "in the situation of mobility." Nogueira and Moraes describe recent research on mobility in Brazil that opens the door for discussions of internal border crossing or short-term movements of people with an emphasis on the "meaning" or "resignification" of these mobilities.[83]

Building on this understanding of interlocation and mobility, *homeless-ness* is construed within the migratory patterns of Brazil, in which the lack of coordinated efforts to absorb migrants in metropolitan areas has resulted in an increase in "people in the situation of the street" (*pessoas em situação de rua*). A profile of the homeless population in São Paulo shows how the displaced population increased steadily from 2000 to 2019, due to a signif-icant number of internal migrants in addition to those from other coun-tries, particularly Venezuela. Naming the transient nature of homelessness as "migration" reframes the question from an individualistic approach to one that examines how the flows of homelessness reflect the larger picture of internal and regional movement of people based on continuing racism and the historical, social, political, and economic reasons for and implications of such mobility.[84] Identifying these various dimensions as *interlocation* pro-vides yet another conceptual tool to map these movements and consider the resignification of "land," "territory," and "space" through a decolonial lens in which locations are expropriated and reclaimed.

The "Landless Movement" (Movimento Sem Terra—MST) has a long history of struggles against coloniality in Brazil and remains one of the few organizations actively working for "land reform."[85] It shares affinities with the Land Ministry (Pastoral da Terra) of the Catholic Church, whose Base Communities (Comunidades Eclesiais de Base) provided the venue for peo-ple to reflect and organize, using the perspective of liberation theology's emancipatory discourses to justify their actions.[86] Based on these discourses, the movement adopted a confrontational stance against the state and the agrarian class, invading unproductive land and demanding the right to form cooperatives.[87] Interpreting the MST in terms of a decolonial migration ethics and interlocation processes sheds light on its mobile and historically situated character: small farmers—many of German and Italian origin—lost their properties to agricultural expansion supported by the military government's development strategy, were expelled, joined the MST, and adopted a normative discourse to reclaim land, often in a different location. However, the work of the MST expands beyond land occupation by a collective of displaced populations to a critique of global capitalism, racism, and exploitation. For this reason, the MST has formed coalitions with groups such as workers' unions, the movement for children "in the situation of the street," the *quilombola* movement, educators, political and social agents, and Indigenous groups.[88] While forming allies internally, the MST has also reinforced the global nature of its claims by building worldwide solidarity with international groups.[89]

Also configured within the umbrella term of "migration" are various forms of *tourism*.[90] Although often punctual in character, tourism is influenced by the global nature of coloniality and continues to reinforce relationships of power established in the past. For instance, the wealthy can cross borders to exercise their touristic gaze or fascination for the exotic side of urban settlements called "favelas" in Brazil, but the poor are not allowed to overstep their boundaries.[91] While many favelas emerged with the travel of northeastern Brazilian migrants to large cities, their provisional settling in makeshift dwellings turned into eventual permanence. In her discussion of *poverty tourism*, Freire-Medeiros argues that the favelas in Rio de Janeiro have a "distinctive socio-geographic character" that stimulates the international imagination and promotes an exotification to attract consumers from North America and Europe.[92] Both private and public tourist agencies have incorporated visits to the favelas, but the *favelados* have been offered limited venues for empowerment and agency to produce their own "meanings" and capitalize on this market. Within this context, Jaguaribe and Heatherington argue that the tourist gaze can be criticized and disrupted by a reflection on the meaning of the very experience of *touring*.[93]

Furthermore, poverty tourism overlaps with *sex tourism*. The erotification of Brazilian women, since the colonial descriptions of the naked Indigenous woman and the alluring qualities of the enslaved African, evolved to portray the syncretic, mixed-race woman as representative of Brazilian feminine sensuality. Contemporary culture mirrors this stereotype in the image of the "mulatta for export" and generates businesses exploiting the female body. Giacomini describes how women develop techniques in "professional seduction" and are required to maintain a globalized body shape that corresponds to the "awaited" rather than their "actual" body type. Sex tourism within Brazil is a consequence of such colonial representations.[94]

Williams and other scholars consider *human trafficking* and *slave labor* as complementary dimensions of mobility but question the tendency to equate them with sex tourism. This conception reinforces the trope of a typical naïve, uneducated, African descendant woman from the South, whose movement is stigmatized under the notion of human trafficking, especially when the mobility of northern tourists or privileged Brazilians goes unquestioned. Equating slave labor with sex work not only obscures the historical reality of African enslavement and current efforts to combat exploitive labor but also can result in the criminalization of migrant workers (including sex workers) and their network of family and friends who may help them find work and housing.[95] Thus, while activists press for the recognition of violence against women, decriminalization of the victims of trafficking, and criminalization of the traffickers, they differentiate these cases from the autonomous activity of sex workers. Alcoff warns that whereas violence against women seems to be a universal phenomenon, the cultural understandings, legal interpretations, and psychological reactions associated with violence against women can vary from place to place and that coloniality may influence these perceptions.[96]

The situation of *Indigenous groups* living near international borders is rarely included in the discussion of migration in Brazil. For instance, the Guarani are present in four countries—Bolivia, Brazil, Paraguay, and Argentina—while the Kaiowá Pa and Terena traverse the borders of Brazil and Paraguay. They have a tradition of spatial *mobility* integrated into their concept of land, family, and cosmovision, motivating agricultural practices of rotating lands, visits to family members, the building of social and political networks, or avoidance of conflicts and violent invasions. The Guarani cosmovision requires staying away from the land of evil spirits, including ecologically degraded areas, and searching for a "land without evil" (*Yvy marã e'ÿ* or *terra sem males*), where they can establish their way of life (*Reko*).[97] The forming of national boundaries and the introduction of agribusiness in Brazil disintegrated and restructured the lives of Indigenous peoples, who were often expelled to other lands across the border. In the case of the Terena, recent land demarcations have "placed" them on the Paraguayan side of the border as their "traditional" place of origin to the benefit of agricultural expansion in

Brazil. While the business and commerce between Paraguay and Brazil has a certain fluidity, this porousness of the border has not been afforded to the Terena.[98] The refusal of nation-states to acknowledge Indigenous history, cosmovision, or spatial mobility further reduces them to small reserves within political boundaries, thereby continuing the colonization process.

Interestingly, these themes emerge even within traditional systems of colonialism. The religious discourses permeating the discussions on migration by many priests and nuns in Brazil refer to liberation theology.[99] Accordingly, the Migration and Human Rights Institute (Instituto Migração e Direitos Humanos) created a "Ministry for People in Mobility" to offer services to migrants and refugees, seafarers, tourists, and other travelers, including the homeless and victims of human trafficking.[100] Likewise, as mentioned above, the Pastoral Land ministry provided the MST with concepts and discourses from liberation theology.[101] The expanded definition of migration and its connection to theological language is not merely rhetorical but indicates the manifestation of what Dussel had defined as prophetic voices that bring to light the suffering and border-crossings practices that are not recognized by state laws and policies but can be justified ethically by the appeal to decolonial liberation.[102]

In terms of the meaning of migration in Brazil, these examples illustrate the dynamic processes involving mobilities and locations within a decolonial perspective. While some forms of migration are forced or coerced, other forms are stigmatized and criminalized; while some are naturalized as invisible forms of privilege, others are subversive and emancipatory. Interlocation captures these dynamics: it reveals the power of coloniality, highlights contemporary forms of mobility that attempt to overcome it, and identifies their connection to different spaces. Interlocation also redefines migratory locations not as fixed territories but as fluid terrains of struggle where opportunities for resistance may emerge. Interlocation prompts us to ask for a *locus enuntiationis* that questions static relations of race, gender, and class by promoting "epistemic disobedience" and criticizing the matrix of power.

B. Ethics and Human Rights: Regional Migration from Bolivia, Haiti, and Venezuela

The struggles and critique by social movements have provoked concrete changes in laws regarding immigrants and refugees entering Brazil, driving policy shifts from an emphasis on national security to a discourse on human rights. In 1997 Brazil enacted its own refugee norms through Law no. 9,474, and in June 2017 the government passed a new immigration law (no. 13,445) revoking the Alien Statute of 1980 (which had focused on national security).[103] This recent law uses the language of human rights and guarantees immigrants humanitarian protections as well as other political and social rights.[104]

Another factor that reinforced the discourses on human rights was the relaxation of migration restrictions among neighboring countries through regional integration. In the last decades of the twentieth century, the Southern America Common Market (Mercosul) emulated the European Union and moved toward a regional framework for trade, commerce, and human rights.[105] The 2002 Mercosul Residence Agreement allows for citizens of member states to reside and work for two years in another member state and provides for basic rights to education, equal working conditions, and family reunification.[106] This represents a change in the conception of immigrants, presenting them not as whitening agents, civilizing influences, or enemies of the state but as human beings with dignity and rights. Consequently, since 2010, most immigrants to Brazil have come from Latin America and the Caribbean, changing the trends seen in the days of Brazilian nation building.[107] However, while the law establishes the humanitarian basis for immigration, the actual experience of immigrants is not always in line with these aspirations.

A case in point is Haitian immigration. Haitians are granted a humanitarian status to enable their immigration to Brazil since they do not qualify as refugees under Brazilian refugee law; however, the state is under no obligation to help them in their resettlement process, leaving them to depend on charitable organizations. From 2015 to 2016, Haitians were the leading source of foreign labor in Brazil, and as of 2015, around thirty thousand Haitians had arrived in the country. Since then, due to the economic downturn following 2016, many Haitians have decided to make their way to Mexico and the United States.[108]

The response to Bolivian immigrants represents yet another experience. Estimates indicate around two hundred thousand Bolivian immigrants to São Paulo, of whom ten to fifty thousand are undocumented. Many labor in garment and textile sweatshops in closed buildings without windows or proper lighting or access to sanitary facilities and are paid by the piece rather than according to minimum wage regulations. Due to the lack of coordinated efforts to support migrants, Bolivian immigrants have had to sift through a disconnected list of agencies, including unions, attorney associations, consulates, and civil and religious organizations.[109]

What is the philosophical relevance of these points? Before we answer this question, we will consider one last case: the unique and puzzling Brazilian response to Venezuelan migration. Despite a slow start, the Brazilian military provided humanitarian aid and integrated 180,000 Venezuelan immigrants in 2019, with almost 130,000 asylum claims.[110] Numerous organizations, including the UN, UNICEF, and USAID, provided on-the-ground support as well as funding to help with relocation assistance.[111] Yet the promotion of this resettlement program as a military matter with the backing of an autocratic political leadership in the United States reveals the ideological affinities of the Brazilian government and its revival of the ideology of national security.

Interpreting these points according to an ethics of decolonial liberation, we consider that Brazil's recent policies do not reflect the normative dimensions defined earlier. Political expedience, economic calculations, and populist nationalism have served as the bases for recent responses to migration, although there is a normative framework for ethical actions based on human rights and constitutional law in place. On the one hand, postcolonial forms of syncretism, nationalist disregard for diversity, and impediments to multiculturalism reveal how both the leitmotif of race, class, and gender and the colonial matrix of power are adapted to new times. On the other hand, scholars have questioned the meaning and significance of migration while social movements and agencies have incorporated the language of human rights in their response to current forms of mobility, thereby questioning the state's negligence in supporting migrant populations. We conclude that although the pernicious complexities of coloniality are still operating in Brazil, there are opportunities to identify and dismantle them.

Conclusion

Our first goal in this chapter was to discuss migration ethics in light of "global plurality." We adopted a broader concept of "migration" to capture worldwide interlocations that may occur within or beyond the borders of nation-states. Due to plurality, migration in each location can have a differentiated philosophical or ideological justification; therefore, we affirmed our *locus enuntiationis* and our option for liberation ethics and decoloniality theory.

This option is more appropriate for the Latin American context, in contrast to political liberalism in Anglo America and critical theory in Europe, whose sophisticated tools are limited in their ability to analyze the various implications of migration considered in this chapter.

Our second goal was to clarify our adoption of liberation ethics and decoloniality theory as the basis for a Latin American ethics of migration. This option implied an ontology, epistemology, and ethics. The *ontological task* was more descriptive and concerned the definition of "Latin America" and the "migrant" as concrete, situated, and embodied "otherness." Based on Dussel and Mignolo, we recognized the ambiguity of the concept "Latin America" but decided to keep it, provided this choice was corrected by a clear ethical principle. Our *epistemic task* led us to Quijano, who revealed the underlying ideology and rationality of coloniality, showing that class, race, and gender are not simply descriptive terms but are, rather, strong Eurocentric epistemic concepts. Alcoff and Lugones demonstrated how these concepts are rigidly applied to "baptize" and name subjects and objects according to preestablished racist and sexist beliefs. Coloniality is, therefore, an epistemic precondition, a powerful and elusive way of thinking that enabled colonization and colonialism and continues to operate as a default system in syncretic postcolonialism. Thus, Mignolo proposes "epistemic disobedience" as the starting point of decoloniality. Finally, our *ethical task* considered the normative claims raised by those oppressed by colonial systems, leading us to affirm our option to focus on the context of exploitation, dismissal, and erasure caused by colonialism. Therefore, we called attention to the interconnection of the leitmotif of class, race, and gender with a matrix of power in coloniality. Combining liberation ethics with decoloniality theory led to a clear normative demand for "decolonial liberation." As a maxim, this could be defined as follows: *We should always ask about who is being oppressed, dismissed, or erased by coloniality.*

Our third and main goal was to utilize this normative framework to reveal, discuss, and criticize the underlying ideologies guiding migration policies in different phases of Brazilian history. Reinterpreting some historiographic material, we provided details on how colonization began as an extractive and agrarian project; how colonialism created systems to explore the geopolitical reality of an interconnected world through interactions with Africa, Asia, and Europe; and how coloniality supplied the ideological basis for forced migration and assimilation into a Eurocentric syncretic identity. This historical background sheds light on contemporary practices. In analyzing the Brazilian material on migration, we did not necessarily ask whether the Terena are originally Paraguayan or Brazilian or how they can conform to "whiteness." Rather, we asked what the underlying colonial motivation is that prompts this racialized question. We did not ask what the requirements are for tourists to visit Brazil but rather how their mobility is permissible and how their visits produce new "meanings" about Brazil.

What are the outcomes of this discussion? First, we applied decoloniality and questioned the economic exploitation, systemic racism, and patriarchal structures imposed by coloniality in Brazil—also observed throughout the Americas. Second, we exposed how coloniality is updated through the assimilatory programs based on postcolonial syncretism, the disregard for the plurality of multicultural identities, and the oppression of migrants for the sake of national security in Brazil—showing how the emphasis on syncretism has negated the possibility of multiculturalism. Third, we identified interlocation processes that promote dynamic mobilities of peoples in fluid spaces. The people in situation of mobility—MST members, *quilombolas*, Indigenous people, homeless, Sem Terra, Latin American migrants—attach new multicultural meanings to multiple locations (territory, land, *quilombos*, streets) and question how certain borders are defined, crossed, or allegedly trespassed in arbitrary ways.

The framework of liberation and decoloniality compels us to ask which identities and perspectives are missing or subjugated by coloniality—thus providing a perspective we cannot find in political liberalism or critical theory. Therefore, we believe that this ethics of migration with roots in Latin America can claim broad normative validity, because the option for "decolonial liberation" is relevant in any global contexts where colonial oppression influences global migration.

Notes

1. Shmuel Eisenstadt, *The Absorption of Immigrants: A Comparative Study Based Mainly on the Jewish Community in Palestine and the State of Israel* (Glencoe, Ill.: Free Press, 1955).

2. Veit Bader, "The Ethics of Immigration," *Constellations* 12, no. 3 (October 2015): 331–61.

3. International Organization for Migration, *Glossary on Migration* (Geneva: International Organization for Migration, 2019).

4. Francisco Vitoria, *De Indis* and *De jure belli*, ed. James Brown Scott (1532; New York: Wildy and Sons, 1917); John Locke, *Two Treatises of Government*,

ed. Peter Laslett (1689; Cambridge, U.K.: Cambridge University Press, 1988), 2.119–21; and Thomas R. Malthus, *An Essay on the Principle of Population*, vol. 2, 6th edition, ed. E. A. Wrigley and David Souden (London: William Pickering, 1986). See also Eric Richards, *The Genesis of International Mass Migration: The British Case, 1750–1900* (Manchester: Manchester University Press, 2018), 250–51.

5. Michael Walzer, *Spheres of Justice: A Defense of Pluralism and Equality* (New York: Basic Books, 1983); Joseph Carens, *The Ethics of Immigration* (New York: Oxford University Press, 2013).

6. William Kymlicka, *Multicultural Citizenship: A Liberal Theory of Minority Rights* (New York: Oxford University Press, 1995); Michael Blake, *Justice, Migration, and Mercy* (Oxford: Oxford University Press, 2020).

7. Immanuel Kant, *Zum Ewigen Frieden*, in *Kants Gesammelte Schriften*, vol. 8 (Berlin: Königlich Preussische Akademie der Wissenschaften, 1902), 358.

8. Hannah Arendt, "We Refugees," in *The Jewish Writings*, ed. Jerome Kohn and Ron H. Feldman (New York: Schocken Books, 2007), 264–74; Jürgen Habermas, *Ach Europa: Kleine Politische Schriften XI* (Frankfurt: Suhrkamp, 2008), 88–95.

9. Seyla Benhabib, *The Rights of Others: Aliens, Residents, and Citizens* (Cambridge, U.K.: Cambridge University Press, 2004), 114–21 and 179–80.

10. Mokoko P. Sebola, "Refugees and Immigrants in Africa: Where Is an African Ubuntu?" *Africa's Public Service Delivery and Performance Review* 7, no. 1 (2019): a285; Yen Le Espiritu, "A Critical Transnational Perspective to Asian America," in *The Oxford Handbook of Philosophy and Race*, ed. Naomi Zack (Oxford: Oxford University Press, 2017), 102–13.

11. Santiago Castro-Gómez, *Crítica de la razón Latinoamericana* (Barcelona: Puvill Editores, 1996), 129–37; Michel Gobat, "The Invention of Latin America: A Transnational History of Anti-Imperialism, Democracy, and Race," *American Historical Review* 118, no. 5 (December 2013): 1345–75.

12. Walter Mignolo, *The Idea of Latin America* (Oxford: Blackwell, 2005), 58.

13. Mignolo, *The Idea of Latin America*, 72 and 94.

14. Walter Mignolo, *The Darker Side of Renaissance: Literacy, Territoriality, and Colonization* (Ann Arbor: University of Michigan Press, 1995), 5–7.

15. Enrique Dussel, *Ética da libertação: Na idade da globalização e da exclusão* (Petrópolis: Vozes, 2000). For a good summary of Dussel's position, see Alejandro Vallega, *Latin American Philosophy: From Identity to Radical Exteriority* (Bloomington: Indiana University Press, 2014), 52–75.

16. Enrique Dussel, *Ética comunitária: Liberta o pobre!* (Petrópolis: Vozes, 1986), 244–47.

17. Enrique Dussel, *The Invention of the Americas: Eclipse of "The Other" and the Myth of Modernity*, trans. Michael Barber (New York: Continuum, 1995).

18. Enrique Dussel, *Política de la liberación*, vol. 1 (Madrid: Trotta, 2008); *Política de la liberación*, vol. 2 (Madrid: Trotta, 2009).

19. Dussel, *Ética da libertação*, 501, 530; idem., *The Underside of Modernity: Apel, Ricoeur, Rorty, Taylor, and the Philosophy of Liberation*, trans. Eduardo Mendieta (Atlantic Highlands: Humanities Press, 2000).

20. Dussel, *Ética da libertação*, 435.

21. Aníbal Quijano, "Coloniality of Power, Eurocentrism, and Latin America," *Nepantla* 3 (2000): 533. See Amos Nascimento, "Coloniality of Power and the Ongoing Intersectional Impact of Eurocentrism," *Neue Politische Literatur* 63, no. 1 (2018): 159–60.

22. Quijano, "Coloniality of Power," 534.

23. Quijano, 551–52, 562, and 566.

24. Quijano, 568.

25. Mignolo, *The Darker Side*.

26. Glória Anzaldúa, *Borderlands/La Frontera: The New Mestiza* (San Francisco: Aunt Lute Books, 1987).

27. Walter Mignolo, "The Geopolitics of Knowledge and the Colonial Difference," *South Atlantic Quarterly* 101, no. 1 (Winter 2002): 57–96; idem., *On Decoloniality: Concepts, Analytics, Praxis* (Durham, N.C.: Duke University Press, 2018).

28. Mignolo, *On Decoloniality*, 223.

29. Mignolo, *On Decoloniality*, 224.

30. Linda Alcoff, "Mignolo's Epistemology of Coloniality," *New Centennial Review* 7, no. 3 (Winter 2007): 83.

31. Linda Alcoff, "Anti-Latino Racism," in *Decolonizing Epistemologies: Latino/a Theology and Philosophy*, ed. Ada M. Isasi-Díaz and Eduardo Mendieta, 107–26 (New York: Fordham University Press, 2011), 124–25.

32. Linda Alcoff, "On Judging Epistemic Credibility: Is Social Identity Relevant?" in *Engendering Rationalities*, ed. Nancy Tuana and Sandra Morgen (Albany: State University of New York Press, 2001), 53–80; idem, "Decolonizing Feminist Philosophy," in *Decolonizing Feminism: Transnational Feminism and Globalization*, ed. Margaret McLaren (Lanham, Md.: Rowman and Littlefield, 2017), 21–36; Amy Reed-Sandoval, *Socially Undocumented: Identity and Immigration Justice* (Oxford: Oxford University Press, 2020), 64–75.

33. María Lugones, "Heterosexualism and the Colonial Modern/Gender System," *Hypatia* 22, no. 1 (Winter 2007): 186–209; idem., "Toward a Decolonial Feminism," *Hypatia* 25, no. 4 (Fall 2010): 744.

34. Lugones, "Toward a Decolonial Feminism," 753.

35. Lugones, "Toward a Decolonial Feminism," 754.

36. Our purpose here is not to consider the variety of detailed arguments on normative validity or the many possible intersections, forms of exclusion, or resistance within migratory processes and iterations of coloniality in Brazil but to examine how liberation ethics and decoloniality theory could be applied to the Brazilian context.

37. Amos Nascimento, "Colonialism, Modernism and Postmodernism in Brazil," in *Latin American Philosophy: Currents, Issues, Debates*, ed. Eduardo Mendieta

(Bloomington: Indiana University Press, 2003), 124–49; idem., "Syncretism as a Form of Multicultural Politics?" *Journal of Latin American and Caribbean Ethnic Studies* 7, no. 2 (2012): 115–36; Amos Nascimento and Josué Sathler, "Black Masks on White Faces: Liberation Theology and the Quest for Syncretism in the Brazilian Context," in *Liberation Theology and Postmodernity in the Americas*, ed. Eduardo Mendieta et al. (New York: Routledge, 1997), 95–124.

38. José Eisenberg, "Cultural Encounters, Theoretical Adventures: The Jesuit Missions to the New World and the Justification of Voluntary Slavery," *History of Political Thought* 24, no. 3 (Autumn 2003): 1.

39. Caio da Silva Prado Jr., *Evolução política do Brasil* (São Paulo: Brasiliense, 1980); Boris Fausto, *A Concise History of Brazil* (Cambridge, U.K.: Cambridge University Press, 1999).

40. Voyages: The Trans-Atlantic Slave Trade Database, Emory University, 2009, https://www.slavevoyages.org/assessment/estimates.

41. Pierre Verger, *Artigos* 1 (São Paulo: Corrupio, 1992); *Fluxo e refluxo do tráfico de escravos entre o Golfo do Benin e a Bahia de Todos os Santos: Dos séculos XVII a XIX*, trans. Tasso Gadzanis (São Paulo: Corrupio, 1997); João José Reis, "Identidade e diversidade étnicas nas irmandades negras no tempo da escravidão," *Tempo* 2, no. 3 (1997): 7–33; Mariza Carvalho Soares, "Descobrindo a Guiné no Brasil Colonial," *Revista do Instituto Histórico e Geográfico Brasileiro* 161, no. 407 (April–June 2000): 71–94; Cristiane Batista Da Silva Santos, "A África Central e os lugares de memória do tráfico Atlântico na Costa de Maraú: Etnônimos, etnicidade e diáspora," *Sankofa* 6, no. 10 (January 6, 2013): 63–95; Mac Cord, "Identidades étnicas, irmandade do rosário e rei do Congo: Sociabilidades cotidianas recifenses (século XIX)," *Revista Campos de Antropologia Social* 4 (2005): 51–66; Linda Heywood, *Diáspora negra no Brasil* (São Paulo: Contexto, 2008); Habeeb Akande, *Illuminating the Blackness: Blacks and African Muslims in Brazil* (London: Rebaak, 2016).

42. The 2010 census shows 50.74 percent of the population as Afro-descendant and 0.43 percent as Indigenous. See also Justin Bucciferro, "A Forced Hand: Natives, Africans, and the Population of Brazil, 1545–1850," *Journal of Iberian and Latin American Economic History* 31, no. 2 (September 2013): 285–317; idem., "Racial Inequality in Brazil from Independence to the Present," in *Has Latin American Inequality Changed Direction?* ed. Luis Bértola and Jeffery Williamson (Cham: Springer Open, 2017), 171–94.

43. Gilberto Freyre, *Casa grande e senzala* (Rio de Janeiro: J. Olympio, 1933); B. Feitler, "Four Chapters in the History of Crypto-Judaism in Brazil: The Case of the Northeastern New Christians (17th–21st Centuries)," *Jewish History* 25, no. 2 (May 2011): 207–27; Jeffrey Lesser, *Welcoming the Undesirable: Brazil and the Jewish Question* (Berkeley: University of California Press, 1995); Michael Rosenthal, "'The Black, Scabby Brazilian': Some Thoughts on Race and Early Modern Philosophy," *Philosophy and Social Criticism* 31, no. 2 (March 2005): 211–21.

44. Reis, "Identidade"; Cord, "Identidades étnicas"; Stephen Selka, "The Sisterhood of Boa Morte in Brazil: Harmonious Mixture, Black Resistance, and the Politics of Religious Practice," *Journal of Latin American and Caribbean Anthropology* 13, no. 1 (April 2008): 79–114.

45. Vicente d'Eça Almeida, *Lições de história marítima geral* (Lisbon: Imprensa Nacional, 1895), 179.

46. Sonia Giacomini, *Mulher e escrava: Uma introdução histórica ao estudo da mulher negra no Brasil* (Petrópolis: Vozes, 1988); Maria Lúcia de Barros Mott, *Submissão e resistência: A mulher na luta contra a escravidão*, 2nd ed. (São Paulo: Contexto, 1991).

47. Fausto, *A Concise History*, 57.

48. R. K. Kent, "Palmares: An African State in Brazil," *Journal of African History* 6, no. 2 (July 1965): 161–75; Stuart B. Schwartz, *Slaves, Peasants, and Rebels: Reconsidering Brazilian Slavery* (Urbana: University of Illinois Press, 1992); Robert N. Anderson, "The Quilombo of Palmares: A New Overview of a Maroon State in Seventeenth-Century Brazil," *Journal of Latin American Studies* 28, no. 3 (October 1996): 545–66; Paulo Funari, "Conflict and the Interpretation of Palmares, a Brazilian Runaway Polity," *Historical Archaeology* 37, no. 3 (January 2003): 81–92.

49. Kent, "Palmares"; João José Reis, *Slave Rebellion in Brazil: The Muslim Uprising in 1835 in Bahia*, trans. Arthur Brakel (Baltimore: John Hopkins University Press, 1993); Yusuf A. Nzibo, "The Muslim Factor in the Afro-Brazilian Struggle Against Slavery," *Institute of Muslim Minority Affairs* 7, no. 2 (July 1986): 547–56; Mott, *Submissão*; Selka, "The Sisterhood"; Akande, *Illuminating*.

50. Amos Nascimento, "Inter-(African-Latin-)American: An Experiment in Inter-Location," in *The International Turn in American Studies*, ed. Marietta Messmer and Armin Paul Frank (Frankfurt: P. Lang, 2015), 173–207.

51. Jeffrey Lesser, *Immigration, Ethnicity and National Identity in Brazil, 1808 to the Present* (New York: Cambridge University Press, 2013), 8, 17–39; Flávia de Ávila, *Brasil e trabalhadores estrangeiros nos séculos XIX e XX: Evolução normativo-legislativa nos contextos histórico, político e socioeconômico* (São Paolo, 2011).

52. Dussel, *Política*, 119–32.

53. Nascimento, "Colonialism," 130–33; idem., "Syncretism as a Form of Multicultural Politics?," 115–36.

54. Giralda Seyferth, "The Diverse Understandings of Foreign Migration to the South of Brazil (1818–1950)," *Vibrant: Virtual Brazilian Anthropology* 10, no. 2 (July/December 2013): 129; Lesser, *Immigration*, 33–34; Ávila, *Brasil e trabalhadores estrangeiros*, 86–89.

55. Andrey Cordeiro Ferreira, "Borders, Histories and Identities: Symbolic Struggle in Indigenous Land Demarcation Processes," *Mana* 15, no. 2 (October 2011): 377–410.

56. Fausto.

57. Tavares Bastos, *Os males do presente e as esperanças do futuro* (São Paulo: Cia. Ed. Nacional, 1976), 51. Cited by Seyferth, "The Diverse Understandings," 131.

58. Cited in Thomas E. Skidmore, *Black into White: Race and Nationality in Brazilian Thought* (Durham, N.C.: Duke University Press 1993), 30.

59. Skidmore, *Black into White*; Marshall C. Eakin, "Race and Identity: Sílvio Romero, Science, and Social Thought in Late 19th Century Brazil," *Luso-Brazilian Review* 22, no. 2 (Winter 1985): 151–74.

60. Cited in Skidmore, *Black into White*, 37.

61. Skidmore, *Black into White*.

62. Freyre, *Casa grande e senzala*.

63. Nelson W. Sodré, *Ideologia do colonialismo* (Petrópolis: Vozes, 1984).

64. Luis Felipe Alencastro and Maria Luiza Renaux, "Caras e modos dos migrantes e imigrantes," in *História da vida privada no Brasil: Império*, ed. Luis Felipe Alencastro (São Paulo: Companhia das Letras, 1997), 220–57.

65. Nascimento and Sathler, "Black Masks on White Faces," 95–124.

66. Ronald Raminelli, "Eva Tupinambá," in *História das mulheres no Brasil*, ed. Mary Del Priori (São Paulo: Contexto, 1997), 11–44; Manuela Carneiro da Cunha, "Introdução a uma história indígena," in *História dos Índios no Brasil* (São Paulo: Companhia dos Letras/Secretaria Municipal de Cultura/ FAPESP, 1992), 9–24.

67. Verger, *Artigos*; Giacomini, *Mulher e escrava*; idem., "Mulatas profissionais: Raça, gênero e ocupação," *Revista Estudos Feministas* 14, no.1 (January–April 2006): 85–101.

68. Maria Odila Leite da Silva Dias, *Cotidiano e poder em São Paulo no século XIX* (São Paulo: Brasiliense, 1984); Eni de Mesquita Samara, *As mulheres, o poder e a família: São Paulo, século XIX* (São Paulo: Editora Marco Zero, 1989).

69. Zuleika Alvim, "Imigrantes: A vida privada dos pobres do campo," in *História da vida privada no Brasil: República*, ed. Nicolau Sevcenko (São Paulo: Companhia das Letras, 1998), 215–87; Lesser, *Immigration*.

70. Prado, *Evolução*, 241–42; Aníbal Quijano, "Colonialidad y Modernidad/Racionalidad," *Perú Indígena* 13, no. 29 (1991): 11–20; Ávila, *Brasil e trabalhadores estrangeiros*, 129–40.

71. John C. Dawsey et al., *Americans: Imigrantes do velho sul no Brasil* (Piracicaba: Editora UNIMEP, 2005).

72. Fausto; Alencastro and Renaux, "Caras e modos"; Alvim, "Imigrantes"; Lesser, *Immigration*, 93.

73. Lesser, *Immigration*, 101–2; Rosana Barbosa Nunes, "Immigration, Xenophobia and the Whitening of the Brazilian Population," *Journal of Transatlantic Studies* 2 no. 1 (March 2004): 59–74.

74. Lesser, *Immigration*, 109–10; Ávila, 92–109.

75. Ávila, 123, 133; see also Jeffrey Lesser, *Welcoming the Undesirable: Brazil and the Jewish Question* (Berkeley: University of California Press, 1995).

76. Lesser, *Immigration*, 153, 155; Kioshi Riachi, "De São Paulo para Mato Grosso: A imigração Japonesa na região de Dourados," in *História, região e identidades*,

ed. Jérri Roberto Marin and Cláudio Alves de Vasconcelos (Campo Grande: Editora UFMS, 2003), 75–100.

77. Artur Hehl Neiva, "O problema imigratório Brasileiro," *Revista de Imigração e Colonização* 5, no. 3 (1944): 468–591.

78. Seyferth, "Diverse Understandings," 137; Jesiane Debastiani, "A política imigratória Brasileira na revista de imigração e bolonização (1940–1945)," *Em Tempo de Histórias* 32 (January–July 2018), https://doi.org/10.26512/emtempos .v0i32.14704.

79. Maria Aparecida de Moraes Silva, *Errantes do fim do século* (São Paulo: Editora UNIP, 1998), 64–67; Verena Stolcke, *Coffee Planters, Workers, and Wives: Class Conflict and Gender Relations on Sao Paulo Plantations, 1850–1980* (New York: St. Martin's, 1988); Ávila, 229–35.

80. Francesca Lessa, "Justice Beyond Borders: The Operation Condor Trial and Accountability for Transnational Crimes in South America," *International Journal of Transitional Justice* 9, no. 3 (November 2015): 494–506; J. Patrice McSherry, *Predatory States: Operation Condor and Covert War in Latin America* (Lanham, Md.: Rowman and Littlefield, 2005); Thomas E. Skidmore, *Brasil: De Castelo a Tancredo* (Rio de Janeiro: Paz e Terra, 1988).

81. Skidmore, *Brasil*; Joan Dassin, *Torture in Brazil: A Shocking Report on the Pervasive Use of Torture by Brazilian Military Governments, 1964–1979* (Austin: University of Texas Press, 1998).

82. Nascimento, "Inter-(African-Latin-)American," 176–80; idem., "Placing Brasilia on the Map: On the Global Inter-Location of a Postcolonial City," *City* 10, no. 2 (July 2006): 149–66.

83. Maria Alice de Faria Nogueira and Camila Maria dos Santos Moraes, *Brazilian Mobilities* (New York: Taylor and Francis, 2020).

84. Prefeitura de São Paulo and FIFE (Fundação Instituto de Pesquisa Econômica), "Produto IX: Relatório final da pesquisa amostral do perfil socioeconômico," in *Pesquisa censitária da população em situação de rua* (São Paulo: Prefeitura de São Paulo, July 2015), https://www.prefeitura.sp.gov.br/cidade/secretarias/upload /00-publicacao_de_editais/0004.pdf; Prefeitura de São Paulo and Qualitest, "Produto IX: Relatório final da pesquisa amostral do perfil socioeconômico," in *Pesquisa censitária da população em situação de rua* (São Paulo: Prefeitura de São Paulo, 2019), https://www.prefeitura.sp.gov.br/cidade/secretarias/upload /Produtos/Produto%209_SMADS_SP.pdf.

85. Cezar Benevides, *Camponeses em marcha* (Rio de Janeiro: Paz e Terra, 1985); Bernardo Mançano Fernandes, *A formação do MST no Brasil* (Petrópolis: Vozes, 2000); Anthony Pahnke, *Brazil's Long Revolution: Radical Achievements of the Landless Workers Movement* (Tucson: University of Arizona Press 2018).

86. Fernandes, *A formação*, 44.

87. See João Pedro Stédile, *A reforma agrária e a luta do MST* (Petrópolis: Vozes, 1997); Pahnke, *Brazil's Long Revolution*.

88. Benevides, *Camponeses*; Fernandes; Friends of the MST, "History of the MST," accessed July 1, 2020, https://www.mstbrazil.org/content/history-mst.

89. Breno Bringel, "El estudio de los movimientos sociales en América Latina: Reflexiones sobre el debate postcolonial y las nuevas geografías del activismo transnational," in *Pensamiento crítico y sujetos colectivos en América Latina: Perspectivas interdisciplinarias*, ed. Yamandú Acosta et al. (Montevideo: University of the Republic of Uruguay/Ediciones Trilce, 2011), 55.

90. For a discussion of "pregnant border crossing" and "medical tourism," which could be explored in relation to Brazil, see Amy Reed-Sandoval, *Socially Undocumented*, 99–126.

91. John Urry, "Mobile Cultures," published by Department of Sociology, Lancaster University, Lancaster, U.K., 2003, http://www.comp.lancs.ac.uk/sociology/papers /Urry-Mobile-Cultures.pdf.

92. Bianca Freire-Medeiros, ed., *Touring Poverty* (New York: Routledge, 2013).

93. Beatriz Jaguaribe and Kevin Heatherington, "Favela Tours: Indistinct and Mapless Representations of the Real in Rio de Janeiro," in *Tourism Mobilities: Places to Play, Places in Play*, ed. Mimi Sheller and John Urry (New York: Taylor and Francis, 2004), 155–66.

94. See Giacomini, "Mulatas profissionais"; Erica Lorraine Williams, *Sex Tourism in Bahia: Ambiguous Entanglements* (Urbana: University of Illinois Press, 2013).

95. Marcia Anita Sprandel, "'Vou pra Rua e Bebo a Tempestade': Observações sobre os dissabores do Guarda-chuva do tráfico de pessoas no Brasil," *Cadernos Pagu* 47 (August 2016): e16479; Williams, *Sex Tourism*, 161.

96. Linda Alcoff, "Discourses of Sexual Violence in a Global Framework," *Philosophical Topics* 37, no. 2 (Fall 2009): 123–39.

97. Andréa Lúcia Cavararo Rodrigues et al., "Reflexões acera do direito ao aguatá porã na fronteira Brasil/Paraguai pelos Kaiowá/Pai Tavyterã," in *Fronteiras étnicoculturais: Tráfico e migração de pessoas nas fronteiras de Mato Grosso do Sul*, ed. Antonio Hilario et al. (Campo Grande: Fundação UFMS, 2018), 13–44.

98. Ferreira, "Borders."

99. Alfredo J. Gonçalves, "Uma pastoral de serviço às pessoas em mobilidade," Brasília, IMDH, 2014, https://www.migrante.org.br/pastoral-da-mobilidade -humana/uma-pastoral-de-servico-as-pessoas-em-mobilidade/; see also William O'Neill, "A Little Common Sense: The Ethics of Immigration in Catholic Social Teaching," *American Journal of Economics and Sociology* 71, no. 4 (October 2012): 988–1003.

100. Instituto Migrações e Direitos Humanos, *I congresso de pastorais da mobilidade humana*, Brasília, IMDH, 2014, https://www.migrante.org.br/pastoral-da -mobilidade-humana/i-congresso-de-pastorais-da-mobilidade-humana/.

101. Fernandes, 44.

102. Bringel, "El estudio," 55.

103. Lindsey N. Kingston, "Haitians Seeking Refuge in Brazil," *Peace Review*, 28 (November 2016): 482–89.

104. Presidência da República, Lei nº 13.445, de 24 de maio de 2017, accessed July 29, 2020, http://www.planalto.gov.br/ccivil_03/_Ato2015-2018/2017/Lei/L13445.htm.

105. Diego Acosta, "Free Movement in South America: The Emergence of an Alternative Model," Migration Policy Institute, August 23, 2016, https://www.migration policy.org/article/free-movement-south-america-emergence-alternative-model; Ávila, 71–82.

106. Acosta, "Free Movement"; International Labor Organization, *Mercosur Residence Agreement*, accessed July 4, 2020, https://www.ilo.org/dyn/migpractice/migmain.showPractice?p_lang=en&p_practice_id=187.

107. L. Cavalcanti et al., *Resumo executivo: Imigração e refúgio no Brasil* (Brasília: Observatório das Migrações Internacionais, 2019).

108. Cavalcanti, *Resumo*; Kingston, "Haitians"; Luiz Sugimoto, "O dramático vai e vem dos Haitianos," *Jornal da Unicamp*, August 16, 2017, unicamp.br/unicamp/ju/noticias/2017/08/16/o-dramatico-vai-e-vem-dos-haitianos.

109. Sonia Ranincheski et al., "The Action of the Brazilian State regarding Bolivian Migrants in Brazil: The Issue of (Un)documented Labor, Refuge and Economic Immigration," *Si Somos Americanos* 14, no. 2 (December 2014): 47–79; Simone Buechler, "Sweating It in the Brazilian Garment Industry: Korean and Bolivian Immigrants and Global Economic Forces in São Paulo," *Latin American Perspectives* 31, no. 3 (May 2004): 99–119.

110. UNHCR, "UN Refugee Chief calls for more engagement in areas of Brazil hosting Venezuelans," August 19, 2019, https://www.unhcr.org/news/press/2019/8/5d5a 5b914/un-refugee-chief-calls-engagement-areas-brazil-hosting-venezuelans.html.

111. USAID, "United States Announces New Program to Support Venezuelans in Brazil," January 20, 2020, https://www.usaid.gov/news-information/press-releases/jan-29-2020-united-states-announces-new-program-support-venezuelans-brazil.

CHAPTER 5

Remember When It Was You

Exploring the Relevance of History for Determining What Constitutes Immigration Justice for Displaced Venezuelans in Colombia

ALLISON B. WOLF

My family and I immigrated from the United States to Bogotá, Colombia, in June 2019.[1] From the moment we arrived, we heard the pleas of displaced Venezuelan migrants:

> *Madre, por favor, ayúdame.*[2]
>   *Por favor, no quiero dinero, pero si tienes ropa extra en tu casa (o comida o algo para tomar o pañales) para los chicos.*[3]
>   *Puede colaborarme con un poco de comida?*[4]

And yet, in the not-too-distant past, Colombians were the ones pleading for help on Venezuela's streets. While some went to the oil-rich nation in search of economic opportunity, many were displaced by violence and fleeing political, economic, and social instability in Colombia. In this essay, I explain why this fact is not incidental. More broadly, I argue that the history between the sibling South American nations (both in general and specifically with respect to immigration) is a central factor in determining what constitutes a just Colombian response to displaced Venezuelans within that country today.

Before diving into this analysis, I must offer some preliminary reflections, starting with the recognition that I conduct this inquiry as a scholar and an immigrant from the United States—a nation that has an extensive and problematic history of imperialism and interference in Latin America, including Colombia.[5] People like me have been rightly criticized for their paternalistic, imperialistic, and colonial attitudes toward nations and peoples of the Global South as well as for their hubris in speaking in authoritative ways about other nations and their peoples. I hear and respect those criticisms and note that I am writing this piece from the position of my own concern, befuddlement, and curiosity and not from a position of expertise about Colombian affairs.

That being said, the core question of this inquiry—namely, should the shared history between Colombia and Venezuela matter for determining what constitutes just treatment of displaced Venezuelans in Colombia, and why?—is not simply random, abstract musing. To the contrary, it stems from current Colombian discourse, in which people defend a certain type of treatment toward displaced Venezuelans by appealing to the history between the two nations. Colombia's president Iván Duque, for example, consistently references this shared history—and the sibling relationship it generated—to justify helping displaced Venezuelans and express solidarity with them. In just one of many such pronouncements, Duque said, "Colombia chooses *fraternity* and to act in solidarity with our *Venezuelan brothers and sisters*."[6] And, he continued, while this will cause challenges for Colombia, "the nation is capable of reciprocating what Venezuelans did for us at other times."[7] Opponents of this position justify unjust treatment or not creating certain programs by asserting that Venezuelans mistreated displaced Colombians in the past and that therefore it is not wrong to fail to give them special treatment in the present, as they do not deserve it. More recently, another position has emerged that maintains that history should not matter because Colombia must put Colombians first without regard to the past.[8] This exploration, then, arises out of current Colombian debates on what constitutes just treatment of displaced Venezuelans.

Still, I do not want to obscure my own intellectual interests in these disputes. I have, after all, been exploring immigration justice in Latin America for many years, which predisposes me to wonder what constitutes just treatment of displaced Venezuelans and what factors are relevant to determining it. Based on my previous work on immigration justice in this context—in which I have argued that analyses of immigration injustice in the Americas must center on oppression and its relationship to immigration policies, practices, and enforcement mechanisms—I was initially inclined to argue that displaced Venezuelans are entitled to be treated in ways that do not reflect or perpetuate their oppression.[9] The problem is that this overall way of framing the issue seems incapable of speaking to the specific concern on which Colombians themselves are focusing—namely, the role of history.[10] While it is clear that displaced Venezuelans face various forms of oppression in Colombia, this does not explain why the shared history between Colombia and Venezuela is pertinent to determining what constitutes just treatment (i.e., what must be done to resist the oppression they face) or why is it especially wrong for displaced Venezuelans in particular to endure oppressive treatment from Colombians. Let me state the point differently. My framework provides a bare minimum standard for immigration justice: *all* immigrants are entitled to treatment that does not create, perpetuate, or reflect oppression. But the questions that occupy us here are about whether the shared history between the South American nations requires Colombia to go *beyond* this minimum. It appears, then, that to get the answers we seek in the present inquiry, we must expand beyond the basic framework I have offered. And I think that Jewish ethics, which centers the significance of history, provides the way forward.

I acknowledge that my choice of turning to Jewish ethics may seem odd to some. After all, Colombia is not a Jewish state—in fact, according to the World Jewish Congress, only around forty-five to fifty-five hundred of Colombia's almost fifty million citizens are Jewish.[11] While I understand the hesitation, however, I think it is misguided. For one, I believe it is mistaken to assert that we cannot apply ethical traditions to new contexts. In fact, turning to Jewish ethics is no different than borrowing ethical ideals from various philosophical traditions—like virtue ethics from the ancient Greeks, deontology and utilitarianism from Europe and North America, or Buddhism from India—which we do all the time. If Jewish ethics has insights to offer, we should learn from them.

Beyond this, though, any raised objections would miss the fact that Jewish philosophy and ethics, especially Levinas's ethics, have strongly influenced Latin American ethical thought, especially (but not exclusively) the philosophy of liberation. According to Juan Carlos Scannone, for example, when theorists of the philosophy of liberation originally met in Argentina, they proposed situating it in Levinas's ethics of the face.[12] Similarly, Enrique Dussel, one of the most influential philosophers of liberation, often explicitly notes his debt to Levinas, saying, for instance, in *Liberación latinoaméricano y Emmanuel Levinas*, "When I read Levinas' *Totality and Infinity* for the first time, it completely unsettled everything I had learned up to that point."[13] Indeed, Michael Barber contends that we cannot even understand Dussel's philosophy without understanding its relationship to Judaic ethics as expressed by Levinas, in particular, "through the idea of an 'ethical hermeneutics' that seeks to interpret reality from the viewpoint of the 'Other' . . . which is as the poor, the widow, the stranger, and the vulnerable from Jewish scriptures."[14] So, far from imposing an ethical tradition onto the Colombian context, I am turning to a tradition that already underlies a major Latin American ethical position.

With these preliminaries behind us, I now turn to my arguments. After providing a brief overview of the shared history between the two South American nations, particularly as it relates to immigration, I highlight key elements of the official and unofficial Colombian responses to displaced Venezuelan migrants in their territory. From there I turn to Jewish ethics and propose that it reveals that Colombia has at least two obligations toward displaced Venezuelans that go above and beyond the minimal standard to treat them in ways that do not create or further their oppression: (1) the obligation to remember its own immigration history (broadly speaking) as well as its history with Venezuela, and (2) the obligation to respond to displaced Venezuelans in ways that honor that history. I conclude by suggesting why it is especially egregious for Colombia and its citizens to treat displaced Venezuelans unjustly (i.e., in ways that perpetrate or worsen their oppression). Let us begin reviewing some of the main parts of the history between the South American nations.

I. A Brief Overview of the Immigration History between Colombia and Venezuela

The history between Venezuela and Colombia is long, deep, and complicated. Simón Bolívar—who was born in Venezuela and died in Colombia— liberated both nations from Spanish colonial rule and is still revered in both.[15] Bolívar himself thought Colombia and Venezuela were equally significant and inherently connected, famously declaring, "Si Caracas me dio vida, Cartagena me distes gloria."[16] Indeed, after achieving independence, he created a grand nation, La Gran Colombia, which included Colombia and Venezuela along with Ecuador, Panama, and parts of Peru and Brazil; this country existed from 1819 to 1831.[17]

Since the dissolution of Gran Colombia, Colombia and Venezuela have maintained a complicated relationship, especially in contemporary times. On the one hand, they have often worked together on regional projects (like the "Contadora Initiative," to try to broker peace in Central America during the 1980s) and share food, culture, and traditions, like *arepas, música llanera* or *joropo,* and *coleos*.[18] Their economies have also been intertwined, with Colombia traditionally serving as one of Venezuela's largest trading partners.[19] And until very recently, people freely crossed back and forth across the border to shop or visit family.

On the other hand, the countries have often found themselves on the opposite sides of political and ideological issues, especially since 2002. At that time, for example, then-president of Colombia Álvaro Uribe repeatedly accused his counterpart in Venezuela, Hugo Chávez, of supporting and supplying the Revolutionary Armed Forces of Colombia (FARC), one of the principle leftist guerilla groups fighting against the Colombian government.[20] Not to miss a beat, Chávez accused Uribe of allowing U.S. troops to operate in Colombia so that they could invade Venezuela.[21]

Despite these tensions, though, Uribe did reach out to Chávez in a weak effort to begin peace talks with FARC,[22] though these fell apart in 2008 when Uribe conducted an armed incursion into Ecuador, killing Raúl Reyes, FARC's second-in-command. In response, Chávez sent troops to the Venezuelan border in an act of solidarity with Ecuadoran president Rafael Correa, who decried Colombia's action as a violation of Ecuador's sovereignty.[23] Things did calm down again when the next Colombian president, Juan Manual Santos, normalized relations upon assuming power,[24] and Venezuela played a significant role in the Colombian peace negotiations with FARC. But once Nicolás Maduro assumed power after Chávez's death, relations continued to deteriorate, especially around the subject of immigration.

Before 2016 — the year the Colombian government signed a peace accord with FARC officially ending a fifty-year-plus internal armed conflict — Colombia was largely a country of emigration. According to the Administrative Department of National Statistics of Colombia (DANE), roughly 557,000 Colombians migrated to Venezuela, the United States, Ecuador, Panama, Canada, Peru, Chile, and Bolivia between 1963 and 1973 alone.[25] Eventually this number soared, and according to the Migration Policy Institute, as of 2014, an estimated 1.2 million residents claiming Colombian heritage resided in the United States.[26] As of this writing, a total of roughly five million Colombians have emigrated and still reside outside their home nation, roughly 10 percent of its population.[27]

By contrast, until recently, Venezuela was a stable nation of *immigration*; Venezuelans were not only "the wealthiest people on the continent, but the country had the most equal income distribution, as well as a fiercely patriotic and charismatic leader and ample energy reserves."[28] Beginning in the 1950s, Venezuela saw its wealth soar with an oil boom; the resultant prosperity drew Colombians to its shores in search of better economic opportunities, better living conditions, educational system, and public services.[29] For the most part, these immigrants were welcomed and seen as contributing to the Venezuelan economy and society because they provided a needed source of manual labor and opened businesses (especially restaurants) that allowed them to settle in Venezuela.[30] In other words, the first wave of Colombian immigration to Venezuela was relatively congenial, and the citizens of both countries saw benefits.[31]

The second major wave of Colombian migration to Venezuela began in the 1970s and continued throughout the 1990s. Unlike the first, this wave largely comprised Colombians displaced by the internal armed conflict between the government and several left-wing insurgent groups with Marxist/Leninist leanings, such as FARC, the Popular Liberation Army (EPL), National Liberation Army (ELN), and the 19th of April Movement (M-19).[32] While official records were not kept, Marco Romero Silva, the director of the Consultancy for Human Rights and Displacement (CODHES), estimates that millions of Colombians left for Venezuela during this time.[33] Professor Antonio de Lisio of the Universidad Central de Venezuela approximates that as many as five million Colombians went to Venezuela in the 1980s and 1990s.[34] In the mid-2000s, an estimated 1.8 million Colombians were still living in Venezuela[35]—the same number of displaced Venezuelans now estimated to be living in Colombia. While there are few official sources, those Colombians migrating as part of this wave reported facing more discrimination, xenophobia, harsh treatment, working difficult jobs in harsh conditions, and being called (and treated as) thieves (*ladrones*) by Venezuelans.[36]

The direction of migrant flows from Colombia to Venezuela began to change when Hugo Chávez assumed power in 1998. The first group to leave were wealthy and highly educated Venezuelans. While many of them migrated to the United States and Spain, 28.4 percent of this group immigrated to Colombia, where they were able to find good jobs and were, largely, welcomed by their neighbors.[37] After this, a second wave of Venezuelans, mostly "middle-class professionals departed for nearby Latin American nations with good employment prospects," again with many successfully settling in Colombia as a result of having bachelor's degrees and other training.[38] But all this began to change in 2015, when the third wave of Venezuelans began fleeing their home nation in droves.

The start of this wave of Venezuelan immigration coincided with a distinct change in the relationship between the two South American nations, including around immigration policy. In 2013, Nicolás Maduro assumed control of a nation whose economy was in shambles. Maduro both blamed a Colombian conspiracy for these issues and faced intense criticism from the Colombian government. He also consistently tried to deflect attention from his own government's failures to fix the ailing Venezuelan economy by blaming Colombian "gas smugglers," who were accused of stealing Venezuela's cheap gasoline to sell in other markets.[39] Given this background, "when Maduro faced a drone attack in August [2015], he initially blamed former Colombian President Juan Manuel Santos [because] a few days before, Santos granted permission for 440,000 Venezuelans to stay in Colombia."[40] In response, in 2015, Maduro shut the border and expelled thousands of Colombians along the frontier, among them many members of binational families (i.e., those consisting of Colombian and Venezuelan members) who had only known Venezuela as their home.[41] All in all, it is estimated that over three hundred thousand Colombians were forcibly expatriated from Venezuela.[42]

In August 2016 Santos and Maduro met in Venezuela to work out a solution and agreed to reopen the border and create five monitored checkpoints.[43] When the border did reopen, the current wave of Venezuelan immigration began. As journalist Dylan Baddour explains, "Tens of thousands of Venezuelans poured into Colombia on the first Sunday the border was open. Initially, many simply bought medicine and food and returned home to Venezuela, though some stayed. As the situation worsened in Venezuela, that shift became more permanent: At least 65,000 Venezuelans moved into Colombia in the first 90 days after the reopening; a year later, that figure had risen to 470,000; and in November 2018, it surpassed 1 million."[44] Compared to earlier Venezuelan migrations, this wave is largely constituted by forcefully displaced Venezuelans seeking refuge in Colombia from the violence, economic disaster, and political turmoil of Maduro's regime. In this group, fewer than 40 percent have a high-school education or above, and the vast majority work in the informal economy.[45]

While it began in 2016, most of these displaced Venezuelans arrived in Colombia during and after 2018 (roughly 78 percent). In November 2019, the numbers of Venezuelans in the South American nation surpassed 1.6 million, and over 1.8 million were estimated to be living in Colombia by the end of February 2020.[46] That number continue to surge—even in the midst of the COVID-19 pandemic, a time when tens of thousands of Venezuelans are temporarily returning home—as hyperinflation, starvation, medical care, and violence worsen under the Maduro regime.[47] Consequently, Migración Colombia predicted that over 2.2 million Venezuelans would reside in Colombia by the end of 2020.[48] But, as we saw earlier, unlike their predecessors, the reception these displaced Venezuelans have experienced has been more fraught.

II. Official (and Unofficial) Colombian Responses to Displaced Venezuelan Migrants

In many ways, Colombia is clearly a leader in its response to the country's Venezuelan *hermanas y hermanos*.[49] Other neighboring countries have imposed strict new entrance requirements that most Venezuelans cannot meet, effectively closing their borders to thousands of them.[50] The United States is making it difficult for Venezuelans to go there, too.[51] And while the European Union consistently declares that member nations should accept Venezuelan migrants, because of the distance and the resources needed to get to Europe from Latin America, the bloc reports only receiving about 18,400 applications, which does not do much to alleviate the crisis.[52]

By contrast, with the exception of the COVID-19 crisis, Colombia has kept its borders open. In fact, according to Trisha Bury, deputy director for the International Rescue Committee, "I've never seen a government trying this hard to register people and leave the borders open."[53] Beyond this, Colombia has extended citizenship to children born to Venezuelan parents on Colombian soil and, in January 2020, announced a plan to work with local authorities to help Venezuelans get regularized, receive increased humanitarian assistance, and become socioeconomically integrated into Colombian society.[54] In February 2021, Colombia gained international praise for regularizing all Venezuelan migrants in its territory by granting them a path to obtain Temporary Protective Status. And Columbian authorities have often made these overtures without actually having the necessary resources, as the country faces its own economic challenges and aid from the international community is nowhere to be found.[55]

While there are multiple reasons for this response—including a pragmatic approach to immigration and a desire to thwart the Maduro regime—a principal one is that the shared history between the two nations has created "a heartfelt affection for Venezuela."[56] As Daphne Panayotatos, an advocate and program officer with Refugees International, observes, "Many Colombians see [welcoming displaced Venezuelans now] as returning the favor" for what Venezuela did for them in the past.[57] This is reflected in comments from Colombian officials and ordinary citizens alike, such as the following:

We cannot have rivalries between Colombians and Venezuelans because we are siblings. They took us in there when we needed them the most when the internal conflict intensified, they gave us job opportunities.[58]

—Senator Efraín Cepeda

Twenty years ago, when the opposite was happening . . . they actually welcomed us. So for all Colombians, this is a very emotional issue.[59]

—Sergio Guzman, the founder of Colombia
Risk Analysis, a political risk consultancy

Venezuela helped many Colombians . . . Now it's Colombia's turn to help Venezuelans.[60]

—Rossana Tua, resident of La Magdalena, where she's lived for almost
a year since moving back to Colombia from Venezuela

Of course, this is not a position universally held by Colombians. As mentioned earlier, many believe that Colombian immigrants, especially displaced Colombians, were actually treated very poorly in Venezuela and that, as a result, Venezuelans do not deserve better treatment.[61] Put differently, while they may concede that the immigration history between Colombia and Venezuela is relevant to determinations of what constitutes just treatment of displaced Venezuelans, some maintain that the history indicates that displaced Venezuelans do not deserve treatment that goes beyond the minimal obligations of immigration justice. This is reflected in increased anti-Venezuelan sentiment by Colombian officials and citizens. A December 2019 Gallup poll found that most Colombians view displaced Venezuelan immigrants as a problem and 69 percent view them "unfavorably."[62] Seventy percent think that Venezuelans are a threat to their job prospects or salary, and 80 percent think they have caused public service systems, like health care and education, to collapse.[63] Most Venezuelan workers work longer hours and are paid less than Colombians for the same job, with the Colombian Ministry of the Treasury reporting a wage gap of 34.9 percent.[64] Thousands of Venezuelan women, including educated professionals, have been forced to turn to sex work to survive, and those who do find other employment, for example, in a restaurant, factory, or as a domestic employee, are vulnerable—often being fired if they become pregnant or have an accident.[65] In June 2018, a car drove through neighborhoods south of Bogotá projecting the following message from a loudspeaker: "We are giving the Venezuelans an ultimatum—you have two weeks to leave . . . [and if you do not] we will kill each and every one of you that we find in Subachoque, whether you work or not, whether you steal or not. We do not want you here anymore—get out!"[66] In the same vein, in the summer of 2019 a pamphlet circulated in Las Águilas Negras ordering everyone to fire Venezuelan immigrants and hire Colombians within forty-eight hours; the pamphlet also promoted deporting displaced Venezuelans (or worse) in order to "clean up" northern Colombian cities from the "delinquency" Venezuelans bring to the country.[67] These are just a few specific instances of the general treatment these migrants endure, which includes police brutality, physical violence, threats of extortion and kidnapping from criminal groups, and murder. Since 2017, Colombia's Institute of Legal Medicine reports that at least 2061 Venezuelan migrants have been killed, with two being murdered each day.[68]

* *

I am confident that the path taken by those who support displaced Venezuelans is morally right, and that the described abuses against displaced Venezuelans are morally wrong. It strikes me as correct for Colombians to think their shared history requires them to lend a hand to their brethren in need, and it is wrong to dismiss, ignore, and/or forget that history or use it to justify unjust treatment.[69] But why is this the case? That is what I explore in the remainder of the essay.

III. The Role of History in Immigration Justice

I maintain that the shared history between Colombia and Venezuela generates specific obligations of immigration justice for Colombians toward displaced Venezuelans. To be clear, though, I am not using the term "obligation" in ways that conform to mainstream Western moral and political thought. When I assert, for example, that the Colombian government and its citizens have unique obligations and responsibilities toward displaced Venezuelans, I am *not* arguing that they must behave according to the dictates of abstract principles of immigration justice—such as the prohibition of violating human rights, Wilcox's Global Harm Principle, Higgins's Priority of Disadvantage Principle, or my own arguments barring oppression.[70] Nor am I arguing that these historically rooted obligations and responsibilities are contractual or transactional; Colombia does not owe Venezuelans certain rights or benefits because of some sort of deal made between the nations; neither must the country uphold end of some bargain or repay its end of a tit for tat or quid pro quo. Finally, when I argue that Colombia has unique obligations of immigration justice toward displaced Venezuelans, I am not suggesting that these duties are based on retributive justice or guilt; I do not think that Colombia must treat displaced Venezuelans a certain way in order to heal past wrongs or because they need to "repay" some sort of debt.

Instead, when I assert that Colombia has additional obligations of immigration justice toward Venezuelans, I mean that their shared history requires them to go beyond the minimal requirements of immigration justice. In particular, I think that Colombians are obligated to *remember* their shared history with Venezuela, and in doing so, it will become clear that the Colombian government and its citizens must *respond* to the needs of displaced Venezuelans in front of them in ways that honor that history. To defend these contentions, I provide an overview of the core Jewish ethical ideas on which I am drawing.

Jewish ethics is a diverse and vast tradition that I do not have the space to adequately detail here. Traditionally, it is seen as being based on foundational biblical texts—largely the exodus from Egypt—and other verses of the Torah, Talmudic texts, and rabbinical commentaries.[71] Central to the entire system is respecting the dignity of all human beings (*kvod hibryot*), which includes both negative rights (leaving people alone) and positive ones (of proactively helping people develop). Combining the duty to respect dignity with heeding lessons from Jewish texts and scholars then leads to the requirement that people live in ways that uphold fundamental ethical ideals: *mishpat* ("justice"), *chesed* ("kindness"), *rachamim* ("compassion"), *teshuvah* ("repentance"), and *tikkun olam* ("repairing the world").[72]

The central aspect of Jewish ethics most relevant to our discussion, though, is how it centers history and is deeply influenced by the histories of Jews around the world—in their experiences, in their responses to the histories, in the stories they pass down. A foundational aspect of Jewish ethics, especially post-Holocaust, is the obligation to remember, or "not to forget." Of course, there are various interpretations of this dictum, but I will only highlight three that appear most relevant to our inquiry.

First, we must remember and honor the sacrifices people have made to be Jewish. For example, we are obligated to remember the many Jews who practiced their religion in secret or who died for doing so, under thousands of years of anti-Semitism that included pogroms, inquisitions, and demands of forced conversion. For many Jews whose ancestors migrated to the United States, there is also an obligation to remember the emotional and economic sacrifices their ancestors made to give their children and grandchildren better opportunities and the ability to practice their religion openly.

Second, we must remember the suffering of the Jewish people (past and present) and respond by repairing the world to prevent and alleviate the suffering of vulnerable others—Jews and non-Jews alike. In this way, history is connected to the obligation of *tikkun olam*—part of repairing the world is remembering our history so that we learn what must be done. Specifically, we must remember the historical injustices perpetrated against Jews through the centuries and use that memory to fight injustice against all people.

Third, and related, living a just life requires remembering tragic histories so that they do not repeat themselves—not only against one's own group but also against other communities. But we cannot simply remember that the events happened or lament the tragedies they caused. To the contrary, as Levinas pointed out, we must explore that history from the perspective of the victims and the vulnerable, not the victors, to understand what went wrong and take action to prevent history repeating itself. In this way, remembering history allows us to fulfill our obligation to protect human life and dignity and, again, to do our part to repair a broken world. Beyond this, though, the command to remember from the perspective of the victims reminds us that the viewpoints and experiences of the oppressed are to be afforded increased epistemic authority.

A. Remember Our History

The ideas expressed previously provide insight into why the history between Colombia and Venezuela matters for determining what constitutes just treatment of displaced Venezuelans. First, a central piece of Jewish history that we are commanded to remember is Jewish enslavement in Egypt and the exodus to the land of Israel that followed. Of course, there are multiple interpretations of these events and the ethical significance of remembering them in Jewish life—to instill and reinforce faith in an almighty G-d, to demonstrate gratitude to G-d for our freedom, to reinforce one's commitment to their Jewish roots, and to remember all who are still oppressed in the world. In all these interpretations, though, we must remember that history to orient ourselves ethically—to remind ourselves of Jewish values so that we act in accordance with them. These historical events do not provide general moral guidance, however. To the contrary, they are invoked precisely to orient moral action in specific cases, including the treatment of immigrants. For example, the book of Exodus declares, "You shall not wrong a stranger or oppress him, for you were strangers in the land of Egypt" and "You shall not oppress a stranger, for you know the feelings of a stranger, having yourselves been strangers in the land of Egypt."[73] Similarly, the book of Leviticus states, "When a stranger resides with you in your land, you shall not wrong him. The stranger who resides with you shall be to you as one of your citizens; you shall love him as yourself, for you were strangers in the land of Egypt."[74] In all these, and other, examples, the point of remembering history is to morally orient ourselves on how to act in specific cases in order to improve the world and prevent injustices specifically against immigrants and refuge seekers. And I think the same is true for Colombia; remembering their history—both as immigrants themselves and specifically with Venezuela—helps morally orient Colombians to create just policies toward displaced Venezuelans.

Recall, though, that we must not simply remember history, but do so in a specific way—namely, from the perspective of the vulnerable and the oppressed. Doing so helps us perceive aspects of the situation we have missed, while developing empathy and connection to the vulnerable so that we want to help. In the case under consideration, this means that Colombia must remember its immigration history through the lens of the vulnerable immigrant and not through that of the powerful receiving state. In other words, Colombians must remember what it was like to need refuge; the difficulties they experienced in seeking it or asking for help; and the deep fear, sadness, and betrayal they felt when it was denied. Doing this—recalling this history from the perspective of the vulnerable, including when *they* were vulnerable—will show that it is the *immigrant* to whom they must justly respond, not other parties. And this will, again, open their eyes to various ways that they must treat their Venezuelan brethren.

Furthermore, as discussed earlier Jewish ethics also requires remembering history in order to fulfill our ethical commitment of repairing the world (*tikkun olam*). In other words, we must remember history in order to improve the world and prevent past injustices from repeating themselves in the future.[75] In my view, this idea is also operative in the case of displaced Venezuelans: Colombians must remember their immigration history in order to prevent perpetrating future injustices against others. When Colombia and its people recall this history, both the positive ways they were treated and the difficulties they endured, they can learn what would constitute just treatment of displaced Venezuelans and avoid repeating mistakes of the past that they experienced.

Based on core tenets of Jewish ethics, then, Colombia must remember its history for at least three reasons. First, remembering history orients Colombians morally; it reminds them *why* they have unique obligations of justice toward displaced Venezuelans. Second, doing so connects Colombians to the experiences of displaced Venezuelans in ways that position them to respond to their needs and treat them justly; in other words, seeing the situation from the position of the vulnerable (and recalling their own past vulnerability) helps develop empathy and a desire to help. Third, it helps prevent immigration injustice going forward. If Colombians treat displaced Venezuelans better than they were treated (for those who believe they were treated poorly) or as they were treated (for those who believe they were treated well), then they will be able to respond now in ways that prevent past injustices from being repeated.

B. Responding to the Displaced Venezuelan Migrants in Ways That Respect History

I have now shown *why* Colombia is obligated to remember its history with Venezuela. But recall that I said Colombia has *two* obligations: to remember the history and to respond to displaced Venezuelans in ways that honor it. What does the second obligation entail? I must confess that I do not have concrete answers to this question, in large part because the specific responses required depend on particular circumstances; there is no easy or universal answer. That being said, I think that we can get some clarity on what it means to respond to displaced Venezuelans in ways that honor history by discussing its opposite—what kinds of responses are absolutely *not* honoring the history.

First, Colombians should not determine how to respond to displaced Venezuelans simply by applying rational, ahistorical, abstract principles to the exclusion of responding at a visceral, bodily, and emotional level to demonstrate empathy and compassion. That is, the government should not try to create one-size-fits-all policies for displaced Venezuelans based on abstract moral principles; rather, it should create policies and practices that respond to the needs of particular groups of displaced migrants and their circumstances. Similarly, Colombian citizens should not determine how to respond to the Venezuelan on the street asking them for help by simply consulting rules of ethics; rather, they should respond in ways that demonstrate compassion and heart. As Levinas notes, failing to respond in such a way (and instead, focusing on abstract rules) could lead us to "descend, at best, into an empty legalism, and at worst, as we have seen throughout our history, the most atrocious barbarism"; we will get so caught up in rational deliberations that we will lose people to rules and procedures.[76]

Allow me to provide a brief example. A really positive thing that Colombia has done for displaced Venezuelans has been to create a program—Permiso Especial de Permanencia (PEP)—allowing Venezuelans to work and access health care, education, and other benefits for themselves and their children. The problem is that if someone did not enter the country at an authorized port of entry and have their passport stamped, they are ineligible. Venezuelans who entered the country via *trochas* (as most do) cannot qualify for PEP.[77] While this may appear to be reasonable—after all, most nations require documents—in this case, it creates major problems, since over half of displaced Venezuelans—between 790,000 and 850,000—are undocumented.[78] Worse, it is nearly impossible for these migrants to obtain what they need to become regularized, since (1) there are no guidelines for how documents (like high-school diplomas) can become recognized in Colombia; (2) most people cannot afford to get the documents; (3) it is almost impossible to get certified documents from Venezuela; and, related, (4) the Venezuelan government is basically refusing to issue passports, with some Venezuelans waiting months, or even years to obtain them.[79] Thus, in focusing on the rational or abstract requirements for Venezuelans to qualify for assistance we fail to respond to the needs of hundreds of thousands of people, leaving them vulnerable to exploitation, abuse, violence, and xenophobia. Part of responding to displaced Venezuelans, then, is doing so in ways that respond to the demand and not calculated rational action.

Feminist ethical ideas combine with Jewish requirements to always honor human dignity to point to a second type of unacceptable response—namely, one that fails to recognize displaced Venezuelans as full, unique, human beings. In other words, responses that treat displaced Venezuelans as derivatives of Colombian needs and imaginaries are unacceptable. Ann Cahill explains that to derivatize someone is to fail to recognize them as a distinct being, instead apprehending them as a mere extension of another. She states, "To derivatize something is to portray, render, understand, or approach a being solely or primarily as the reflection, projection, or expression of another being's identity, desires, fears, etc. The derivatized subject becomes reducible in all relevant ways to the derivatizing subject's existence."[80] The derivatized subject does not matter in her own right and is not recognized as having her own interests, traditions, identities, or goals; she is simply a projection of another's will, desires, identity, and fears. The problem with derivatization is failing to recognize the subjectivity of the other apart from oneself; it is failing to recognize someone as a distinct ontological subject rather than as an ontological extension of another. In the context under discussion, responding to displaced Venezuelans in ways that remember and honor history requires *not* derivatizing them; it means not erasing their humanity, for example, by lumping all Venezuelan immigrants together into an amorphous, oversimplified, generalized, group: "immigrants" or *venecos*.[81] Doing so—treating all displaced Venezuelans according to stereotypes rather than seeing them as vulnerable individuals with needs, fears, desires, and dreams—dishonors the shared history between the two countries by erasing it. The displaced Venezuelans are no longer *hermanos* with a shared history, culture, food, and language; they are merely ideas and stereotypes of whatever the Colombian imagination conceives them to be. In this way, derivatizing displaced Venezuelans erases their history and their humanity.

C. A Brief Reflection on Failing to Respond

Before concluding, I want to briefly return to the final question that moti-vated this inquiry: Why is it so much more egregious for Colombians to treat displaced Venezuelan immigrants unjustly compared to other groups? I think our discussion of Jewish ethics and the role of history, again, helps us answer this question.

In one sense, treating displaced Venezuelans unjustly is more problematic because it violates both the command to remember and the command to use this memory to prevent future injustice. And, in doing so, it opens the door to the kinds of injustices we are increasingly witnessing in Colombia. Treating displaced Venezuelans unjustly does not only perpetrate injustice but also violates commands to remember in ways that impede efforts to learn lessons from that history and prevent future injustice.

Still, there is another issue at play here, one that more readily acknowl-edges the emotional component of the issue. Specifically, a significant reason why it is more egregious for Colombia and its citizens to treat displaced Ven-ezuelans unjustly is precisely that there is a long and deep history between them that matters. And forgetting the history or acting as if it does not mat-ter is, to put it bluntly, a painful betrayal for the one on the receiving end.

Allow me to explain what I mean with an overly simplistic analogy. If I pass by a person on the street whom I do not know and fail to greet them, then I have done nothing wrong—after all, I have no relationship with them and there is no history between us that would create an expectation of a greeting. But if I pass one of my best friends on the street and deliberately do not greet her, then I have done something wrong. I have hurt her by acting as if she were a stranger I have never met. Worse, especially if our friend-ship is long and involved trusting each other in various ways, to act as if she did not exist constitutes a betrayal of that relationship. I think something analogous is going on here. Because of the long and deep history between Colombians and Venezuelans, if Colombians do not respond in a way that meets the expectation that common history has engendered, it is hurtful. It constitutes a betrayal of trust, relationships, and history. Treating displaced Venezuelans unjustly causes emotional injuries that are not involved in the treatment of groups with whom one has no history, as such making the fail-ure to respond with empathy an even worse offense than mistreating other immigrant groups.

I actually think that this is even recognized by Colombians who believe that Venezuelans deeply mistreated them in the past that they thus do not deserve special treatment now. I submit that as part of *their* deep feeling of anger is a sense that Colombians were betrayed by their Venezuelan brothers, who did not fully recognize them as *herman@s* and instead treated them as mere *ladrones*, despite the shared history between the two nations. This in turn feels like an act of disloyalty precisely because of the history that we have discussed here, one that led Colombians to believe that *they* would be received in Venezuela differently from other immigrant groups or, at least, treated with respect.

If I am right about what I just said, then my point is reinforced: history matters. The disagreement is not about that fact but rather over what that history requires of Colombians toward displaced Venezuelans now—namely, some Colombians appear to think Venezuelans deserve some sort of tit-for-tat response. Given the discussion about feelings of betrayal, though, I think even that is too simplistic a reading. I do not believe these Colombians are really expressing the desire for revenge that they claim to be; rather, they are expressing their deep pain that Colombians were treated unjustly, as if history did not matter, and their need for that to be recognized and addressed too. In that case, while these real and justified feelings of betrayal deserve a response, they reinforce why Colombia has special historically based obligations toward displaced Venezuelans and why failing to meet the moment is especially wrong, painful, and potentially dangerous to future generations' relationships.

Concluding Reflections

A friend of mine recently taught me a Colombian phrase: "Donde comen dos, comen tres"—when there is enough food for two, there is always room for one more.[82] Colombians have a tradition of helping people, being generous, and being welcoming. And this has surely been my experience— Colombians have been so wonderful to my family and me. Whether it be countless offers of assistance in finding housing, employment for my spouse, and good schools for our children or the steady stream of invitations for playdates, lunches, and wine drinking, I have seen firsthand that Colombians live out a deep commitment not only to "*not* oppressing a stranger" but also to treating them kindly, compassionately, and justly.

While Colombia has done a lot to welcome its Venezuelan *hermanas, hermanos, y hermanes*, it is clear that the treatment I have received differs profoundly from theirs. As we have seen, too often, they endure exploitation, violence, xenophobia, and, since Covid-19 began, growing calls for their deportation. This strikes me both as clearly unjust—nobody should be subjected to that kind of oppression and abuse—and as especially egregious and painful given the history between the two South American giants. In this essay, I have shown why this is the case. Colombia and Venezuela share a storied and complicated history that connects them and engenders unique obligations of immigration justice that require going beyond avoiding oppressive treatment. Colombians must remember this history and respond in ways that honor it. To fail to do so is not only immoral but also hurtful, willfully ignorant, and painful. Worse, it not only violates the norms of Jewish ethics I discuss in this essay but also violates the very moral ideals to which my own experiences have clearly shown Colombians subscribe. So, while I am grateful for the wonderful reception I have received, I hope Colombians remember that history and respond to it in ways that provide my Venezuelan counterparts with even more.

Notes

1.   I want to sincerely thank Gaile Pohlhaus Jr., Alison Bailey, Catalina González Quintero, as well as the editors of this volume, Amy Reed-Sandoval and Luis Ruben Díaz, for reading earlier drafts of this essay and for providing invaluable comments that clearly led to its improvement.
2.   "Ma'am, please help me."
3.   "Please, I don't want money, but if you have some extra clothes, you could bring me for my children (or food or water or diapers)."
4.   "Could you give me a bit of food?"
5.   I am deeply aware of this power dynamic and the relations of coloniality, imperialism, and interference of the United States in Colombia—interference that continues to this day. I am also very cognizant of the perils of someone from the United States criticizing—or appearing to criticize—the actions of Latin American nations. For this reason, I was honestly reticent to write this essay. However, as I hope will become apparent to the reader, the intention of this paper is not to criticize—it is to engage and better understand something that is troubling in my newly adopted home. I am not aiming to critique and condemn as much as I am hoping to better understand what is happening and why. I hope the chapter is taken in the spirit of humility, affection, and cooperation that is intended.

6.   "'Colombia optó por la fraternidad': Iván Duque sobre el éxodo de los venezola-nos," *Revista Semana*, September 2, 2018, https://www.semana.com/nacion /articulo/colombia-opto-por-la-fraternidad-ivan-duque-sobre-el-exodo-de-los -venezolanos/581791, emphasis added.

7.   "'Colombia optó por la fraternidad.'"

8.   Silvia Ruiz Mancera, "Primero nosotros, los colombianos," *El Tiempo*, Janu-ary 27, 2019, https://www.eltiempo.com/mundo/venezuela/analisis-sobre-la -xenofobia-de-los-colombianos-hacia-los-venezolanos-319166.

9.   See, for example, Allison B. Wolf, "Dying in Detention as an Example of Oppres-sion," *APA Newsletter on Hispanic/Latino Issues in Philosophy* 19, no. 1 (Fall 2019): 2–8; Allison B. Wolf, *Just Immigration in the Americas: A Feminist Approxima-tion* (London: Rowman and Littlefield International), 2020.

10. To be clear, I also find most traditional Anglo philosophy, including philosophy of immigration, unable to provide guidance on the current discussion given that it has tended to ignore questions of history. As Amy Reed-Sandoval notes in her essay "The New Open Borders Debate" (in *The Ethics and Politics of Immigration: Core Issues and Emerging Trends*, ed. Alex Sager [Lanham, Md.: Rowman and Littlefield, 2016], 13–28), traditional approaches to immigration justice largely focus on answering two abstract questions: (1) Can states justly exclude perspec-tive migrants? and (2) Is there a universal right to migration? Furthermore, they do so by searching for general philosophical principles from liberal, democratic, political thought rather than by engaging specific immigration issues in par-ticular nations or their histories. By the same token, thinkers who are part of a more recent trend in philosophical discussions of immigration justice—one that does focus on particular borders and policies using feminist theory, critical race theory, Latin American philosophy, and nonideal theory—also tend to ignore history. Of course, there are some exceptions. For example, José Jorge Mendoza and Grant Silva both incorporate the history and development of the concept of "whiteness" in the United States to argue that anti-immigration sentiments and projects in the United States are connected to racism and Shelley Wilcox pres-ents a nonideal approach to prioritizing immigrant admissions that considers past harms the receiving nation has committed against the sending nation. But, on the whole, history does not feature prominently in the New Open Borders literature either, especially beyond the United States and Mexico.

11. "Colombia," World Jewish Congress, accessed July 20, 2020, https://www.world jewishcongress.org/en/about/communities/CO.

12. Juan Carlos Scannone, "La filosofía de la liberación: Historica, características, vigencia actual," *Teología y Vida* 50 (2009): 60.

13. The original Spanish reads: "Cuando leí por primera vez el libro de Levinas Totalidad e infinito se produjo en mi espíritu como un subversivo desquici-amiento de todo lo hasta entonces aprendido." Enrique Dussel and Daniel E. Guillot, *Liberación latinoaméricano y Emmanuel Levinas* (Buenos Aires: Edi-torial Bonum, 1975), 7.

14. Michael Barber, "Preface," in *Ethical Hermeneutics: Rationality in Enrique Dusell's Philosophy of Liberation* (New York: Fordham University Press, 1998), ix.

15. There is even currently a popular telenovela, *Bolívar*.

16. Hermes Figueroa Alcázar, "Caracas, una cita con la historia," *El Universal*, September 2, 2009, https://www.eluniversal.com.co/sociales/caracasuna-cita-con -la-historia-NLEU12719. In English: "While Caracas gave me life, Cartagena gave me glory."

17. This is how we refer to the nation today to distinguish it from present-day Colombia. But at the time the polity was referred to as "Colombia," according to Joseph M. Parent, "Bolívar's Dream of Gran Colombia," in *United States: Voluntary Union in World Politics* (Oxford: Oxford University Press, 2011), 111. See also "Así fue la Gran Colombia de Bolívar," https://www.colombia.co/pais -colombia/historia/asi-fue-la-gran-colombia-de-bolivar/.

18. Michael J. LaRosa and Germán R. Mejía, *Colombia: A Concise Contemporary History*, 2nd edition (Lanham, Md.: Rowman and Littlefield, 2017), 207. *Arepas* is a typical food eaten in both countries, made of a ground corn dough that is often stuffed or covered with eggs or meat. *Música llanera joropo* is music popular in the Colombian plains and Venezuela characterized by the small harp. *Coleos* is a type of Colombian-Venezuelan rodeo.

19. David Smilde and Dimitris Pantoulas, "The Venezuelan Crisis, Regional Dynamics and the Colombian Peace Process," Norwegian Peacebuilding Resource Center, August 2016, 4, https://www.alnap.org/system/files/content/resource/files /main/noref-venezuela-and-colombian-peace-process.pdf.

20. In Spanish: *Fuerza Armada Revolucionaria de Colombia*. See LaRosa and Mejía, *Colombia*, 221–22.

21. Smilde and Pantoulas, "The Venezuelan Crisis," 3.

22. LaRosa and Mejía, 242.

23. LaRosa and Mejía, 101–2.

24. LaRosa and Mejía, 101–2.

25. Administrative Department of National Statistics of Colombia (DANE), accessed June 12, 2021, https://www.dane.gov.co/.

26. Dayra Carvajal, "As Colombia Emerges from Decades of War, Migration Challenges Mount," Migration Policy Institute, April 13, 2017, https://www.migration policy.org/article/colombia-emerges-decades-war-migration-challenges -mount.

27. LaRosa and Mejía, 215.

28. Dylan Baddour, "Colombia's Radical Plan to Welcome Millions of Venezuelan Migrants," *Atlantic*, January 30, 2019, https://www.theatlantic.com/inter national/archive/2019/01/colombia-welcomes-millions-venezuelans-maduro -guaido/581647/.

29. "Así se vivía cuando la ola migratoria era de Colombia hacia Venezuela," *El Tiempo*, February 11, 2018, https://www.eltiempo.com/mundo/venezuela/anteriormente -la-ola-migratoria-era-de-colombianos-hacia-venezuela-181258.

30. "Así se vivía."
31. "Así se vivía."
32. In Spanish, Ejército Popular de Liberación (EPL), Ejército de Liberación Nacional (ELN), and Movimiento del 19 de Abril (M-19).
33. Megan Janetsky, "Here's Why Colombia Opened Its Arms to Venezuelan Migrants—Until Now," *Foreign Policy*, January 14, 2019, https://foreignpolicy.com/2019/01/14/heres-why-colombia-opened-its-arms-to-venezuelan-migrants-until-now/.
34. Janetsky, "Here's Why."
35. LaRosa and Mejía, 221.
36. Personal communication.
37. Economía y Negocios, "3 de cada 4 venezolanos trabajan en Colombia sin un contrato laboral: Cifras del empleo que ocupan, según estudio de la U. Externado. Menguó afluencia de empresarios," *El Tiempo*, February 26, 2020, https://www.el tiempo.com/economia/sectores/realidad-laboral-de-venezolanos-en-colombia -466664.
38. Economía y Negocios, "3 de cada 4 venezolanos."
39. LaRosa and Mejía, 222.
40. Janetsky.
41. Baddour, "Colombia's Radical Plan."
42. Gustavo Andrés Castillo Arenas and Patrick Ammerman, "A Country That Welcomes Migration," *Yes!*, February 19, 2020, https://www.yesmagazine.org/issue /world-we-want/2020/02/19/colombia-venezuela-migration/.
43. LaRosa and Mejía, 222.
44. Baddour, "Colombia's Radical Plan."
45. Economía y Negocios.
46. Economía y Negocios; "Response for Venezuelans," last accessed July 20, 2020, https://data2.unhcr.org/en/situations/platform/location/7511; IOM, "Venezuelan Refugee and Migrant Crisis."
47. Tamara Taraciuk Broner and Kathleen Page, "Stuck at Venezuela's Border with Covid-19," *Human Rights Watch*, July 15, 2020, https://www.hrw.org/news/2020 /07/15/stuck-venezuelas-border-covid-19-all-around#; Michael Stott and Gideon Long, "Venezuela: Refugee Crisis Tests Colombia's Stability," *Financial Times*, February 19, 2020, https://www.ft.com/content/bfede7a4-4f44-11ea-95a0-43d1 8ec715f5.
48. Ricardo Ajiaco, "Migrantes Velozolanos llegarían a 2 milliones en 2020," *El Tiempo*, January 22, 2020, https://www.eltiempo.com/politica/partidos-politicos/lo-restos -de-colombia-frente-a-una-migracion-venezolana-que-no-cesa-453616.
49. United Nations, "UN Refugee Agency Ramps Up Support for Venezuleans, Praises 'Extraordinary Solidarity' of Colombia," *UN News*, October 9, 2018, https://news.un.org/en/story/2018/10/1022682; Shabia Mantoo, "UNHCR Welcomes Colombia's Decision to Regularize Stay of Venezuleans in the Country," *Relief Web*, February 4, 2020, https://reliefweb.int/report/colombia/unhcr-wel comes-colombia-s-decision-regularize-stay-venezuelans-country.

50. Anastasia Moloney, "Is South America Closing Its 'Open Door' on Venezuelans?" *Reuters*, August 8, 2019, https://www.reuters.com/article/us-venezuela-migration-analysis/is-south-america-closing-its-open-door-on-venezuelans-idUSKCN1UY27D; Joshua Collins, "Venezuelans Stranded as Ecuador Imposes New Visa Rules," *Al Jazeera News*, August 26, 2019, https://www.aljazeera.com/news/2019/08/venezuelans-stranded-ecuador-imposes-visa-rules-190826134509203.html; Dylan Baddour, "Ecuador Shuts Its Border to Venezuelan Refugees amid Historical Exodus," *Washington Post*, August 20, 2018, https://www.washingtonpost.com/world/the_americas/ecuador-shuts-its-border-to-venezuelan-refugees-amid-historic-exodus/2018/08/20/28223fec-a48c-11e8-ad6f-080770dcddc2_story.html.

51. Molly O'Toole, "Venezuela, Now a Top Source of U.S. Asylum Claims, Poses a Challenge for Trump," *Los Angeles Times*, June 5, 2019, https://www.latimes.com/politics/la-na-pol-trump-venezuela-asylum-immigration-20190605-story.html.

52. Francesco Guarascio, "Asylum Applications in EU Rise as More Venezuelans Seek Refuge," *Reuters*, June 24, 2019, https://www.reuters.com/article/us-europe-refugees/asylum-applications-in-eu-rise-as-more-venezuelans-seek-refuge-idUSKCN1TP0LQ; Mirra Banchon, "EU lawmakers Issue Call to Take in Venezuelan Migrants," *DW.com*, June 7, 2018, https://www.dw.com/en/eu-lawmakers-issue-call-to-take-in-venezuelan-migrants/a-44556414.

53. Trisha Bury cited in Baddour, "Colombia's Radical Plan."

54. Jenny Bartsfield, "Colombia Gives Venezuela Newborns a Start in Life," United Nations Refugee Agency, October 14, 2019, https://www.unhcr.org/en-us/news/stories/2019/10/5da42be64/colombia-gives-venezuela-newborns-start-life.html; Anatoly Kurmanaev and Jenny Carolina González, "Colombia Offers Citizenship to 24,000 Children of Venezuelan Refugees," *New York Times*, August 5, 2019, https://www.nytimes.com/2019/08/05/world/americas/colombia-citizenship-venezuelans.html; Ricardo Ajiaco, "Migrantes Venozolanos."

55. In 2019, for example, the United Nations High Commissioner for Refugees (UNHCR) and International Organization for Migration (IOM) requested $738 million from the international community to assist migrant-receiving countries in Latin America and the Caribbean, but as of July 2019, it had only received 23.9 percent of the funds needed. And even though the World Bank estimates that Colombia "had to spend roughly $900 million last year to meet only the basic needs of Venezuelan migrants . . . a 2019 campaign by the World Bank to help raise funds to assist Colombia in settling Venezuelan migrants raised $152 million." See Oriana Van Praag, "Understanding the Venezuelan Refugee Crisis," Latin American Program Woodrow Wilson Center, Sept 13, 2019, https://www.wilsoncenter.org/article/understanding-the-venezuelan-refugee-crisis.

56. Baddour, "Colombia's Radical Plan"; idem., "This Country Is Setting the Bar for Handling Migrants: The Conservative Government of President Iván Duque

in Bogotá Is Offering Citizenship to Colombian-Born Babies of Venezuelan Mothers," *Atlantic*, August 16, 2019, https://www.theatlantic.com/international /archive/2019/08/colombias-counterintuitive-migration-policy/596233/.

57.   Castillo Arenas and Ammerman, "A Country That Welcomes Migration."

58.   Senator Efraín Cepeda.

59.   Baddour, "This Country Is Setting the Bar."

60.   Baddour, "This Country Is Setting the Bar."

61.   While I know for a fact that she herself completely rejects this position, I want to thank Catalina González Quintero for helping me see this other perspective.

62.   Stott and Long, "Venezuela."

63.   Oxfam, *Yes, But Not Here*, October 2019, https://oxfamilibrary.openrepository .com/bitstream/handle/10546/620890/bp_yes_but_not_here_en_xenophobia -migration-venezuela-251019-en.pdf.

64.   Economía y Negocios.

65.   Julia Zulver, "At Venezuela's Border with Colombia, Women Suffer Extraordinary Levels of Violence," *Washington Post*, February 26, 2019, https://www .washingtonpost.com/politics/2019/02/26/venezuelas-border-with-colombia -women-suffer-extraordinary-levels-violence/; International Refugee Committee, "Needs Assessment Report: Venezuelan Migrants in Colombia," November 6, 2018, https://reliefweb.int/report/colombia/needs-assessment-report -venezuelan-migrants-colombia-expansion-november-6-2018; Ramirez and Gómez, "Explotación al migrante," *Revista Semana*, https://especiales.semana .com/desprotegidos-la-vida-de-los-migrantes-en-colombia/explotacion-laboral -al-migrante-venezolano.html.

66.   In Spanish: "Este es un ultimátum para los venezolanos. Tienen dos semanas para retirarse . . . Daremos muerte a cada uno de los que se encuentren en Subachoque, trabajen o no, roben o no. No los queremos más, fuera de aquí." See "Alerta por xenofobia en contra de los venezolanos en Colombia," *Revista Semana*, June 2, 2018, https://www.semana.com/nacion/articulo/xenofobia-en -colombia-contra-los-venezolanos/569808.

67.   CNN Español, "Denuncia amenazas en panfletos contra inmigrantes venezolanos en Colombia," August 1, 2019, https://cnnespanol.cnn.com/2019/08/01/denuncian -amenazas-en-panfletos-contra-inmigrantes-venezolanos-en-colombia/.

68.   Justice Desk, "En primer cuatrimestre 2 venezolanos murieron al día de forma violenta," *El Tiempo*, May 20, 2020, https://www.eltiempo.com/justicia/investi gacion/cifras-de-migrantes-venezolanos-asesinados-en-primeros-meses-de-2020 -497738?cid=SOC_PRP_POS-MAR_ET_WHATSAPP.

69.   Let me be clear: there are many reasons why the unjust treatment endured by displaced Venezuelans is wrong, especially the fact that such treatment creates and perpetuates oppression against this group in the form of exploitation, cultural imperialism, systemic violence, and derivatization. But I think there is another level of wrongness in light of the shared migration history between the nations, and that is the focus of this work.

70. As I will discuss later, I do not reject that these principles can play a role in the treatment of immigrants. In fact, I myself, strongly maintain that a nation's immigration policies, practices, and norms cannot create, further, or reflect oppression. What I am saying here is that these are not the ideas guiding the current discussion.

71. The Torah comprises the Five Books of Moses, which serve as the foundational sacred text in Judaism. The Talmud is the central text of Rabbinic Judaism and the primary source for Jewish law.

72. "Jewish Ethics Here and Now," last accessed July 20, 2020, http://www.applied jewishethics.com/.

73. Ex 22:20; Ex 23:9.

74. Lv 19:33–34.

75. Theologically, this is based in a different understanding of the Creation story and the human relationship with G-d. According to the Judaic version of this story, G-d never finished creation, instead purposefully leaving part of the world unfinished so that human beings would have a purpose in life—namely, being partners with G-d in creating a better world. But as with the other ideas presented here, accepting that we must help improve the world does not require this theological commitment.

76. William Large, *Levinas's* Totality and Infinity: *A Reader's Guide* (NY: Bloomsbury Academic, 2015), 12.

77. These are the hundreds of informal paths created by migrants to cross into Colombia.

78. UNHCR, "Response for Venezuleans," https://data2.unhcr.org/en/situations /platform/location/7511; María Lucia Torres Villareal, Paola Marcela Iregui Parna, and Alejandra Lozano Amaya, "Una mirada a los derechos de la población migrante en el Distrito Capital: Retos de una creciente realidad," in *Migración y derechos humanos: El caso Colombiano, 2014–2018*, ed. María Teresa Palaxios Sanabria y Beatriz Londoño Toto (Bogotá: Editorial Universidad del Rosario, 2019), 207; Santiago Torrado and Jorge Galindo, "Colombia busca regularizar a un millón de venezolanos indocumentados," *El País*, February 8, 2021, https:// elpais.com/internacional/2021-02-08/colombia-se-propone-regularizar-a-un -millon-de-venezolanos-indocumentados.html.

79. Torres Villareal, Parna, and Amaya, "Una mirada," 222; Mariana Zuniga, "'I'm Stuck Here': The Desperate Search for a Passport in Venezuela," *Independent*, September 21, 2018, https://www.independent.co.uk/news/world/americas/venezuela -passport-leave-economy-maduro-colombia-border-immigration-a8548806.html.

80. Ann J. Cahill, *Overcoming Objectification: A Carnal Ethic* (New York: Routledge, 2012), 32.

81. *Veneco/a* is a xenophobic slang term against Venezuelans.

82. Thank you, Catalina González Quintero.

CHAPTER 6

Rule by the Bodies

*Biological Citizenship and Politics of Life
in Times of Migration in Chile*

RAÚL VILLARROEL

Introduction

In this chapter, I examine philosophical grounds that allow for a better understanding of the phenomenon of migration that has occurred in Chile in recent
years and the way in which it has revealed the existence of certain apparently
racist traits in the behavior of Chilean citizens in reaction to the increasing arrival of foreigners on national soil. Such behavioral expressions can be
understood by drawing on Michel Foucault's concept of termed *biopolitics*.
More specifically, Foucault explicates how attempts are made to justify death
within the *biopower* economy, in which the proclamation of an entire race or
population as inferior leads some to think that the disappearance of those
who are thus deemed "other" (i.e., strangers, outsiders, immigrants) would
strengthen us biologically.[1]

It is necessary to consider that biopolitics refers to the fact that *politics is
exercised over and through the bodies,* as the French theorist Didier Fassin
says. In the particular case that we want to analyze here, this takes place
especially in the bodies of immigrants, on whom the expressions of racism
or discrimination fall, based on the biological differences allegedly existing
between nationals and foreigners. Since it is particularly in the bodies and
on them where inequalities are registered, violence is imprinted and norms
of conduct and misconduct are registered in a corporeal way. It can be said,

then, that politics governs lives, as politics manifests itself in bodies and, depending on what kind of practices politics applies to those bodies, defines diverse moral choices for them.[2] At the same time, Italian philosopher Giorgio Agamben's notion of the *bare life* will be central in understanding the differences that can be established by the power between different kinds of lives and different kinds of human beings in the contemporary world—those who are protected and those who are abandoned. In this last case, the very lives of immigrants are certainly abandoned. The Spanish philosopher Adela Cortina addresses this issue as well. Her concept of *aporophobia* (fear of the poor, from the Greek *aporos*) describes the attitude of rejection toward poor immigrants, in contrast to the enthusiastic welcome given to foreigners who arrive as tourists eager to spend their euros or dollars. Due to a variety of reasons, ranging from unsafe living conditions to corrupt governments, these immigrants are forced to leave their homes and then encounter many difficult and oftentimes unjust legal situations. According to Cameroonian philosopher Achille Mbembe they end up being victims of *necropolitics*, a politics of death.[3]

I. Migration in Chile

International migration has been a fundamental element in the demographical evolution of Latin America and the Caribbean. Almost all countries in the region received significant migrant flows during the nineteenth and twentieth centuries. Currently, the area is emerging as a scene of mass migration. In the case of Chile, political stability and relative economic growth have maintained the retention of its own population, while attracting numerous migrants from the region in search of jobs and opportunity.[4] As early as the 1990s, when immigration was slowly becoming a reality in Chile, some people began to despise, humiliate, or even physically attack migrants in some cases. At the same time as newcomers were arriving from Peru, Bolivia, Ecuador, Colombia, the Dominican Republic, Haiti, or Venezuela, a racist construction based on myths and stereotypes (traits, color of skin, nationality) was progressively identifying them as responsible for unemployment, illness, crime, or prostitution in Chile.[5]

In the second decade of the twenty-first century, the phenomenon of accelerated immigration in Chile sparked a surge in public awareness and occupied political and citizen debate. The Chilean people witnessed the massive arrival of foreigners with surprise and uncertainty, as the local press coverage of this period attests. However, the immigration of this decade was not a new phenomenon, as it had happened in the previous decades, albeit on a smaller scale. For this reason, it is striking to note the treatment of such immigration as if it were an unprecedented development in national history.

According to Canales, in less than a year, the Chilean government presented two estimations of the volume of immigrants residing in Chile: the first one on December 31, 2018, and the second one on December 31, 2019.[6] The first study estimated the number of immigrants to be at 1,119,267. This figure was almost 50 percent higher than the number recorded eight months prior by the 2017 population census in Chile, which reported an estimated 783,282 migrants. The second study estimated that the number had risen to 1,251,225. Both studies were supported by the same methodology and the same type of primary information: the 2017 Census and Policía de Investigaciones (PDI, or the Investigative Police) records of temporary and permanent visas.

The media's portrayal of this event, which includes both the official discourse of political authorities and the approach of social science experts and the opinion of various actors of the civic world, demonstrated the existence of certain behavioral dispositions as well as xenophobic, classist, and racist beliefs among the Chilean people. Prior to this episode, such exclusionary dispositions and views were not believed to exist. Obviously, this constitutes a dangerous reproduction of issues that tend to trigger internal conflicts in nations and critically fragment or divide contemporary societies.

In the case of Chile, this discrimination and unease in the face of immigration and the increasing presence of new migrants in the country are even statistically verified in the qualitative analysis that the authorities undertake of demographic figures for the "objective" understanding of the current national reality. Part of the problem originates in the logic underpinning the construction of the figure of the "migrant" as susceptible to quantification, because it operates in the form of social and mainly political categories, which identify some individuals, so-called immigrants (those from Peru, Bolivia, Ecuador, Colombia, Haiti), while failing to focus on those who are defined by means of the higher status of "foreigners" (mainly Europeans and Americans). Thus, the relevant social inequality that underlies the raw data is hidden.[7]

It could be said, then, that recent migration policy in Chile has been focused mainly on the former ("immigrants") and, to a much lesser extent, on the latter ("foreigners"). There is a classist bias derived from racism and xenophobia present in the policy design. This is because speech that stigmatizes immigrants ("There are too many," "The situation is out of control," "High crime rates matter," "They constitute a true invasion," etc.) is used in reference to certain immigrants in particular (those from Latin America), while tending to make others entirely unproblematic (European, North American, etc.). This inequality of classes among immigrants is also manifested as a process of residential segregation. Extraregional migrants are concentrated in richer districts, in the *barrios altos* (literally, the "high neighborhoods") of Santiago. Regional migrants are concentrated in middle- and lower-class districts. Residential segregation of immigrants reproduces the segregation pattern of the Chilean population at large, as in big cities, Chilean citizens tend to be territorially divided, isolated, and segregated according to economic status.[8]

This perspective seems to have reinforced an image of migration that is treading upon dangerous grounds, one that is entering a phase that may not be controlled. The threat has given sustenance to new immigration policies, such as the restriction of visas available to Haitian immigrants or the "democratic visas" offered to Venezuelan immigrants. In other cases, these policies have included the use of force against immigrants as well as deportations, attracting significant media interest. As Canales indicates, we are witnessing a well-developed anti-immigration discourse, the objective of which is "to put the house in order."[9]

Similarly, at the level of the general population, there does not seem to be particular interest in determining the causes or consequences of migration, or in the attention that should be given to the actual magnitude of this phenomenon. The discomfort surrounding immigration means the focus of concern falls primarily on the migrant subjects and on their configuration as strangers, or their status as excluded, since it is this objective determination that makes differentiation and distinction schemes operate very clearly based on racial, ethnic, and class prejudices.

It is worth stopping here to consider a few antecedents that link Chilean history with the current crisis.

Immigration in Chile has a long history. Since the sixteenth century, as established by the Chilean historian Celia Cussen, and in a period exceeding three hundred years, "twelve million men, women and children were captured in innumerable locations within the African continent and forcibly transported to America." She affirms that after initially docking in Cartagena de Indias, some groups of slaves were transferred to Panama and then by land or sea to Lima, the capital of the Viceroyalty of Peru. From there they began the journey to Chile, "until finally arriving in Valparaiso, after seven months of losing sight of the coast of the continent of their ancestors."[10]

Since then, successive generations of Africans were progressively integrated, but always into the less-favored strata of Chilean society. However, this incorporation process allowed them to generate not only personal but also commercial connections with people of various social levels. Because of these connections, they were able to acquire goods and properties. Moreover, as Cussen relays, some of them excelled in in the development of certain minor trades. Therefore, immigrants in Chile likely saw better prospects at social mobility than immigrants to other parts of the American continent. Unlike economies such as those of Brazil, Cuba, or Haiti, which were mainly producers of crops destined for the European market, and which depended on slaves, Cussen argues that "the Chilean economy was not built on their backs."[11]

An important distinction that the Chilean historian highlights, with respect to the situation in the rest of Hispanic America at that time, is that slavery was already known in the Kingdom of Chile, through its encounter with the Indigenous population, specifically Mapuches captured at south of the Bio-Bio river. Indeed, Mapuches incorporated as servants in the richer houses of Santiago would have coexisted with their black slave counterparts, an arrangement that persisted from the early sixteenth century until the beginnings of the republic in the first decades of the nineteenth century. As Cussen writes, "According to the census of the Bishop of Santiago in 1778–79, 12% of the population from Copiapó to Maule was described by his pastor as 'mulatos,' 'blacks' or 'browns'" ... They most often worked in the cities and, eventually, in the surrounding farms as domestic servants, sellers, seamstresses, muleteers and as trusted men and women of the Chilean elite.[12]

As this early history demonstrates, the phenomenon of migration to Chile cannot be reduced to the significant arrival of foreigners into the country during the last decades, which is what the current population of Chilean citizens somehow seems to assume, judging by the concern the issue has generated and by how it is portrayed in the mass media. As the Chilean sociologist Josefina Correa confirms, relevant episodes in the history of Chile, which have defined her national identity, have been linked to multiple and diverse migration experiences. These can be seen in "selective migration policies of people from Germany to southern Chile in the late nineteenth century to 'enhance the Chilean race'; in the Chileanization processes in the north of the country after the Pacific War and in the presence of Patriotic Leagues against the Peruvian population; in the emigration processes during the military dictatorship of Pinochet, both for the forced and voluntary exile of Chileans."[13]

Toward the end of the previous century, Chile began to experience economic prosperity and made significant advances in a modernization process that placed the country in a position of certain indisputable supremacy in the Latin American context. Accordingly, we can observe that Chile began to exercise a significant gravitational pull on regional migratory process, on a larger scale than had occurred in previous periods of its history. Individuals seeking work that requires lower qualification levels became increasingly attracted to Chile as a source of jobs; simultaneously, Chileans themselves became less and less inclined to seek this type of "lower" employment.

These factors contributed to a climate of political and institutional stability that other countries of the continent have considered exemplary. As Correa indicates, this has favored an immigration process "of an intra-regional or south-south nature." Until very recently (it could even be said until the moment just before the outbreak of social protests on October 18, 2019, a fact that has radically and uncertainly altered the future of national society), Chile sought to identify itself as a culturally homogeneous, European, and exceptional nation in the Latin American context.[14]

However, it should be reiterated that in recent years, a plague of racism has begun to spread within the Chilean population, which has been the subject of analysis and debate. Particularly problematic are the speech used and the perceptions surrounding the massive recent arrival of immigrants from Latin America and Afro-Caribbean nations. These people have left their countries in search of less precarious living conditions than those they have abandoned, spurred by the social vulnerability derived from the shortage of productive work options existing there. This generates within them high expectations of accessing better job prospects in Chile and considerably higher income than they received before, with the promising possibility of even just a gradual increase in their well-being.[15]

However, these expectations are frequently unmet. Many factors are at play here, of which the most important is that once settled in the country, the immigrants are subject to discrimination and even criminalization in some cases, and it is these circumstances that place them in the context of marginality. This is a condition that, in agreement with Stefoni, can hardly be explained as being sought or generated by the migrants themselves; nor is it derived from their personal deficiencies or failures. It is only a result of their forced displacements, which can be clearly understood as a phenomenon related to the operation of the global economic structure. Therefore, "it is the economy['s] operation that requires workers at the lowest possible cost, since without them the economic development of the first world and of many countries in the region simply could not exist."[16] In contexts of the global economy and temporary employment, which is unprotected, flexible, and exploitative, the worker, provided by the increasing migratory flows, becomes cheap and affordable. This is how "migrants have been incorporated as workforce, who face precarious job conditions, low wages and insecurity as a result of working market conditions and migratory policies."[17]

A simple but paradigmatic example of the situation described above is the case of the recent and vast incorporation of Latin American immigrants, mainly Afro-Caribbean, into the building industry in Chile. As Stefoni describes, this sector tends to prioritize migrant labor forces, which, due to global outsourcing processes, is characterized by severe irregularities in their treatment. In other words, these migrants are not always protected by the existing institutional and legal-control systems in the country. Further, "the more progress in the outsourcing chain, the greater presence of job insecurity, this defined in terms of low wages, absence of contract, long hours of work and absence of social security." This is because "immigrants tend to concentrate on the lowest links in this chain."[18]

Many other examples of this type serve to illustrate how hidden and veiled racism seems to have manifested itself in the Chilean experience of immigration during the last two decades, in a process that reveals an overlap in the racist personal attitudes of the common people and the official politics of the authorities. As indicated, although it is not a new phenomenon, in recent years the conscience of Chileans seems to have forgotten its past experiences related to migration and now seems to be shaken, awakening a set of confused feelings that oscillate between bewilderment and outrage, surprise and repulsion at the arrival of citizens from other latitudes. Consequently, immigrants are often received with fear and perceived as a threatening presence, especially now that Chileans and immigrants are forced to share the same living space.

In the following pages, I consider some of the deeper and most significant reasons for this singular response, exploring the kind of philosophical insights that I believe should sustain a critical reading that allows for an understanding of this peculiar human, political, and social phenomenon beyond the simple ethnographic descriptions.

II. The Government of the Bodies

As stated previously, politics is exercised over and through bodies. In particular, inequalities are recorded, and violence is imprinted upon them. Politics governs lives, manifests itself in bodies, and defines moral choices.[19]

French philosopher Michel Foucault posited that the entry of life into the field of politics constituted the threshold of biological modernity.[20] However, if we refer to the etymology of the word "biopolitics," his term for this phenomenon, we see that, paradoxically, it does not concern life so much as the regulation of populations through various technical knowledge, such as demography and epidemiology or family planning and public health. With this in mind, in 2014, Didier Fassin referred to a formula presented by Georges Canguilhem, in his text *La connaisance de la vie*,[21] to understand the meaning of the *politics of life itself*. According to Fassin, if each society had in mind not the mortality that suits it but rather the life it must preserve, social events would unfold differently. Which leads us to think that the political choices of each society in matters of social justice and protection always mean an ultimately fatal judgment about the lives of its members. For example, one might believe that the distribution of social resources by the state has to do with preserving the life of the population, but this is not the case, because it is done only insofar as it is rationally and economically possible to do so, not because *life itself* is the primary interest.[22]

This is one of the most radical contradictions of the contemporary world. On the one hand, life, if we understand life as a mere fact of living that becomes the object of a kind of sacralization, this leads to the recognition of life as a supreme good. Yet, lives, this time mentioned in the plural, receive very different value assignments; one set of lives is worth more than others. Such inequality would be marked not only in quantitative terms, for example, according to the number of years of life expectations, but also qualitative, related to the diverse material conditions of population existence. Millions of individuals are absolutely abandoned to extreme poverty and famine, whereby life ends up being inevitably linked to a politics of death, to a *necropolitics*, as Achille Mbembe would say.[23]

Fassin's examination of Foucault's philosophy leads him to conclude that his reflections on biopolitics, begun in the mid-1970s, constitutes an unfinished work, which Foucault did not resume after the course he taught at the Collège de France in 1978–1979, "Naissance de la Biopolitique."[24] Curiously, and unlike what was proposed in its title (something already widely commented on otherwise), the lessons of that year were entirely dedicated to the study of liberalism, not to biopolitics properly, except for some sparse collateral references. The "specific problems of life" did not appear again in the subsequent courses given until his death in 1984. Life would not have been his main concern, as Fassin thinks, "neither as *bios* nor as *zoé*." Foucault would have been interested only in the way in which impersonal living beings were converted into populations or individuals; that is, in the way in which governmentality and the processes of subjectification came to constitute the modern vision of the world and of humanity.

With this understanding, Fassin seems to pursue Foucault's lost steps to develop some "implications of the concept of biopolitics," those envisaged but abandoned by the philosopher in his late work, by addressing the question of what (in coincidence with the British Nikolas Rose) he calls *life itself*: "life that is lived through a body (not only through cells) and as a society (not only as a species)."[25] Such a conception seeks to escape the usual restriction that reduces life to a simple biological phenomenon (although it is also that) and the fact that living beings are reduced to populations (although they certainly are, from a state's perspective). In short, he seeks to return "to where Foucault himself left the biopower, before reducing politics to his technologies and morals to ethics."[26]

Fassin makes us notice the fact that Foucault's work on biopolitics almost entirely ignores the concept's important consequences in terms of inequalities, as well as the fact that governmentality contributes to huge disparities in the quantity and quality of life and that the processes of subjectification could be brutally different for the dominant and the dominated. Obviously, government technologies produce inequalities of life, while at the same time expunging such processes, making their consequences imperceptible. Fassin addresses the inequality issue in a more specific way in his book *La force de l'ordre: Une anthropologie de la police des quartiers*,[27] wherein he explains how the growing inequality of the contemporary world, both in the comparison of countries and in the internal characteristics of each country, stimulates "migratory flows towards richer nations, while social disparities tend to marginalize those who already belong to stigmatized groups for racial and ethnic reasons."[28]

The final effect of these inequalities, we could say, is the disqualification, as something inferior, of the lives of certain individuals or groups of individuals that society seems to want to reduce to their *bare-life* condition, as defined by Agamben.[29]

III. Bare Life

Agamben, following Hannah Arendt, radicalizes the Aristotelian distinction between *bios* and *zoé*. On the one hand, emphasizing differences and their irremediable separation, Agamben, in fact, contrasts the zoé, "the simple fact of living common to all living beings," with the bios, "the way or way of life proper to an individual or a group," which is also a "qualified life, a particular way of life."[30] Yet he contradictorily shows an eventual fusion of both terms, when he writes that politics is the fundamental structure of Western metaphysics, since it occupies the threshold in which the articulation between the living and the logos is fulfilled. Consequently, "the politicization of the bare life is the metaphysical task par excellence in which the humanity of the living being is decided."[31]

In this way, the Western world from its very origin is marked by an inscription of biological life at the heart of political life. This aporia of separation and confusion of bios and zoé would be the ultimate truth of our modernity. That is why Agamben offers his own development of the Foucauldian biopower paradigm, examining the modalities of inscription of life-forms in that mythical sphere that Benjamin previously called "bare life."[32] The *Homo sacer*, being confined in the margins of society, is presented as the central figure of our world, and in the same way, today we would see it very clearly illustrated in the image and suffering of those whom we are summoned in these pages to think of: immigrants, refugees, displaced people. These people are very clearly represented in all those who have emigrated to Chile in search of a better life in the last two decades. Within all these unique individuals, life manifests itself very concretely in their bodies. Even the very qualification of "homeless" or "wanderers"—terms that are often used to address migrants, refugees, those who are displaced, those who have been forced to move because of their history and have been expelled from their territories—undeniably demonstrates the spirit of inhospitality and exclusion in current laws. What is even worse, this reveals a contradictory situation almost hard to believe in a world supposedly defined by logic and references to "globalization."

It is essential, then, to think about the politics of the body, considering the body in its relation to power. Power etches its authority on the body, from the mark of the slave or the prisoner to the legal norm that allows the use of force to control behavior. The position of politics regarding violence was previously examined, although in a somewhat different manner, by Walter Benjamin and Carl Schmitt,[33] who analyzed the mechanisms of liberalism's administration of violence, understanding it as a denial of the original substrate of politics.

Both the fundamental violence of the state and the potential opposition of social actors manifest in the same place: the body. The allegory presented by Kafka in his tale *In the Penal Colony* illustrates this.[34] The Czech writer shows us how the sophisticated machine used to execute the convicted person inscribes the law that he has violated on his own body through long-term torture. In the real social world, if we follow Kafka's metaphor, the violence of the state takes many forms, which can range from the imposition of restrictions on social protection to budget cuts to the public health-care system to the brutal police repressions exercised against peaceful citizen demonstrations. And, as Fassin warns, violence can be political and appear as the savage exercise of force on bodies, or it can be structural and operate as a progressive inscription of inequality within bodies. Political violence tends to be denounced. Structural violence, on the other hand, tends to be denied.

Hence, politics is what transforms lives, because it acts on bodies and therefore sets in motion all the social mores that underlie the established order. In this case the issue of democracy can no longer be raised exclusively in relation to the problems that refer to the performance of representatives and rulers but must also be raised in relation to the issue of equality and justice, to the problem of treatment that is given to migrant foreigners and minorities. In short, issues of democracy must be related to the problem of recognizing the forms of violence and domination apparently legitimately exercised in society. In this way, politics should not be seen only as the "game of the arts of governing" but should be seen in relation to the issues effectively put into action in government practices. What we should worry about, then, would not be so much about power *over* life as Foucault has said but about the power *of* life as such, and this is precisely what some, such as Adriana Petryna, have defined as the crucial problem of *biological citizenship*.[35]

Thus, if Foucault called the first concept "biopower," the second can be called "biolegitimacy;" it is the latter that has, as just noted, become a crucial issue in the moral economies of contemporary societies. It is this same biolegitimacy that provides the ground of biological citizenship. This is even more obvious in the proclamation of a humanitarian reason for the government of human beings, wherein humanitarianism does not refer to human rights in general but, in particular, to the right to live, to the simple fact of living somewhere in the world, as is common to all living things.

IV. Security and Politics of Life

Today, Fassin's definition of the politics of life is more relevant than ever, as we can see its manifestation within the issue of security, both globally and in Chile in particular. It is a phenomenon whose origin, in accordance with its particular modality of current expression, can be tracked more or less to three decades ago and refers to the process of identification or construction of an internal enemy, in the absence of an external one, to justify the security claim, relating it very centrally and visibly with the immigration issue. The issue of security has easily led to the legitimization of repressive policies, legal limitation of migratory flows, the development of more efficient technologies for border control, increasingly severe procedures for identity verification and a proliferation of confinement and deportation practices affecting undocumented immigrants.

As a result of the global convergence of a dominant control model and a logic oriented toward the dissemination of a concept of public order, policies and practices have become very similar at the transnational level. This new model of governmentality, according to Andrea Cavalletti in his book *La Città Biopolitica: Mitologie della Sicurezza*, is established through this peculiar ability to always define a possible threat and isolate it, illuminating at the same time a level of happiness or common good—that is, to reserve an area for the population, protected and privileged, where insecurity has no place and from which any other segment of the population is finally excluded.[36] That is to say, "The government must distinguish and expose a potential non-society, an enemy of happy society, a risk that—[whether it] comes from outside or inside—is properly a risk of [the] dissolution of society."[37]

We know well that modern racism, according to Foucault's intuition, is nothing more than the extrapolation of the concept of political enemy in a biological mode. Thus, the final place of the political is not the nation-state but the great security space, that positive security threshold that constitutes cooperating islands of intensity and a proximity line operating as a living and impenetrable border. The way we think of the past images of the political refugee and distinguish him from the one who crosses borders for strictly economic reasons today confirms that the real enemy is the latter, because it implies a new and unknown threat to biopolitical security. Cavalletti maintains, "As a new reproof, this absolute fugitive is rejected towards death" in a "device that leaves no possibility of escape."[38]

As the inequities have deepened, the political response has tended to translate into the deployment of punitive actions, essentially directed against those lives and bodies that have been increasingly placed on the social margins. This seems to be how a paradigmatic turn in the democratic order of contemporary societies happens, as Fassin suggests, because they transit almost without any mediation from the "social justice" that they formally declare to pursue to the "social order" that effectively seeks to establish itself through police logic often appealing to a questionable publicity of its actions, which can even reach unfortunate levels of spectacularization.

In this way, a simultaneous double process of subjectification and subjection is established, which consists in the construction of certain identity figures of social subjectivity that, at the same time, are brought to the condition of submission by the state, since in order to obtain the recognition of rights that are supposed to assist them, they must submit to the institutions and the agents that have the power of decision over their very existence. Foucault's points are relevant here yet again. The biopolitical network subordinates bodies to different means of governing, always with reference to emerging (although often hardly specifiable) risks to which they must be linked. This is undoubtedly a practice of power over life, but curiously it is put into practice in the name of life itself. In this way, a fundamental distinction is installed, affecting life and expressing the governance of bodies. Once this distinction is installed, the bodies are governed in a diverse way, as on the one hand the contiguous are granted protection while the distant (foreigners, migrants, etc.) are not guaranteed that same protection.

V. Necropolitics and Aporophobia

We are witnesses to a strange time, in which communicational transparency hides the darkness of the bodies and their claims. One of the clearest and most dramatic areas where this can be verified is in the figure of immigration. The migrant body seems to take the stage of the early twenty-first century to reveal an uncomfortable truth: there is no way out, because there is no inside or outside for the meaning of life that can serve as a refuge for its migration. With no starting point and no arrival point, the migrant body wanders in its desperate flight, carrying with it the trace of misfortune: precarious body, bare life, the victim of necropolitics.[39]

Confined to the margins, stripped of its political component, excluded from every citizen exercise, that naked life becomes the paradigmatic way in which biopower inscribes its mark on the suffering body. However, from that margin, in a world that blurs its center with the same speed that the productive forces displace their territories, the bare life also becomes the privileged target of the biopolitical exercise, as evidenced by the figure of the immigrant, the refugee, the stateless person who is at the center of the government policies of our times. In all of them, of course, life manifests itself very concretely in the bodies. Armies of wanderers, held exclusively under exception decrees used as norms of social control, as Agamben describes, and due to an endless war against difference, end up confined in refugee concentration camps. Agamben wonders, "What is a Camp? What is its legal-political structure, the one which made it possible that such events to occur in them?"[40] It is certainly not a simple historical event or an anomaly but "the hidden matrix, the *nomos* of the political space in which we still live." If in the past the camp referred to a place that marked the inscription of the difference between friend and enemy, now "the camp is the space that opens when the state of exception begins to become the norm,"[41] a space of indistinction between norm and exception where discriminatory practices are usual and depend on the will of the police; according to their civic character or personal ethics, these will be more or less cruel toward the refugees held there.

In a manner akin to the slave, the migrant is forced to leave a home. From this moment, his body is imprisoned in a legal problem of difficult resolution, and often his political status is diffused. Hence the relevance of the appeal of Mbembe as a criterion for understanding the suffering and current status of the migrant.[42]

The starting point of the Cameroonian author rises from the failure of biopolitics as outlined by Foucault to account for the complexity of the processes lived on the periphery of the world, where "sovereignty resides largely in power and the ability to decide who can live and who must die."[43] Unlike Foucault, Mbembe tries to more clearly define the concrete conditions established to let live and, above all, kill when he analyzes the practices that produce death through the use of a systematic exercise of violence and terror on certain populations, which he terms the necropower.[44] If Mbembe understands sovereignty as the right to kill, he does so by linking the classical notion of biopower with the state of exception and the state of siege, which allows him to deepen Foucault's analysis of racism over class considerations—"race has always been the shadow over the thinking and practice of Western politics, especially when it comes to imagine the inhumanity of foreign peoples."[45]

Now, it is necessary to clarify here that when we refer to the foreigner, in this case to the immigrant, we really refer to that already known category of the "foreigner in an irregular situation," migrants who have entered the national territory clandestinely or people already living in a country who have lost their right to residence. These "undocumented" people are those whom Arendt in *The Origins of Totalitarianism* called the "without-rights" and who foreshadowed the "end of human rights."[46]

The Spanish philosopher Adela Cortina offers similar positions in her book *Aporofobia, el rechazo al pobre: Un desafío para la democracia*, distinguishing between those seventy-five million foreigners who stepped on Spanish soil in 2016 and sought out the country as a tourist destination from the "other types of foreigners," who came from the other side of the Mediterranean, risking life, losing it countless times to reach that promised land (that is, the European Union in which Spain is also included).[47] It seems impossible not to compare the enthusiastic and hospitable welcome with which foreigners who arrive as tourists overflowing with euros or dollars are received to the merciless rejection that faces successive waves of poor foreigners.

Cortina clarifies with an indescribable force of irony that this is not a result of simple xenophobia, because rejection does not stem from the fact that they come from outside, or that they are of another race or ethnicity. The foreigner does not bother by simply being. Rather, the cause of aggravation and annoyance is when these people are poor. This is exactly what aporophobia is. "And it is the poor who bothers us," she writes, "the resourceless, the helpless, who seem to be unable to contribute anything positive to the GDP of the country they arrive to or where [they] have lived since ancient times, and to who[m], apparently, it will not bring more than complications. The unscrupulous tells of him that [he] will increase the costs of public health, and take away work from the natives, that [he] is a potential terrorist, [that] he will bring very suspicious values and will undoubtedly remove the '[well-being]' of our societies, in which there is undoubtedly poverty and inequality, but incomparably less than that suffered by [those] who [are] fleeing wars and misery."[48]

Conclusion

Following Nikolas Rose in *Politics of Life: Biomedicine, Power and Subjectivity in the 21st century*, the idea of populations conceived of as a collective that could be undermined from outside by an infiltration of inferior races and from within by an excessive reproduction of degenerates gives rise to a biologized racism that links the characteristics of individuals with those of the general population and seeks to constrain or restrict the rights, sexual reproduction, quantities, or powers of the various groups defined by their racial origin and, at the same time, supports the attempt to control the racial character of the population by imposing restrictions on immigration.[49] This is what many nations have carried out since the beginning of the twentieth century to the present day and what we see today prospering as a potential regulatory idea of public policy in Chile, where authorities are afraid of being overwhelmed by hordes of "degraded" immigrants. Foucault himself had already seen this in *Il faut défendre la société*: the fact that racism justifies the function of death in the biopower economy by appealing to the principle that the disappearance of others strengthens us biologically, as we believe we are members of a particular race or population.[50]

Since the beginning of the present century, which many such as Nikolas Rose have described as the "century of biotechnology," this extension of the notion of citizenship toward its biological dimension becomes particularly relevant. By this I mean the notion of biological citizenship, specifically stated by thinkers like Petryna, Fassin, Rose, or involved in the reflection of Esposito and others, because it unequivocally shows a potential corrective to Marshall's traditional conception of the problem, in which he defined as the assignment of social rights meant to establish an egalitarian social perspective, the same one the liberal democracies and their politics of life have been unable sustain, having established, rather, a regime of unacceptable inequities that have given a purely nominal character to existing rights.[51] Therefore, a fatal difference of statutes can be verified, in which some human beings have been protected by social rights while others have been deprived of them and relegated to the condition of bare life.

Once we understand politics beyond governmentality, to include governing by the bodies, we must by necessity pay close attention to the treatment given to these people and the ways in which their lives are evaluated, specifically in the case of migrant subjects, with special attention to the situation of migration in Chile, as emphasized in this work. What politics is capable of doing with life does not only refer to political speeches, or to strategies and calculation of probable economic value that could be extracted to determine their integration or abandonment and rejection. Rather, it has to do with the real way in which these groups and these individuals are treated, what morals or principles are relied upon to designate them as deserving, and the kinds of inequalities and absence of certain recognitions are determined to exist.

In contemporary society, and even more so in a global context of a pandemic health crisis, the precarious situation of immigrants seems to be critically deteriorating. It can be said that the stigmatization of which they have been victims in the past has now acquired a new figure in the present. In the Chilean case, mass media, for example, has focused its attention mainly on the country's metropolitan region, where the COVID-19 contagion is mainly concentrated. In this context, political authorities interviewed on TV are seen emphatically denouncing those who live in the lowest-income communities, highlighting the seeming lack of concern in their behaviors (disrespect for lockdown, the refusal to maintain social distance, the nonuse of surgical masks, etc.), while reacting in an entirely contrasting manner if those same faults are committed by people who live in the highest-income areas. Migrants, then, especially those racialized and poor, not the "foreigners" as we stated earlier, are now much more subject to stereotypes, forms of social control, and moral sanction.

To illustrate this situation, it can be observed that since the beginnings of the coronavirus pandemic, the lenses of differing television channels have homed in on lower-income people in districts in Santiago populated by large percentages of Haitian migrants, gathering sensationalistic material as support for their news and morning shows. Headlines about "the outbreak of the virus in a Haitian migrant community," for instance, quickly became the most relevant news. Even the presence of the virus ends up being racialized through a strange fusion of disease, ethnicity, and residency of the poorest people. The *campamentos*, very precarious human settlements often peripherally placed and far from downtown, are where many immigrants live in overcrowded situations; these too have suffered similar treatment on the part of the media.[52]

For Chilean people today, a new challenge arises with the presence of the Covid-19 pandemic. It seems it would be difficult for them to imagine that a Chilean national could very well carry and spread the virus, and perhaps that is why an "other" is sought. The other becomes an ideal scapegoat, as it is the body of the "other," which can be considered not only guilty of spreading the infection but also of the resulting unemployment or poverty. When this recurring placement of blame pertaining to the spread of the virus falls on a person deemed other or on a migrant community, it is not by mere coincidence.[53]

Lastly, it can be said that these kinds of prejudices against migrants trigger social violence, feelings of aggression, or evil dispositions that lead to a hatred of differences and produce offensive attitudes that can oftentimes lead to death. In this, the arrival of immigrants is now doubly plagued by not only the existing stigmas toward their very presence but also by the possibility of that other imminent lethality, which is the pandemic virus.

This is precisely why, as argued in this chapter, it is imperative to talk about politics *of* life and not about politics *over* life. Life should always be the subject and never the object of politics, and in no way should it ever be reduced to a simple biological matter, as in the case of precarized immigrant lives.

Notes

1. Michel Foucault, *Defender la sociedad: Curso en el Collège de France (1975–1976)* (Buenos Aires: Fondo de Cultura Económica de Argentina, 2000).

2. Didier Fassin, *Por una repolitización del mundo: Las vidas descartables como desafío del siglo XXI* (Mexico City: Siglo XXI Editores, 2019), 17.

3. Achille Mbembe, *Necropolítica* (Santa Cruz de Tenerife: Editorial Melusina, 2011).

4. Carolina Stefoni, "La nacionalidad y el color de piel en la racialización del extranjero: Migrantes como buenos trabajadores en el sector de la construcción," in *Racismo en Chile: La piel como marca de la immigración*, ed. María Emilia Tijoux (Santiago: Editorial Universitaria, 2016), 65–75.

5. María Emilia Tijoux, "Racismo chileno en tiempos de pandemia," *Indymedia Argentina*, July 6, 2020, https://argentina.indymedia.org/2020/06/06/racismo-chileno-en-tiempos-de-pandemia/.

6. A. Canales, "Migración, inclusión y cohesión social: Viejos y nuevos debates en torno a la xenofobia y la discriminación en Chile," presentation at the interna-

tional seminar "Inclusión y cohesión social en el marco de la Agenda 2030 para el desarroloo sostenible," CEPAL, Santiago de Chile, May 28–29, 2019.

7.   Canales, "Migración, inclusión y cohesión social."

8.   Canales.

9.   Canales.

10. Celia Cussen, "Raza y calidad de vida en el Reino de Chile: Antecedentes coloniales de la discriminación," in Tijoux, *Racismo en Chile*, 21.

11. Cussen, "Raza y calidad de vida," 28.

12. Cussen, 29.

13. Josefina Correa Tellez, "La inmigración como 'problema' o el resurgir de la raza: Racismo general, racismo cotidiano y su papel en la conformación de la nación," in Tijoux, *Racismo en Chile*, 36.

14. Correa Tellez, "La inmigración como 'problema,'" 43.

15. "Coyuntura Laboral en América Latina y el Caribe: La inmigración laboral en América Latina," CEPAL, May 2017, https://www.cepal.org/es/publicaciones/41370 -coyuntura-laboral-america-latina-caribe-la-inmigracion-laboral-america-latina.

16. Stefoni, "La nacionalidad y el color de piel," 68.

17. Stefoni, 71.

18. Stefoni, 71.

19. Fassin, *Por una repolitización del mundo*, 17.

20. Michel Foucault, *Historia de la sexualidad*, vol. 1, *La voluntad de saber* (Mexico City: Siglo XXI Editores, 2011), 173.

21. Georges Canguilhem, *La connaisance de la vie* (Paris: Librarie Philosophique J. Vrin, 1993).

22. Fassin, *Por una repolitización del mundo*.

23. Mbembe, *Necropolítica*.

24. Michel Foucault, *Naissance de la biopolitique: Cours au Collège de France 1978– 1979* (Paris: Gallimard, 2004).

25. Nikolas Rose, *The Politics of Life Itself: Biomedicime, Power, and Subjectivity in the Twenty-First Century* (Princeton, N.J.: Princeton University Press, 2006), 27.

26. Fassin, *Por una repolitización del mundo*, 32.

27. Didier Fassin, *La force de l'ordre: Une anthropologie de la police des quartiers* (Paris: Seuil, 2011).

28. Fassin, *La fuerza del orden: Una etnografía del accionar policial en las periferias urbanas* (Mexico City: Siglo XXI Editores, 2019), 25.

29. Giorgio Agamben, *Homo Sacer: El poder soberano y la nuda vida* (Valencia: Editorial Pre-Textos, 1998).

30. Agamben, *Homo Sacer*, 9.

31. Agamben, *Homo Sacer*, 17–18.

32. Agamben, *Homo Sacer*, 87.

33. Walter Benjamin, *Para una crítica de la violencia*, trans. Héctor A. Murena (Buenos Aires: Editorial Leviátan, 1995), https://aprendizaje.mec.edu.py/dw-recursos /system/content/0c59c97/content/Benjamin,%20Walter%20(1892-1940)

/Benjamin,%20Walter%20-%20Para%20una%20cr%C3%ADtica%20de%20la%20
violencia.pdf; Carl Schmitt, *El concepto de lo político* (Madrid: Alianza Editorial,
1987).

34. Franz Kafka, *En la colonia penitenciaria*, Spanish translation, available at https://
biblioteca.org.ar/libros/11395.pdf.

35. Adriana Petryna, *Life Exposed: Biological Citizenship after Chernobyl* (Princeton, N.J.: Princeton University Press, 2013).

36. Andrea Cavalletti, *La città biopolitica: Mitologie della sicurezza* (n.p.: Testi E Pretesti, 2005).

37. Andrea Cavalletti, *Mitologías de la seguridad: La ciudad biopolítica* (Buenos Aires: Adriana Hidalga, 2010), 158.

38. Cavalletti, *Mitologías de la seguridad*, 259.

39. Mbembe.

40. Giorgio Agamben, *Medios sin fin: Notas sobre la política* (Valencia: Editorial Pre-Textos, 2000), 45.

41. Agamben, *Medios sin fin*, 47.

42. Mbembe, 33.

43. Mbembe, 19.

44. Antonio Fuentes Diaz, *Necropolítica: Violencia y excepción en América Latina* (Puebla, Mexico: Benemerita Universidad Autonoma de Puebla, 2012), 18.

45. Mbembe, 22.

46. Hannah Arendt, *The Origins of Totalitarianism*. Published originally 1951.

47. Adela Cortina, *Aporofobia, el rechazo al pobre: Un desafío para la democracia* (Barcelona: Ediciones Paidos, 2017). See esp. page 11.

48. Cortina, 14.

49. Rose, *Politics of Life*.

50. Michel Foucault, *Il faut défendre la société: Cours au Collège de France 1976* (Paris: Gallimard, 1997).

51. Rose, 21; Petryna, *Life Exposed*; Didier Fassin, "Another Politics of Life Is Possible," *Theory, Culture and Society* 26, no. 5 (August 2009): 44–60; Nikolas Rose and Carlos Novas, "Biological Citizenship," in *Global Assemblages: Technology, Politics and Ethics as Anthropological Problems*, ed. Aihwa Ong and Stephen Collier (Malden, Mass.: Blackwell, 2005), 439–63; Roberto Esposito, *Le persone e le cose* (n.p.: Einaudi, 2014).

52. Carolina Ramírez, "Discursos anti-inmigración y su posición privilegiada en los medios: Una amenaza a la convivencia," *CIPER*, May 20, 2020, https://www.ciper chile.cl/2020/05/20/discursos-anti-inmigracion-y-su-posicion-privilegiada-en -los-medios-una-amenaza-a-la-convivencia/.

53. Tijoux, "Racismo chileno en tiempos de pandemia."

PART III

Mexico and Central America

CHAPTER 7

Ethics of Liberation

Listening to Central American Migrants'
Response to Forced Migration

LUIS RUBÉN DÍAZ CEPEDA

Migration of Central Americans to the United States is not new. In fact, mass migration from the region has occurred since at least the 1970s, originating in a mixture of local corruption and imposed capitalism that has caused economic vulnerability, civil war, and genocide. Indeed, forced migration has been, at least in part, caused by colonial structures and the enactment and legitimization of neoliberal economic policies that only look to increase the profit of the few without any esteem for most people's lives. This disregard for the lives of the poor is unequivocally directed specially toward the racialized and sexed/gendered bodies of indigenous people and dark-skinned mestizos.

In this chapter, I argue that migrants suffer the consequences of colonial structures as reflected in internal colonialism, in which diminishing social and economic structures place them in a disadvantaged position, instantiated in discriminatory social practices and manifested in xenophobia and aporophobia. Clearly these practices are immoral and detrimental to a population's well-being and thus need to be challenged. The research I present here reveals that migrants themselves are already doing so by creating solidarity networks, showing their high levels of agency and resilience. These solidarity networks are amplified by pro-migrant social activists and organization that assist them with shelter, lobbying, and defense services.

In support of my argument, I first explore sociological explanations of poverty in Latin America, referring more specifically to Pablo González Casanova's theory of sociology of exploitation, namely its concept of social relation of exploitation, for its broad explanatory power. I then show how exploitation is instantiated in the migration flows from Central America to Mexico and the United States. The third and final section is normative. Here, based on Dussel's ethics of liberation, I argue that meeting the ethical duty to answer to the Other is a clear and useful answer to discriminatory practices. I conclude by illustrating how migrants help each other and how this effort is supported by social organizations.

I. Theorizing the Causes of Poverty

The conquest of Abya Yala by Europe and its consequent transformation into what is now known as Latin America marked the beginning of a new era. For the first time, the entire world was connected. This juncture was brutal, as in the process the native peoples of America were denied human dignity and identity.[1] This disdain for native Americans had the disastrous consequences of decimating them and forcing most of the survivors into a position of serfdom through a social and economic system designed to keep them under the control of the colonial powers. Even after the achievement of independence, these colonial structures continue to exist through internal colonialism, which systematically leaves out a large segment of the population not considered worthy of a better life by the political and economic elites. This discrimination is based on race and gender, wherein the further a person is from a European likeness, the more they are discriminated against. As I will show in this section, colonial structures are not only instantiated in macro frames of reference— they are reflected in social relations of exploitation and domination.

After the independence wars in the first decades of the 1800s, Latin American countries gained their political independence from Spain and Portugal. Yet, over the following century, they remained socially and economically dependent upon Europe, as the local elites continued abusing their colonial privileges and looking at Europe as superior. As a result, indigenous and dark mestizos lived in deplorable conditions, which led to several civil wars in the search of social justice in the 1900s. The outcome of these conflicts were, in some cases, military dictatorships and, in others, a civil government.

After World War II and in the context of the Cold War, Latin America increased its industrialization and urbanization. The decades of the 1950s and 1960s saw political change in Latin America, during which some of the most prominent philosophical theories from the region were developed. These include the theology of liberation, philosophy of liberation, and dependence theory. It was at this time that a new generation of thinkers, which included philosophers, sociologists, and economists, attempted to understand Latin America's poor social and economic condition. Far from homogeneous, these efforts led to the emergence of at least two different and opposing positions: modernization theories and dependence theory.

On the one hand, the theories of modernization argued that poverty in Latin America was due to its lack of an urban middle class. In Roitman's words, "Its difference lies in highlighting the landowning oligarchy as the cause of the backwardness and therefore a rural society whose social structure is characterized by the low level of social mobility and elective rationality."[2] According to this position, once an urban middle class was developed, there would be a state with enough legitimacy to enforce the rule of law and remove power from the former oligarchy. In the process, the urban middle class will modernize the industry and the countryside. In short, the path to follow is the one set forth by the United States and Canada. Once Latin American countries reached the same level of modernization and democracy as their northern neighbors, they would also reach the same level of development.[3]

As it became clear that modernization theories offered neither a sound explanation nor a path to end or at least lessen poverty, a novel approach closer to Latin America's circumstances emerged: critical sociology. This latter claims that social scientists should not remain strangers to their realities but, on the contrary, should actively work to assist the poor. Further, they must attempt to understand the reality and inner lives of individuals. As Mill writes, "The sociological imagination allows us to capture the history and the relationship between the two within society."[4] Critiques of modernization theories continued, resulting in the development by the 1970s of dependency theory by Fernando Henrique Cardoso and Enzo Faletto, among others. They argue that "the social and political structure change as different classes and social groups manage to impose their interests, their strengths and their command on the whole of society."[5] In other words, from the point of view of dependency theory, economic inequalities between the industrialized countries and so-called underdeveloped countries were due not to distinct technological progress but to class struggle. These theorists also argued that the economic system was set up in such a way that Latin America would always be dependent upon the countries of the "Center" (especially the United States) as long as the region continued to import out-of-date technology and export labor and raw material.

While these theories have certainly influenced not only the theoretical development of Latin America but also its political and economic circumstances, I posit that in the case under consideration, which is the current situation of Central American migrants in Mexico, Pablo González Casanova's theory is more apropos, as his sociology of exploitation offers a broader explanatory power. Specifically, González explains that colonial domination implies an unfair appropriation of resources from the colonized country. In a colonial relationship, the dominant country monopolizes the resources of the colonized, blocking other countries from trading with them. Clearly, even in the circumstances of economic liberalism, this action deprives colonies from looking to other partners for better deals. At the same time, colonies are forced to serve as a supplier of the natural resources to the metropolis. In consequence, their industrialization has slowed down to the rhythm that is convenient for the colonizers. Finally, the same mechanism of control over natural resources is used to obtain cheap labor. Unfortunately, these conditions did not disappear with the end of the colonial period; instead, they continued to persist in the form of internal colonialism.

B. Internal Colonialism

The colonial period in Latin America was characterized by a hierarchical system, with Spaniards in the highest position. The encomienda system provided encomenderos with free labor. As the indigenous people's physical constitution was not fit to work in the mines, people from Africa were kidnapped and forced into slave work in the extraction of resources. Both black slaves and indigenous people received no payment and were given barely enough food to survive. It is of significance to note that not all native people suffered in equal measures, as some made alliances with the colonial powers and thus held privileges over other natives. Those privileges never matched those of native Spaniards or Spaniards' descendants, yet were fundamental to spread and sustain the structures of domination by naturalizing them in the form of social relations.

Relevant to my argument, González points out that colonial structures do not disappear with political independence but quite often remain in the form of *internal colonialism*, defined as "a structure of social relations of domination and exploitation between heterogeneous cultural groups."[6] González elaborates that the exact form internal colonialism takes emerges from the colonial structure left when a country gains political independence. In the *plural society*, for example, one ruling class is substituted by another (Spaniards, Creoles, and white mestizos); at the same time, there is no substantial change in the deplorable conditions in which indigenous and darker mestizo people live. In the case of Latin America, the self-entitled elite have ruled our countries without a real democracy. Another manifestation of the persistence of colonial structures is *marginalism*, the phenomenon of underdevelopment, wherein the ruling elite excludes a large part of the population from political, economic, and social development processes.[7]

In furthering his project of developing a sociology of exploitation, González argues that "asymmetry is linked to the idea of power and dominance; it is indirectly analyzed as predominance or dependency, as monopolization of the economy, power, culture of one nation by another; or directly as an economic, political and psychological influence that men or nations with power, wealth, prestige exercise over those who lack them or have them to a lesser degree."[8] This postulation signified a major development in the analysis of the reasons for poverty in Latin America, for it includes not only the social and economic structures that cause systemic poverty in people of color but also the social relations of exploitation between rulers and citizens, elites and peasants, and so forth. Quijano explains that "internal colonialism corresponds to a structure of social relations of domination and exploitation between heterogeneous cultural groups," wherein the powerful use the higher social and economic positions they took over from the former colonial powers to keep colonized groups subjugated under the same social dynamic as prior to independence.[9]

These colonialist structures are instantiated in the way individuals makes themselves present in the world; this is to say in their personalities. Furthering this point, González points out that one of the most relevant features of a colonialist personality is the complicated web of attitudes toward other people according to the place individuals are ascribed on the social scale. Even as internal colonialists may be servile to people higher than themselves in the social hierarchy, they dehumanize the colonized. To the colonialist, the colonized can be ignored, humiliated, or, even worse, killed, as the latter are perceived as "things" at the disposition of the former.[10] Clearly, migrants are among those most affected by these colonial structures, as they are forced to leave their countries because they cannot find the material conditions necessary to support their lives.

To summarize, Latin American countries suffer from among the highest levels of economic inequity in the world, as evidenced by both external differences as compared to the United States and Canada as well as by internal inequalities when the income of the lowest to the highest economic decile is compared. Modernization theories have explained this phenomenon as a failure of Latin American countries to follow the same path of the United States—the development of a middle urban class able to bring democracy and modernize industry. Counter to this explanation, dependency theory maintains that economic inequalities are due to class struggles and an unfavorable trade relationship with the industrialized countries. While both theories were popular in their time and to some extent remain valid, I prefer González's sociology of exploitation, as it considers the social and economic conditions together with social relations to explain the endemic oppression of people of color. I argue that this colonial structure and social relation of exploitation creates a large group that has no access to material resources and suffers discrimination on a regular basis, which forces them to leave their countries. They embark first to other countries in Latin America, then to the United States and, in fewer numbers, to Canada. In the following section, I present a brief description of how these processes manifest themselves in the lives of Central American immigrants on Mexico's territory.

II. Central American Immigrants in Mexico

Contrary to widely held belief, the migration of Central Americans to the United States is not a new phenomenon but has occurred since the 1970s. According to Jonas and Rodríguez, the origins of this migration can be traced to a mixture of civil war, genocide, violence, radical capitalism, and economic vulnerability.[11] It has been, at least in part, caused by the implementation and legitimization of neoliberal and globalization policies that deny ways of life and survival that diverge from those required by the market, which privileges individualization over the collective. These policies have created a surplus population, which tends to be seen as inferior by the dominant powers.[12]

This disregard for the lives of the victims of the system can be seen in both overt and covert forms of discrimination against migrants from the Global South. Within this broader context, I proceed to expose the particularities of the Central American migrants' stay and transit through Mexico on their way north.

A. Southern Border

Connections between Mexico and Central America trace back to colonial times, during which both belonged to the Spanish Empire. The borders between Guatemala and Belize in Central America and the states of Chiapas, Tabasco, Campeche, and Quintana Roo in Mexico were established in 1882, after several wars and territorial disputes. Within this context, Mexico and Guatemala share nearly 80 percent of the total borderline. Historically speaking, Chiapas is the Mexican state with the most connections to Guatemala, followed by Tabasco. While there were national differences, it is possible to argue that at a local level there was a relatively high trade connection, usually beneficial to Mexico.[13]

Manuel Ángel Castillo and Mónica Toussaint document three large immigration waves from Central America to Mexico after the achievement of independence.[14] The first one was seasonal and dates to the turn of the twentieth century, when farmworkers from Guatemala migrated to work on coffee plantations in the zone known as the Soconusco in Chiapas. This workforce was not only welcomed but also promoted by the coffee plantations' owners, who actively sought cheap labor. Most immigrants were young adults with little to no formal education; they were not perceived as outsiders, as they played a vital role in the economy and did not create social antagonism. As time progressed, this migration movement diversified, and immigrants began to work in other areas, such as construction and domestic services in the cities.

A second immigration wave resulted from the armed conflict in Central America from 1981 to 1983. Fleeing from this turmoil, thousands of farmworkers found refuge in Mexico, mostly in Chiapas, with a smaller number relocating to the states of Campeche and Quintana Roo. Even though Mexico was not a signatory country of the United Nations Convention and Protocol Relating to the Status of Refugees, it provided asylum to immigrants from the region.[15] By the decade of the 1990s, the "Mexican government's implementation of the Program of Migratory Stabilization led to the progressive, definite settlement of those who had decided to stay in Mexican territory, nearly one third of the total 'recognized refugee population.'"[16]

The third immigration wave is ongoing and consists of in-transit migrants whose goal is not to stay in Mexico but to continue their way to the United States. For the most part, this migration comprises young adult males, but it also includes some women and unaccompanied children. I elaborate on this type of migration in the following section. For now, it is enough to add that in addition to the aforementioned stabilization program, the Mexican government has passed new laws protecting the rights of people beyond their citizenship. For example, the Immigration Law passed in 2011 (but implemented in 2013) holds, among other things, the principles of "recognition of the acquired rights of migrants and equity between nationals and foreigners."[17] The legislation then attempts to protect migrants regardless of their legal status, giving precedence to their human rights before their legal status. In that sense, it is important to note that since the creation of the Office of the United Nations High Commissioner for Human Rights (OHCHR), human rights have been a powerful tool to better the migrants' material conditions, as they have prompted the promulgation of laws to protect persons regardless of their immigration status.[18]

The combination of former seasonal migrants, refugees, and in-transit migrants who decide to stay in Mexico has created a transnational population with connections on both sides of the border. It is only fair to say that this immigrant population receives fairly decent treatment on the part of the government in Mexico, as they have access to education, medical services, and family reunification and can present complaints against wrongful behavior on the part of government authorities. At the same time, it is vital to not forget that this treatment is still contingent on national security concerns and economic conditions.[19] In that sense, difficulties arise when nondocumented migrants reach legal adulthood (eighteen years old in Mexico), at which point they cannot acquire full legal rights. As a direct consequence, they have no access to a college education and/or better jobs. Clearly these disadvantages condemn them to a low social and economic status, which leaves them vulnerable to discriminatory attacks from others. Women and children are especially vulnerable to such assaults.

To elaborate upon the harmful circumstances that women face because of migration, it is important to recognize the reality, which is that they often succumb to these conditions. If a woman decides not to migrate, she is often left with domestic responsibilities, especially that of childcare. Usually this means that she cannot pursue a professional career of her own and consequently becomes dependent upon the ability and willingness of her partner or relatives to support her and their family. Clearly this violates her own personal aspirations and may force her to endure abusive behavior. On the other hand, if women do decide to migrate, they risk facing harsher traveling conditions than men do, including the possibility of sexual harassment and abuse. As one migrant named Helena shared, "When I cross the border, I try to do it during my menstrual period, so they do not rape me."[20] These conditions do not end upon the completion of travels. Rather, they are a permanent menace that persists when migrant women become settled in their destination. As Lindsey Carter writes, "Immigrant women are blocked, delayed, and discouraged from accessing their rights to legal identity, health care, and regularization of their immigration status, not because of restrictive laws, but as a result of negative and confusing institutional interactions with low-to-mid level officials."[21] Unlike openly restrictive laws, these harassing behaviors are subtler and hard to detect, as they have been normalized in the form of abusive social relations. Moreover, in those instances where they are detected and denounced, they are rarely prosecuted.

In sum, similar to other migration patterns in South America, seasonal migrant workers first went from the Guatemalan countryside to the coffee plantations in the rural areas of Mexico. From there, some moved to the cities, creating networks and a transnational community, which served as a supporting social network as they adjust to living in Mexico. Immigrants living in Mexico receive degrees of government protection as their children have access to education, medical services, family reunification, and legal personality. To acknowledge this fairly good treatment is not to ignore that it is still subordinated to issues of national security. Beyond government treatment, it is possible to observe that most discriminatory practices come at a micro level, from either the general population or government officers (acting on their own will, not under government directives). These discriminatory social practices affect mostly, but not exclusively, women and children. Further, these trying conditions are an example of how immigrants are tolerated in as far as they are functional to the system and are used to support the privileges of the few.

B. Transit to the United States

Historically, for the most part, Central American migration has occurred across the Texas borderline between the United States and Mexico. Some immigrants have sought to enter the United States clandestinely, while others have turned themselves in to immigration authorities for the purpose of seeking political asylum. The number and demographic composition of this migratory flow was stable for a long time. However, at the end of 2013, a notable increase occurred, reaching its climax in the summer of 2014. Since then, there has been an oscillation in the numbers of migrants. The composition of this migratory flow also changed, with an increase in the number of unaccompanied minors as well as family groups (mainly women with children), who turned themselves in to be arrested by immigration officials to later request political asylum.

It should be noted that at the same time there was an increase in Central American migrants, there was a decrease in the number of Mexicans seeking to enter the United States in an unauthorized manner. Consequently, the overall balance of migrants seeking to enter the United States illegally has in fact declined to levels unseen since the 1970s. Josiah Heyman, Jeremy Slack, and Emily Guerra question why, despite this decline in actual migration flow, border surveillance has not only not decreased but in fact has increased. They conclude that "recent empirical evidence has linked these contending discourses about borders and immigration to niche right-wing media, and to the election of Donald Trump," fostering hate speech and rejection of the Other on the part of American citizens toward marginalized groups, including immigrants.[22]

C. The Emergence of the Caravans

Seeking to protect themselves from the predatory practices of criminal organizations and in the hope that the U.S. government will grant them political asylum if they show in numbers, some migrants decide to complete the journey from Mexico's southern border to the United States in large groups. This change in the form of the migratory flow first manifested itself dramatically on October 12, 2018.

Historically, migrants seeking to reach the United States traveled in isolation or in small groups. However, on that date, a message on Facebook led to the departure of three hundred people from San Pedro Sula, Honduras. The originating Facebook page had only two hundred members. The message read, "Every day 300 people leave Honduras, we better make a caravan, as a single family, to take fewer risks to the north," which at first did not have much impact. However, its dissemination by the local HSH television station—ironically, as a criticism of the caravan's endeavor—allowed the message to reach a much wider audience, inspiring approximately three thousand people to join the group within a few days.[23] In less than two weeks, the caravan had grown to around seven thousand people, who arrived at the border bridge between Guatemala and Mexico on October 19, 2018.

The immigration authorities of Mexico did not prevent the entry of this first caravan to Mexico, although they did not help in an organized way. One of the causes of this lack of attention was the transition of federal government administrations. The outgoing administration, headed by Enrique Peña Nieto, initiated a weak response with the "You Are at Home" (Estas en tu casa) program. At the same time, the elected administration of Andrés Manuel López Obrador, which was not yet in office, also did not take control of the situation. Since then, it has been religious organizations and human rights organizations that have put pressure on the state to safeguard the best interests of migrants, especially infants and women. The relative ease and support that this first caravan had in entering Mexico, as well as the migrants' minimal exposure to attacks and extortion, inspired other people to do the same. Consequently, several more caravans were organized to the United States, only to find the most obstacles at precisely the end of their journey.

The transit from Mexico to the north was not what the immigrants expected. Far from their expectations of finding a relatively easy entry to the United States, they encountered adverse circumstances. Due to the Trump administration's harsh immigration policies, immigrants who did manage to reach U.S. territory and request political asylum were sent to detention centers to wait for a migration judge to hear their case. This waiting period can take years and has involved the separation of families, including the removal of infants and toddlers from their parents.

Unfortunately, being in these detention centers under the Trump administration was not the direst situation that an immigrant could face, since, as immigration policies hardened, they were not even allowed to apply for political asylum in U.S. territory. In their article "Blockading Asylum Seekers at Ports of Entry at the US-Mexico Border Puts Them at Increased Risk of

Exploitation, Violence, and Death,"[24] Heyman and Slack documented that the U.S. government had implemented various strategies to deny immigrants access to the asylum system:

> US border officials have refused to allow many asylum seekers who are subject to expedited removal to pursue asylum claims, even when they request asylum or express a fear of return. The [Trump] administration has criminally prosecuted and detained asylum-seekers in order to deter others from coming. It has separated children from parents at the border, and it now proposes to reunify these families, albeit in detention facilities. It has even raised the possibility of declaring Mexico a "safe" third country, thus barring asylum claims from migrants that first pass through Mexico.[25]

More than this, as of February 2019, the Trump administration began to promote more subtle and aggressive strategies to limit immigration. One of these was to prevent immigrants from even reaching the ports of entry at the immigration checkpoints. This was accomplished by posting immigration officers on the international bridges that connect Mexico and the United States. These officials were then tasked to question people, especially colored immigrants, before they enter U.S. territory about their immigration status. If they could not prove a legal immigration status, they were not allowed to proceed further to the established checkpoint.

Facing this situation, migrants were soon no longer attempting to enter the United States via caravans, reverting to the practices of crossing through nonauthorized ports by themselves or in small groups. However, the stiffening of border security forced them to go through more distant and more dangerous paths. In Ivan's words, "I am going through this place that I know, where there is no fence. Now [May] is a good time to do it, for I cannot carry too much food. However, because of the rain season, there is water. I already know the route."[26] In addition to the dangers inherent in going through the desert, unauthorized access to the United States is now considered a felony by the United States justice system. Formally speaking, this criminalizes migrants, which in turn will make it difficult for them to establish their case before an immigration court, as they would already have criminal records. A third alternative that migrants have chosen is to remain in Mexico waiting to be called to apply for political asylum, which can take several months or even years. Obviously, rejection at the ports of entry and forced settlement in the border cities of northern Mexico puts migrants at risk of being kidnapped and forcibly put to work by drug cartels, whether as marijuana farmers or cocaine producers, hit men, or prostitutes. Clearly, the policy subjects them to the very risks from which they fled in the first place.

On January 20, 2021, Joe Biden was sworn in as the forty-sixth president of the United States. The first hundred days of his administration brought some favorable changes for immigrants, yet, as of this writing, serious challenges remained. The improvements include the reactivation of the Temporary Protected Status program to the benefit of certain national groups, the narrowing of immigration enforcement in the interior of the United States (including the removal of the public charge rule and the focus, in enforcement, on those noncitizens who represent a national security risk), the end of the Muslim and African travel ban, the freezing of regulatory fees and excessive bureaucratic and sometimes duplicated procedures, and an increase in the budget for the United States Citizenship and Immigration Services. These changes taken together mean that immigrants who are already in the country have a fair and human path to gain legal status. However, the situation south of the border line has not improved that significantly.

The enumerated changes are necessary but not sufficient to properly respond to the migration situation on the border with Mexico. It remains, for example, to increase the refugee ceiling. In his platform statement "Reassert America's Commitment to Asylum-Seekers and Refugees," President Biden pledged to start with a ceiling of one hundred twenty-five thousand refugees, a number he promised to increase during his administration.[27] Yet, on February 12, 2021, the Department of State declared that Biden would propose a ceiling of 62,500 refugees for the fiscal year 2021. This number further decreased and has remained around fifteen thousand, allegedly because of the COVID-19 pandemic and the previous changes made by the Trump administration. Biden's administration resettled only 647 refugees during its first two months, and if it continues at this rate this will most likely mean a resettlement number lower than during any fiscal year under the Trump administration.[28] A second improvement that has yet to materialize is the end of family detention: while long-term detention has come to an end and short-term detention centers are slated to become processing centers, as of May 2021 these latter were still operating.

Most importantly, while it is true that, officially, unaccompanied children and asylum seekers with an open case are now allowed into the United States to apply for asylum, the fact is that the U.S. government is not prepared to let them do so. Consequently, some migrants must still wait for their hearing in Mexico, alongside Central American migrants whose cases were denied. According to Ana Laura Ramírez-Vázquez, a feminist activist living in Ciudad Juárez who focuses on issues relating to children and adolescents, children who remain in Mexico do not find an integral process that may channel them to a better life, causing a best-case scenario in which they may receive secondary education and get a low-paying job that makes them victims of capitalism.[29] In the worst-case scenario, migrants can be killed or kidnaped by criminal groups. In short, some of the problems that migrants faced during the Trump era are still apparent and very real under the Biden administration.

Throughout, Mexican social and religious organizations have played a vital role in protecting the immigrants' lives, beginning with providing safe shelters. Immigrants' houses such as El Buen Pastor (The Good Shepherd), la Divina misericordia (The divine mercy) at the southern border, or La Casa del Migrante (Migrants' house) and Annunciation House at the northern border offer places where migrants can stay and rest. In the case of the southern border, migrants tend to stay in the shelters for only a few days, to get some rest, wash their clothes, and heal their injuries. As soon as they are ready, they resume their journey to the north. In the case of the north, migrants stay for longer periods, with some waiting for hearings in the U.S. courts of their asylum claims. In either case, shelters serve as a safe place, as there is a tacit agreement by migratory authorities to not conduct any raids in shelter facilities or their vicinities. They also serve as an intermediary between Mexican authorities and immigrants seeking to obtain a humanitarian visa, by providing evidence that the claimant is injured.

I argue, then, that as capital is no longer restricted by state limits, "the relation Center-periphery is becoming a social relation, instead of a geographical relation."[30] As in the case of Central American migrants, these social relations can be of exploitation and discrimination. This mistreatment commences at their place of origin, where they do not make enough money to survive or are direct victims of gang-related violence. This is an important distinction, for it points out that they are not necessarily being pulled by the "American Dream" but, rather, are pushed out of their homes by the hostile colonial conditions they live in. In this exodus from Central America, some migrants opt for staying in the southern borderlands, as they can keep some level of contact with their relatives. Others decide to continue traveling to the north. Once they reach the Mexico-U.S. border, some turn themselves over to immigration officials in the hopes of gaining political asylum. However, this process became increasingly difficult because of the Trump administration's cruel and challenging policies, which continue to reverberate under Biden's tenure. Consequently, some migrants have decided to stay in Mexico, where they may continue to suffer the same discrimination from which they were fleeing.

It is important to notice that migrants are not passive subjects. On the contrary, as Jaime Rivas argues, immigrants are active participants who receive and interpret information and design strategies in their relationships with various local actors, as well as with external institutions and their staff.[31] In the following section, then, I analyze the factors and ethics that keep them going despite the harsh conditions of the exodus. In doing so, I demonstrate that migrants show agency and solidarity to create solidarity networks among themselves, even as they receive the support of pro-immigrant social organizations and activists. This solidarity is exemplary of the ethical duty proposed by both Emmanuel Levinas and Enrique Dussel.

III. Solidarity

I begin this section with the idea that the modern notion of the nation-state was built from the dichotomy of a "we-they," a friend or an enemy.[32] I maintain that, within a close community, people with shared identity help those inside of what I call their fraternal circle; that is to say people who are part of the same. As I will show, unlike this "we-they" system based on fraternal relationships within the imaginary community, some people go beyond their fraternal circle to engage in a relationship of solidarity with the Other, who by his mere presence questions the I. This questioning awakens a subjectivity in the I, wherein his duty toward the Other is recognized and fulfilled. This is because the I carries a preontological duty to the Other, which is an intrinsic part of the subjectivity of the individual. Let me delve into this process of the genesis of a political subjectivity.

In his conversation with Philippe Nemo, Levinas reassures his interlocutor that the responsibility toward the Other is addressed by the I as a face, as the exteriority.[33] The I is full when it responds to the calling of the Other, since its own subjectivity is already occupied by its responsibility before the stranger. Responsibility is not an option for the I. However, this does not mean a condemnation. On the contrary, in the ethical encounter with the Other,[34] the I finds its freedom, because "freedom is in charge of the responsibility that it cannot assume, an elevation and an inspiration without complacency."[35] This responsibility is there because the nature of the good is prior to being and has chosen the I to receive the command of the Other in which to respond. The very pronoun *I* means "Here I am" for you, in the voice of the I that answers the claim of the other without asking for anything in return.

When assumed, this responsibility translates into an obsession, which Levinas's philosophy does not shy away from. On the contrary, he embraces the idea, because an obsessed person is not capable of indifference to the Other. In Levinas's words, "This obsession with the other translates not to who should be blamed but to the question 'What should I do?'"[36] It is important not to lose sight of the fact that this obsession with the Other is not the voluntary act of an isolated individual; rather, in the ethical act of taking the place of the Other, the I grows in freedom, because by recognizing the command of the Other, the I is. Responsibility toward the Other is a responsibility that does not obey the acts of the I; it is a responsibility that is not imposed but is made to be invited. In the words of Levinas, "It is on this figure of being that is possessed in the equality, about being *ápX'n* where the obsession that we have recognized in the proximity bursts." In other words, this obsession does not require that the I already has a relationship with the Other; rather, it is awakened by the very presence of the Other, especially that of the widow, the orphan, and the stranger.

This responsibility for the Other, impelled by the presence of the Other in the subjectivity of the I, prevents the I's consciousness from completing itself. For Levinas, "subjectivity is defined by the responsibility of others and not by being."[37] That is, subjectivity is not the identity of the self to itself, but its responsibility for the other. This responsibility comes as a presence that overflows, a presence that does not allow consciousness to identify with itself. For Levinas then, the I must respond to the face of the Other, the stranger. This is the source of solidarity when migrants have nothing material to give away, as they are in challenging conditions, yet still are there for others, including strangers, with whom they cross paths.

This solidarity is beyond the line of duty marked by liberalism and its preference for selfish individual interest, as immigrants help each other, even though this means risking their own well-being. In the course of research for this work, many instances of solidarity were encountered.[38] During field research on the border line between Tabasco, Mexico, and Guatemala, we waited by the railroads of the Beast (La Bestia), which is the train that Central American migrants board at Mexico's southern border to get to Mexico City. From there, they look for other routes and ways to get to the northern border. They do so illegally, under a considerable risk of being captured by Mexican authorities or criminal group. At the railroad, we witnessed firsthand as migrants who had just met on their trip in the Beast were waiting for one of them (whom, for privacy reasons, I will call Pablo) to heal from a wounded ankle, an injury caused by jumping from the train to avoid a checkpoint set up by Mexico's Migration National Institute. They told us, "No, we are not going to leave this dude here, we met him a few days ago, we came together on the train, in the Beast, we were doing good, but we saw a checkpoint, and we jumped. It was his turn, bad luck, we were doing good, f . . . k. But it is what it is, how are we going to leave him alone? No, we wait. We all are together."[39]

As we continued the research, it was possible to establish that behavior like this was not the exception but the rule among most migrants. It is important to highlight that opposite to quid pro quo practices—for example, in exchange-sex where women accept to have sexual intercourse with a male who protects them through the trip up north—in most cases the answer to the Other was not conditional on immigrants having something to give back. Again, they all were traveling with extremely scarce resources. Yet they shared the little they had, even if this little were to keep Pablo company even when doing so meant losing time and precious resources.

This sense of solidarity was manifested not only by immigrants but also by people who were moved by a feeling of solidarity to go meet people beyond their immediate circle to help the Other. I refer here to social activists and their organizations whom we encountered assisting migrants both in their journey and at the border.

A. Social Organizations

Using Levinas's philosophy as a starting point, Enrique Dussel developed a conception of how an ethical subjectivity is present in the world from both a political and an ethical perspective. Dussel writes that "the 'being-subject' is a way of being aware or awake, that the birth of subjectivity (and embodiment) is placed in a position in which events appear phenomenally."[40] In other words, being is having a body, but more importantly, being aware of the world and the exploitation relations that exist in it. True subjectivity, which necessarily occurs within a community, occurs just as in Levinas, when the I is at the service of the Other. However, moving beyond Levinas's ideas, Dussel maintains that personal action is not enough; solidarity with the Other must be offered in a collective, organized, and institutional way.

The first step, then, to create a legitimate social organization is critical awareness. Undeniably, many groups of people never rebel against oppression. However, there is also the case of those who, while they do not directly suffer oppression, unite in solidarity with the victims and fight alongside them. It is possible then to affirm that only certain groups of people go "from non-conscience . . . to critical ethical conscience."[41] Since the condition of being oppressed is not a sufficient or necessary reason for the emergence of a social organization, the question arises, "Where is the spark that starts them?" Based on Dussel's philosophy, I propose that the answer lies in the consciousness of oppression, not in oppression itself, since once people realize that oppressive conditions are not natural but are a consequence of human actions, they begin to fight them together.

Contrary to the liberal conception of men who take the individual as an independent being in constant war with other individuals for control of resources, ethical social organizations arise when there is a sense of community, when a "we" and not an "I" is created. To take this step from I to us, it is vital to recognize that human beings are not isolated but are always part of a community. The community begins to establish itself when a person goes from being just a person to being a political actor and understands politics as the creation of conditions in which all people can have a dignified life. This political actor comes from experiencing oppression firsthand, but also from the presence of the Other. From this, he begins to search for answers to his questions and makes the suffering of the Other his own and offers himself in substitution of the Other.

This step is taken when, in addition to the political community in which a person is born, there are strong ties that go beyond the limits of fraternity to become bonds of solidarity. As Dussel argues, "We are born into a political community . . . however, from a political point of view, this remains an abstraction that lacks the contradictions that always run through a community . . . we move from the political community to the people."[42] This movement occurs due to the mutual recognition of the oppressive condition of life of the victims of capitalism. When people are united in their grief and anger, they will fight together to overthrow the status quo that denies their right to *buen vivir*. For the fight to be successful, it is necessary to strengthen the bonds of co-responsibility and solidarity between the victims and the people who have come to their call for aid.

As I have already established, the link that unites these groups is solidarity defined as "critical emotionality directed at the suffering externality of the victim . . . [Solidarity] is, [then] the metaphysical desire of the Other as another."[43] In other words, while fraternity is a feeling that is promoted within a closed political community, solidarity seeks to alleviate the pain of the Other as Other, allowing the I to shed the restrictions imposed by a state in order to assist the Other wherever he is. In fact, the ethical I does not wait for the Other to appear but is eager to meet him. It is important to reaffirm that solidarity is not limited to the territory of a state or a political community but extends to the communion between the victim and the I, which not only responds to the questioning of the Other that is presented to it but also actively seeks be close to the victim. By doing so, the I leaves the privileges that come with membership in the oppressive system and fights alongside the Other.

Clearly, if a person is not close to the Other, he will hardly develop a sense of ethical duty toward him. At first, it is an action in which the I searches the Other for the origin of the relationship between signified and signifier, but later it becomes a living relationship in which the I is exposed to the suffering of the Other. In other words, for the individual to perform her ethical duty, it is necessary to shorten the distance between them. As Dussel says, "shortening the distance is a praxis, it is acting towards the other [while Other], it is an action directed towards the neighborhood, the praxis is this and nothing else: a proximity approach."[44] To feel the pain of the Other, the I must leave the ivory tower and see the suffering of others face-to-face.

This movement is a conscious act of the I that goes beyond its borders, because it recognizes the suffering of the Other and therefore rushes to alleviate it: "Proximity is [then] the word that best expresses the essence of people, their first (archaeological) and final (eschatological) incarnation, an experience whose memory mobilizes people and their most ambitious and highly-minded projects."[45] It is important to note that proximity is not limited to physical focus, as people may be physically close to each other but may not be emotionally close. That is, despite being physically close, they may lack the sense of solidarity with others that occurs when they recognize themselves in the suffering of others. In Dussel's words, "This closeness to things, this physical proximity is proxemic (people to being), not proximity (person to person)."[46] This means that physical proximity is a necessary but not sufficient condition to establish the relationship of solidarity between the oppressed and the one who has recognized the alleviation of their unpleasant condition as an ethical duty.

This proxemic proximity movement, that is, the passage from just being physically near to actually establishing a relationship with the Other, is carried out by both migrants and social activists who live in solidarity with the oppressed, either because they are part of them or because they fight alongside the Other. An ethical person loses his innocence and realizes that it is he who is in the prison of totalization and not the Other, because the Other, despite the oppressive social conditions, is already free in its alterity. Both the ethical I and the Other fight a system that has led individuals to view exploitation as natural and to place blame on an impersonal economic system instead of on the people who promote it. A fair person is then one who recognizes that "ethical conscience [is] defined as the capacity of one to listen to the voice of the other, the trans-ontological word that springs beyond the current system to respond to the voice of the other, which is justice."[47] This answer comes from a community as life potential.

The ethical concepts introduced by Levinas but expanded by Dussel are not mere abstractions but have had real and tangible effects on the world. Liberation philosophy has been in constant dialogue with so-called progressive governments. This has led to the development of other forms of government, such as the plurinational state of Bolivia as, well as to the conceptualization of obediential power (described by Dussel). Likewise, liberation theology has implemented ecclesiastical practices close to the base community. Certainly, these practices promote the idea of a living church that is close to the material needs of those in need. In it the ethical principles of solidarity with the Other are lived. Religious and social organizations on the border share these principles of obedience to the ethical duty toward the victims of the system.

The examples of these organizations, as well as of the migrants themselves, demonstrate that when people fulfill their ethical duty towards the Other, it is possible to create fairer societies that allow life to flourish. This is due to the expansion of relationships based on ethics, responsibility, and solidarity, which occurs first between the Other and the I, and then among all people. This is an example of how, even under the harshest conditions, a fairer society is possible when the value and dignity of the other is recognized through advocacy, lobbying, and assistance on a wide spectrum of migration issues.

Conclusion

Oppression in Latin America is due to social and economic structures that were created and developed in colonial times. Gaining political independence from Spain and Portugal did not erase these structures that keep indigenous people and dark-skinned mestizos in material conditions of exploitation. This structural racism increased with the implementation of neoliberal economic policies throughout Latin America since the decade of the 1980s. The free market and a for-profit economy were promoted and implemented as the way to modernize the Latin American economy and end poverty. However, as predicted by dependency theory, this did not occur. Rather, structural poverty consistently increased in the countries where these policies were applied. Poor economies and armed conflicts have, since then, forced Central Americans to migrate to the north. Some of them have Mexico as their final destination, while others are looking to reach the United States and, in fewer cases, Canada.

The structures that force people to migrate must be examined and theorized, as they have been by others. However, in this chapter, through Pablo González Casanova's sociology of exploitation, I have focused on the social relations that are enabled by those structures. As González theorizes, these two dimensions are mutually caused. Once this is understood, given its detrimental effect on living conditions it is necessary to offer a normative theory that aids in warding off these oppressive conditions and relations. This search does not need go very far, as migrants are already practicing solidary relationships, as indicated in Dussel's expansion of Levinas's ethical theory. These are manifested in the support networks and assistance migrants provide to each other during their dangerous path to the north. This ethical behavior is also shared by social activists and organizations supporting migrants through shelter, legal assistance, and lobbying services.

Finally, I would like to clarify that by emphasizing the agency of immigrants and their ethical behavior, together with social activists and organizations that succor them, I am not discussing the conditions where this possibility of agency is null. Such is the case when immigrants are captured by criminal organizations and forced to work in illegal farms, mines, or prostitution centers. Clearly, under these conditions, migrants have very little room to exercise their will without taking a high risk of being raped or killed. Again, this is, of course, a serious issue that needs to be addressed. Yet possible solutions to the crisis need to have migrants as the central speakers of the discussions; for this purpose, their ability and knowledge needs to be recognized. In short, oppressive social relations are instances of colonization; reversing those practices is both a form of decolonization and a way to build a fairer system.

Notes

1. Enrique Dussel, *1492: El encubrimiento del Otro* (La Paz: Plural editores, Facultad de Humanidades y Ciencias de la educación–UMSA, 1994).
2. Marcos Roitman Rosenmann, *Pensar América Latina* (Buenos Aires: CLACSO, 2008), 35. In Spanish in the original [Su diferencia estriba en subrayar como causantes del atraso a la oligarquía terrateniente y por ende a una sociedad rural cuya estructura social se caracteriza por el escaso nivel de movilidad social y racionalidad electiva.]
3. For more on the debate between the *laissez passer* and goverment-driven modernization approaches see José Medina Echavarría, *Consideraciones sociológicas sobre el desarrollo económico de América Latina* (San José: Educa, 1980).
4. C. Wright Mills, *The Sociological Imagination* (New York: Oxford University Press, 1959).
5. Fernando Henrique Cardoso and Enzo Faletto, *Dependencia y desarrollo en América Latina* (Mexico City: Siglo XXI, 1977), 18. [La estructura social y política se va modificando en la medida en que distintas clases y grupos sociales logran imponer sus intereses, su fuerza y su dominación al conjunto de la sociedad].
6. Pablo González Casanova, *Sociología de la explotación* (Buenos Aires: CLACSO, 2006), 183. [Una estructura de relaciones sociales de dominio y explotación entre grupos culturales heterogéneos, distintos]. Casanova's contemporary Anibal Quijano describes this phenomenon as "coloniality." For more on the relation between coloniality and migration see Luis Rubén Díaz Cepeda, "Consideraciones éticas de las organizaciones sociales fronterizas en defensa de los Migrantes," in *Migrantes, refugiados y derechos humanos*, ed. Francisco de Jesús Cepeda Rincón and Guadalupe Friné Lucho González (Mexico City: Tirant lo blanc, Paso de la Esperanza A.C., 2019), 63–78.

7.   For more on coloniality and social division see Anibal Quijano, "Colonialidad del poder y clasificación social," in *El giro decolonial: Reflexiones para una diversidad epistémica más allá del capitalismo global* (Bogotá: Siglo del Hombre Editores, 2007), 93–127.

8.   González Casanova, *Sociología de la explotación*, 18. [La asimetría está ligada a la idea de poder y dominio; es analizada indirectamente como predominio o dependencia, como monopolización de la economía, el poder, la cultura de una nación por otra; o directamente como influencia económica, política y psicológica, que los hombres o las naciones con poder, riqueza, prestigio ejercen sobre los que carecen de ellos o los tienen en grado menor.]

9.   Quijano, "Colonialidad del poder," 241. [El colonialismo interno corresponde a una estructura de relacionessociales de dominio y explotación entre grupos culturales heterogéneos, distintos.]

10. Moving forward with his research, by 1999, González noted that these social relations of exploitation were not exclusive to Latin America; rather, exploitation is global. See Pablo González Casanova, "La explotación global," *Memoria* October, no. 116 (1998): 136–63.

11. Susanne Jonas and Nestor Rodríguez, *Guatemala-U.S. Migration: Transforming Regions* (Austin: University of Texas Press, 2015).

12. Giorgio Agamben, *Homo Sacer: Sovereign Power and Bare Life*, trans. Daniel Heller-Roazen (Stanford, Calif.: Stanford University Press, 1998).

13. Alejandro Chanona Burguete and José Ignacio Martínez Cortés, "Las relaciones de México con América Latina bajo un nuevo esquema de integración comercial," in *México-Centroamérica*, ed. Benítez Manaut and Fernández de Castro (Mexico City: Instituto Tecnológico Autónomo de México, 2001).

14. Manuel Ángel Castillo and Mónica Toussaint, "La frontera sur de México: Orígenes y desarrollo dela migración Centroamericana," *Cuadernos Intercambio Sobre Centroamérica y El Caribe* 12, no. 2 (July–December 2015): 59–86.

15. Alto Comisionado de las Naciones Unidas para los Refugiados (Acnur-México), *Protección y asistencia de refugiados en América Latina: Documentos regionales 1981–1999* (Mexico City: ACNUR, 2000).

16. Manuel Ángel Castillo, "The Mexico-Guatemala Border: New Controls on Transborder Migrations in View of Recent Integration Schemes?" *Frontera Norte* 15, no. 29 (June 2003): 51.

17. Secretaría de gobernación, Instituto Nacional de Migración, "Ley de Migración y Su Reglamento," 2012, http://www.inm.gob.mx/static/marco_juridico/pdf/Ley _de_Migracion_y_Reglamento.pdf.

18. Daniel Vázquez and Sandra Serrano, "Enfoque de derechos humanos y migración," in *Política migratoria y derechos de los migrantes en México*, ed. Velia Cecilia Bobes León (Mexico City: FLACSO, 2018), 26.

19. As it happened in 2019, when the Mexican army was ordered by President Lopez Obrador to prevent Central American migrants from reaching the borderline between Mexico and the United States.

20.   Helena, interview by author, December 15, 2019. (Name changed to protect her identity).

21.   Lindsey Carte, "Everyday Restriction: Central American Women and the State in the Mexico-Guatemala Border City of Tapachula," *International Migration Review* 48, no. 1 (Spring 2014): 114.

22.   Josiah Heyman, Jeremy Slack, and Emily Guerra, "Bordering a 'Crisis': Central American Asylum Seekers and the Reproduction of Dominant Border Enforcement Practices," *Journal of the Southwest* 60, no. 4 (Winter 2018): 755.

23.   Jenaro Villamil, "Cómo se gestó el multitudinario 'desplazamiento forzado,'" November 4, 2018, *Proceso*, https://www.proceso.com.mx/558263/como-se -gesto-el-multitudinario-desplazamiento-forzado.

24.   Josiah Heyman and Jeremy Slack, "Blockading Asylum Seekers at Ports of Entry at the US-Mexico Border Puts Them at Increased Risk of Exploitation, Violence, and Death," Center for Migration Studies, June 25, 2018, https://cmsny .org/publications/heyman-slack-asylum-poe/.

25.   Heyman and Slack, "Blockading Asylum Seekers."

26.   Ivan, interview by author, May 27, 2020. Name has been changed to protect the identity of the interviewee. [Me voy a ir por ese lado, ya sé que ahí no hay muro. Estos días es un buen momento para hacerlo, pos como no puedo cargar mucha comida, aprovecho que hay agua en las montañas por las lluvias. Ya me la sé.]

27.   Joe Biden for President, "The Biden Plan for Securing our Values as a Nation of Immigrants," accessed June 12, 2021, https://joebiden.com/immigration/.

28.   Jorge Loweree and Aaron Reichlin-Melnick, "Tracking the Biden Agenda on Legal Immigration in the First 100 Days," American Immigration Council, April 29, 2021, https://www.americanimmigrationcouncil.org/research/tracking-biden -agenda-legal-immigration-first-100-days.

29.   Ana Laura Ramírez Vazquéz, interview by author.

30.   Ankie Hoogvelt, *Globalization and the Postcolonial World: The New Political Economy of Development* (Baltimore: Johns Hopkins University Press, 1997), 145, as cited in Fernando Coronil, "Naturaleza del poscolonialismo: Del Eurocentrismo al globocentrismo," in *La Colonialidad del saber: Eurocentrismo y ciencias sociales. Perspectivas Latinoamericanas*, ed. Edgardo Lander (Buenos Aires: Consejo Latinoamericano de Ciencias Sociales, 2000), 101.

31.   Jaime Rivas Castillo, "¿Víctimas nada más?: Migrantes Centroamericanos en El Soconusco, Chiapas," *Nueva Antropol [Online]* 24, no. 74 (2001): 9–38.

32.   Carl Schmitt, *El concepto de lo político* (Madrid: Alianza Editorial, 1991).

33.   Emmanuel Levinas, *Ethics and Infinity*, trans. Richard A. Cohen (Pittsburgh: Duquesne University Press, 1985).

34.   Emmanuel Levinas, *Totality and Infinity*, trans. Alphonso Lingis (Pittsburgh: Duquesne University Press, 1969), 24.

35.   Emmanuel Levinas, *Autrement qu'être ou au-delà de l'essence* (Paris: Le livre de poche, 1978), 178.

36.   Levinas, *Autrement qu'être ou au-delà de l'essence*, 168.

37. Emmanuel Levinas, *El humanismo del otro hombre* (Mexico City: Siglo XXI editores, 1974), 132.
38. The author wants to express his gratitude to Lily Lara Romero and José Manuel Hernández Franco for their generous hospitality and assistance to conduct this research.
39. Migrant group, interview by author, December 6, 2019. [No, no vamos a dejar a este bato aquí, lo conocimos hace unos días, veníamos juntos en el tren, en la Bestia, veníamos bien, pero ahí estaba un retén y pos brincamos. Le tocó a él, mala suerte, ya veníamos muy bien. Pero así esto, ¿Cómo lo vamos a dejar solo? No, aquí esperamos. Vamos todos juntos.]
40. Enrique Dussel, "Sobre el sujeto y la intersubjetividad: El agente histórico como actor en los movimientos sociales," *Pasos*, no. 84 (July–August 1999): 85.
41. Enrique Dussel, *Ética de la liberación en la edad de la globalización y de la exclusión* (Madrid: Trota, 1998), 309.
42. Enrique Dussel, *20 tesis de política* (Mexico City: Siglo XXI, 2006), 72.
43. Enrique Dussel, "De la fraternidad a la solidaridad," in *Pablo de Tarso en la filosofía política actual y otros ensayos* (Mexico City: Ediciones Paulina, 2012), 106.
44. Enrique Dussel, *Philosophy of Liberation*, trans. Martinez Aquila (New York: Orbis Books, 1985), 17.
45. Dussel, *Philosophy of Liberation*, 19.
46. Dussel, *Ética de la liberación*, 30.
47. Dussel, *Philosophy of Liberation*, 47.

CHAPTER 8

The Justice of the Other

*Mexicans, Palestinians, and Saharawis on
the Same Side of Different Walls*

SILVANA RABINOVICH

Introduction

Contrary to expectations, thirty years after the emblematic fall of the Berlin Wall, physical barriers that impair the free circulation of peoples have multiplied. Today, at least seventy such walls stand in various places around the globe. In this chapter, we will focus on three of them: the one stopping Mexicans and Latin Americans from entering the United States; the one that the state of Israel built to prevent the *return* of Palestinians to their homes and lands; and the one the Moroccan kingdom built to annex the Saharawi territories and assimilate the occupied Western Sahara population. I chose these three walls because they are all related to Mexico. The first one stops immigration from Latin America and blocks out from the United States even other migrants originating from faraway places, such as Africa. I chose the second because the Israeli technology that we call here "the Wall," and which is "tested" in Palestinian territories, is sold in Latin America.[1] Finally, the wall that the Moroccan kingdom built in Western Sahara is an issue that unites Mexicans and Saharawis both as states (Mexico recognizes the Saharawi Arab Democratic Republic since 1979) and as peoples, as the many joint cultural activities show.[2]

We approach these three walls, symbols of colonial and neocolonial policy, from the perspective of Emmanuel Levinas's heteronomous ethics. We propose to translate *heteronomy* not as a subjugation to dominance but as the duty to let oneself be taught by the justice *of* the other. Unlike altruism, which intends to apply its own idea of justice to others that do not obtain it in the form of justice *for* the other, heteronomy implies a change of perspective. Striving to listen to the justice *of* the other means recognizing that what we consider acquired rights are, in fact, privileges from a decolonial point of view. As a key to heteronomous ethics, we analyze here the role that *vulnerability* plays in the discourse that justifies the construction of illegitimate walls as well as in the figures of immigrants and refugees. These pages explore the political potential of heteronomous ethics beyond Levinas. This is achieved by introducing other thinkers into the dialogue—beyond the philosopher's decisions about his own work, and as Levinas himself proposes, "beyond my death." They are invited here as necessary voices from a decolonial perspective.[3] Furthermore, we consider the idea of *right of return*, invoked both by Palestinians and Saharawis, and reflect on its meaning in the case of Mexico. Lastly, we review the meanings of *exile* in relation to the mentioned walls.

I. The Wall or Your Life: Heteronomous Reflections

Allegedly built to protect the lives of inhabitants of certain places, "frontier" walls put life under threat. They threaten all forms of life (including the lives of those they are supposed to protect). While their aim is to prevent danger, the walls produce precisely what they claim to avoid. In a world that boasts about "globalization," the walls are multiplying in a polymorphous, rapid way.

Life, like water, flows. The official aim of walls is *stopping*. They stand in the way of animals (most obviously the human kind), but they also divert water and stagnate life. Water does not recognize political frontiers, and it does not lack memory.[4] In addition to preventing the passage of those people the governments in charge consider "undesirable," walls act as membranes that distract attention in order to manage prohibited dealings: it is well known that the international drug trade passing through Mexico is not limited to the land border at all, but is rather conducted by sea and even through submarine operations, involving private companies and state legal organizations.[5] However, this wall also acts as a membrane when it comes to clandestine labor, which is let in "invisibly," according to needs, so as to deny these people their rights.

According to Évelyne Ritaine,[6] walls (emblems of decision-making power, control, and categorization) are always built unilaterally in order to territorialize *asymmetrically*.[7] Built as identity-enclosure devices that humiliate others, walls lock the ones they intend to protect inside, so as to prevent the entrance of people deemed "undesirable," who are paradoxically locked outside. In the context of the "militarization of contiguity,"[8] the great frontier fences deepen technological asymmetry because they deploy permanent control devices (increasingly sophisticated cameras, radars, satellite networks, sensors, and identity-recognition devices). And we are supposed to believe they are only looking at one side. . . . The efficacy of this complex device exceeds the mere physical, spectacular presence of the walls, which evidently fulfills a symbolic function. Israelis call this contiguously militarized space *kav hatéfer*, which means seamline, a phrase that sounds like a public confession of the desire to annex territory. Asymmetries are promoted to subject the other and implement either a colonial (Israel with Palestine, Morocco with Western Sahara) or a neocolonial model (the United States with Mexico).[9] Social and economic asymmetry lies at the heart of every system of discrimination.

The discrimination device is deployed at checkpoints. Indeed, according to Damien Simonneau, the wall is no more than a corollary of the *checkpoint*, which is the actual control laboratory.[10] From the point of view of those subjected to this experience, like Palestinian writer Azmi Bishara, each checkpoint is an abyss that blocks access to public space: "It is a place of domination and despotism. It is a site and a fortress only visible from the outside. Seeing it is allowed, passing through it or touching it is forbidden. It is not a public space. It is a space that controls public space."[11] I will be referring to the subversion of public versus private in this context later, in relation to private capital invested in a public matter.

The asymmetry and unilaterality of walls are expressed in the fact that they usually do not bear the same name on both sides. For example, the wall termed the "safety fence" or "separation fence" by Israel is called "annexation," "segregation," or "apartheid wall" in Palestine. The one Moroccans call "Sand Wall," "defensive wall," or *Berm* (and which fails to name the millions of landmines that impair the return of the exiled) is known among Saharawis as the "wall of shame."[12] As for former president Trump, he doesn't resort to any euphemisms and prefers to call it simply "the wall."[13] Indeed, in the era of Twitter, political words are increasingly less euphemistic: both the former U.S. president and former Israeli prime minister Benjamin Netanyahu talk shamelessly about *annexation* (whether referring to the Syrian Golan Heights or the Palestinian Jordan Valley).[14]

Let's concur with Ritaine that the Wall (in upper case) designates a territorial segregation policy made up of devices that exceed the mere physical wall (in lower case).[15] In short, we could say that "the Wall or your life" is a false choice. This expression reminds us of the robber's threat: "your money or your life," which makes it preferable to lose your belongings rather than risk your neck. However, what the state's voice is actually hinting at is "the stock exchange or your life." The astronomical earnings of the defense and espionage industry (among other companies listed on the Stock Exchange) involved in the construction of a "border" wall, or more specifically in the Wall policy, threaten peoples' lives. We are in a situation where public space is adapted to the privileged protection of private capital to the detriment of public life, in two ways. Firstly, it undoubtedly threatens the lives of the excluded, who are besieged, exiled, deprived of their lands, and condemned to poverty. Secondly, to an incomparably lesser extent, it ruins the lives of the "included" who, for fear of the other, let certain totalitarian elements enter interpersonal relationships. This eliminates hospitality as a way of life. Hospitality is downgraded to the mode of globalized tourism. This raises the question of how insiders let the Wall negatively affect *life*.[16]

II. Vulner-Abilities

As we attempt to answer the question of why there is a consensus regarding the construction of the walls studied here, two closely related factors come up and intertwine in the scene: fear and vulnerability. Since these concepts appear in different, even opposite forms on both sides of the wall, it would be more appropriate to name them in the plural: fears and vulnerabilities.

On this side of the walls, on the excluded side, fears are related to threats of a territorial segregation policy.[17] These are well-founded fears caused by the terrible situation facing the populations concerned, who are deprived of their lands, under the terror of occupation by another state (in the case of Palestine or Western Sahara), or terrorized by organized crime (in the case of

Mexico and Central America, among many others). These fears drive people's desire to pass through these barriers even at the risk to their lives, because they feel "there is nothing else to lose." *On the other side* of the same walls, the builders' side, lies what Paul Virilio called "the Administration of Fear."[18]

Regarding the achievement of consensus to build walls in two of the compared cases, Arizona and Israel, Simonneau describes it as a three-act play in which a state besieged by certain "invaders" builds a protective barrier.[19] In the *first act*, the porosity of the territory and discourse mobility among the wall's advocates become political problems. In the *second act*, this interest group demands that the government solve these already defined "political problems" through security measures. And in the *third act*, this same group spreads its perspective as an indisputable truth, demanding through the public sphere and institutions (the judicial branch, the mass media) that the state should proceed with construction. By the end of the play, the state "gives in" to the demands. Through the promulgation of a public, and realistic, fear, dissidence is automatically delegitimized and considered irresponsibly utopian. Radical Israeli leftist Roy Wagner describes his experience of failing to talk to Israelis who uncritically defend soldiers because they feel protected by them against oppression, persecution, and the perils that have "never stopped lurking Jews": "That to survive, us Jews must strike—strike hard and first—is what we're taught since we're old enough to be taught anything at all. And it always comes down to that, and so details like whose land the wall cuts through, and who said what in court, and who it was that cast some stone or shot some bullet, and at whom—are nothing anyone really should, at bottom, ever mind."[20]

Fears relate to an inescapable human characteristic: *vulnerability*—that is, literally, the potential of being harmed. In the context of a globalized, virile order, vulnerability (degraded to weakness) is experienced as an anomaly that should be fought, a failure, a deficiency, an effeminacy. Going back to the three-act play, vulnerability is acted out in different, even antagonistic ways. Supporters of the Wall consider vulnerability a security gap that should be combated and hidden from others. The excluded, from the point of view of the justice *of* the other, embrace vulnerability as their very own; even when facing the other, they demonstrate it to avoid suspicion and to elicit solidarity, if possible. The wall's panoptic control mechanisms are aimed at preventing empathy and the feared spirits of hospitality. Nevertheless, hospitality appears in lodgings along the way. The case of Las Patronas in Mexico is emblematic: for over twenty years, a group of women has been giving food and water to migrants passing swiftly northwards on the train known as "the Beast." Fortunately, the Wall policy does not intimidate everyone "on the other side," and the rebels, who are aware of the fact that they live in a voluntary ghetto, embrace their vulnerability (more or less visibly according to their possibilities) to extend hospitality to those who manage to infiltrate through the wall. In Israeli society, Anarchists against the Wall dare express their fears regarding the policy that is supposed to defend them. In a context governed by fear, the disobedient cultivate hospitality toward those who are hegemonically perceived as threats. This hospitality is expressed in the form of listening to the demands for justice of the people affected by the Wall policy: in the Jordan Valley, small groups of Israeli pensioners accompany Bedouin shepherds every day to mitigate and denounce harassment by settlers. Many Palestinian farmers' olive trees remain "on the other side" of the wall, and the restrictions make harvest impossible, since only one member of each family is allowed to pass the checkpoint during that season and the wall doors open only three times a day. In this case, "on the other side," groups of volunteers have organized themselves to help the Palestinian families with these tasks.[21] In comparison with the enormous demonization mechanism in place, these acts that stem from embracing vulnerability may seem minimal. However, by detecting the blind spots of the panopticon, they can humbly make life sustainable. In addition, there are lawyers "on the other side" who provide legal counsel and represent the "Area C" Palestinians in court when they seek redress against the various forms of harassment they suffer by the state of Israel.[22] Israeli women in the Machsom Watch group are constantly watching for human rights violations at the checkpoints.[23] Likewise, Active Stills photographers on both sides of the fence have been documenting the wall's construction since 2005, after it was declared illegal by the International Court of Justice in 2004.[24]

I would like to call these acts of disobedience "vulner-abilities" to show the agency capacity of the disobedient, diviners of the justice *of* the other. This term is inspired by Levinas's heteronomous ethics, which suggests that the "exposure" of vulnerability before the other means assuming responsibility for them. Thus, in the middle of the word describing the ability to be hurt (from the Latin *vulnerus*), we insert a hyphen to highlight the power that lies in what is usually presented as weakness. *Vulner-ability* inspired by Levinas can be described as the *shudder* produced by the "relaxation of virility without cowardice . . . for the little cruelty our hands repudiate, which characterizes *the just war waged against war*."[25]

III. On the Same Side of Different Walls

> The contemporary "armour-plating" of territorialised limits appears as an asymmetric response to the perception of an asymmetric peril.
>
> —Évelyne Ritaine, "La barrière et le checkpoint"

In 1989, the world knew fifteen frontier walls, including the famous Berlin barrier; tragically, even though the collapse of the latter seemed to augur a new era, more than forty countries have built either physical or virtual (technological) frontier fences since then, to the point that today there are more than seventy separation walls around the globe.[26] A number of authors consider it paradoxical that the globalization era—which is supposed to promote the free circulation of capital, goods, and labor—is characterized by walls that block the movement of certain majoritarian populations.[27] Worse, these excluded majoritarian populations come from lands exploited in the service of wasteful expense "on the inside of the wall."[28]

Each wall has its own peculiarities, but there is something in their nature that is inherent to the territorial policy they support: asymmetry. This characteristic can be noticed in the disproportionate power of the builders and the exposed vulnerability of the excluded. Again, this asymmetry is radicalized in the widely accepted perception of the *others*' vulnerability exposure as a *danger* among those who feel protected. Here, I briefly outline the three "wall" cases examined in this chapter, prior to moving to a deeper analysis of their meaning and interconnections.

The first case involves the barrier between the United States and Mexico. Despite the notoriety gained by the efforts by former president Donald Trump to "build the Wall" under his administration, an actual wall has existed between the two countries since 1990, when it was first built by the United States, with various materials. In 1992 it was reinforced with steel plates that had been used during the Gulf War.[29] A significant part of the wall is in fact a river. Strangely enough, former president Trump, who was interested in fortifying the fence with concrete panels, wanted to "militarize" the border wall with a water-filled trench, stocked with green alligators.[30]

The declared reason for the existence of this wall, even amid the enthusiasm for globalization, is stopping illegal migration and smuggling. However, as I mentioned before, the wall fails to impair drug smuggling in particular.

The second wall examined is in Africa. It spans 2,720 kilometers and is made of sand, rocks, barbed wire, checkpoints, radars, antitank ditches, and more than seven million antipersonnel and antitank landmines. Morocco built it in six stages between 1980 and 1987, in the context of a military conflict.[31] Specifically, the Polisario Front, designated by the Saharawi people as the representative authority for the decolonization of Western Sahara by Spain in 1975, was excluded from the Madrid three-party agreement entered into by Spain with Morocco and Mauritania.[32] A Bedouin popular army, the Polisario Front, sustained an active struggle until 1991, when a cease-fire was declared in order to hold a self-determination referendum. The MINURSO (United Nations Mission for the Referendum in Western Sahara) has been charged with conducting this referendum, but it hasn't succeeded in this mission in the thirty years that have passed since 1991. The Saharawi people on both sides of the wall (half of it under Moroccan occupation and the other half in refugee camps of an exiled republic) are still waiting for their moment. *On this side* of the wall, the refugee camps that have been situated in the Algerian Hamada for forty-five years continue to run into countless difficulties in spite of their admirable, dignified social and political organization. On *the other side* of the wall, under Moroccan occupation, the people suffer cruel discrimination, torture, and consistent violation of human rights. Unlike the U.S. intention of excluding Mexicans, the Moroccan kingdom strives to annex the Saharawi territory by denying its right to independence and offering "autonomy" instead.[33] Yet, the Mexicans and Saharawis share, in spite of their different circumstances, the excruciating pain of forced disappearance and clandestine mass graves.[34]

The third wall is in Asia and surrounds a divided country. I refer here to the wall continually being built by Israel in the West Bank since 2002 with a wide range of materials and technologies; its peculiarity lies in the fact that it measures twice the length of the perimeter it is intended to cover. The construction of barriers had started in Gaza after the Oslo Accords. By the mid-nineties, Israel started to place high-security metal fences and watchtowers to surround this coastal strip of Palestinian territory. This was followed by the unilateral dismantling, as of 2005, of all Israeli settlements that were located in Gaza. This was known as the "Gaza disengagement." In this way, Ariel Sharon, the author of this initiative, managed to besiege this 365 km² area by land, air, and sea and present it in the media (and the memory of many Israelis) as a pacifist act.[35] Since 2017, clandestine tunnels dug by the besieged, overcrowded inhabitants of Gaza have been countered by Israel with a forty-meter-deep underground wall.[36] The idea of an underground wall is astonishing: how far can domination fantasies go?

Even though the Israeli wall is supposed to be a defensive fence against "terrorist" attacks, it is actually a colonial device for territorial annexation, which is widely accepted in the Israeli society, convinced as it is that "there is no one to talk to on the other side." There is still one more aspect to consider: there had been a debate in the Zionist movement from its inception around the need and the morality (or immorality) of striving to become a demographic majority on that land. In 1944 philosopher Martin Buber expressed his strong disagreement with this idea, because he considered it immoral, precisely because Jews had always been a minority.[37] However, the obsession with attaining demographic majority was deeply engraved in the history of political Zionism. Today, the Wall acts as a demographic control device for the Palestinian people and serves the purpose of inventing an impossible— and undesirable—majority. Israeli architect Eyal Weizman explains that the possibility of reaching a consensus around such an oppressive and depriving structure is a consequence of the elastic management of space (due to the various changes during the wall construction that he details in his book) paralleling the prolonged state of exception period:[38]

> Barriers are indeed different to borders: they do not separate the 'inside' of a sovereign, political or legal system from a foreign 'outside,' but act as contingent structures to prevent movement across territory. Such measures are legally tolerated precisely because they are temporary. However, the very logic of military rule in the West Bank and Gaza has always perpetuated itself through ever-new, seemingly 'temporary' facts. It is the very definition of the occupation as 'temporary,' and the definition of every violation of rights as merely 'temporary' evils, that has allowed Israeli society and its courts to ignore these ongoing acts . . . What the temporary 'state of emergency' is to time, this elasticity became to space.

Here, Walter Benjamin's thesis about the *state of exception as a rule* becomes apparent.[39] The state of exception involves the suspension of fun-

damental rights, and indeed the Wall policy infringes the right to freedom
of movement (article 13 of the Universal Declaration of Human Rights). And
it does so hegemonically, using the public consent achieved by the three-
act play I described before. In 1940, Benjamin wrote, "The tradition of the
oppressed teaches us that the 'state of emergency' in which we live is not the
exception but the rule. We must attain to a conception of history that accords
with this insight. Then we will clearly see that it is our task to bring about
a real state of emergency, and this will improve our position in the struggle
against fascism."[40] This disturbing Benjaminian call to create "a genuine state
of emergency" is the call by the disobedient on both sides of the Wall, whose
transgressions against the injustice unveil its *illegitimacy*.

On the other side, they are paving the way for "a genuine state of emergency" (or "of exception") by exercising hospitality and disobeying the man-
date to dehumanize those who live *on this side*. On this side, this state of
exception is anticipated by those who expose their vulnerability (migrants,
martyrs, all of them *exiled*) and make the well-meaning *on the other side*
shiver, while the Wall's mass media machinery rushes into coopting them
and doping their minds. The term "exiled" is not restricted here to its usual
meaning, being also associated with the notion of "exiled at home"; that
is, encompassing those people who have not been displaced but have been
deprived of the land under their feet.[41]

Before we dive into the description of some acts of disobedience demonstrating the illegitimacy of the Wall,[42] let's analyze the beginning of Weizman's
quote: "Barriers are indeed different to borders." As shown in his book, the
West Bank "wall" adopts abstruse forms, such as bridges and tunnels that
are not intended to communicate but rather to divide, thus legitimating an
"archipelago of extraterritorial sovereign spaces" with illegal Israeli settlements in the middle of Palestinian territory.[43] Weizman mentions a "parti-
tion in three dimensions," which would imply an absurd "territorial border"
passing through columns and bridge crossbeams, for instance.[44]

Indeed, these walls are not frontier barriers, because they annex land, and
what we arguably call "Nature" reacts to this. The title of Weizman's book,
Hollow Land, is a pun on the colonial political theory promoted as "Holy
Land." And, since we are evoking political theology, it would be interesting
to approach two divinities that are contested in the colonial scenario: Yahve
(whose promise of the land is used as an excuse for the settlements and the
dispossession of land) versus Gaia (the theogonic power that Bruno Latour

evokes as the announcer of the "New climate regime" in his criticism of modernism and its war of humans against nature, causing a catastrophe called the Anthropocene).[45]

IV. Walls as the Earth's Prosthetic Devices

In this section, I consider walls from the point of view of what we call "Nature," as if humans were not part of it. Hence the controversial figure of a prosthetic device—a human creation that is intended to solve bodily flaws—in order to consider the wall in relation to the Earth. They are both forms of inhabiting marked by the "Promethean shame" that leads to an artificial correction of the body or of the soil. Philosopher Günther Anders coined the concept of Promethean shame to name the perception that humans are inferior to their technical products. This is both because they consider nature as inferior to artifice and because they are incapable of controlling it.[46] This mismatch between the producer and their product resonates in the discrepancy between what the walls intend to do and what they actually do. As mentioned earlier, they act as membranes and filters (the Mexico-U.S. fence does not stop drug smuggling) and as embodiments of annexation of territories to exploit "resources" (the Moroccan wall facilitates the access of European companies to the phosphates in the Saharawi soil and to fishing on Saharawi coasts).

Vallet and David refer to "Walls of Money" in relation to the security industry and its militarization of markets.[47] The "carnal" relationship between the private security industry and the Israeli army,[48] for instance, shows that the Wall industry is at the heart of the country's economy. Indeed, Weizman notes this solidarity of public-private capital in the very architecture of the wall.[49]

What's "natural" and shared among different animal species, including humans, is migration (nomadism). Material walls' purpose in the globalized era is to manage this movement, by frantically encouraging movement for an enriched minority and impairing the movement of the vast impoverished majority. Walls also affect the environment, in part (but not exclusively) because they are used to tame its backbone, water.

In the case of Mexico and the United States, in 1944 the countries entered an international water treaty concerning two rivers: the Colorado River (Baja

California and Sonora) and the Rio Bravo (Chihuahua, Coahuila, Nuevo León, and Tamaulipas). The 1944 water treaty establishes that Mexico allocates water to the United States from the Rio Grande River, and the United States allocates water to Mexico from the Colorado River. In 2017, the signing of Minute 323, an international agreement that establishes how the United States and Mexico share water in the Colorado River,[50] alarmingly compromised water supply in Sonora by reducing Mexico's part of the Colorado waters, even though, as a temporary measure, it does not override the 1944 treaty.[51] Water shortage in Sonora (mostly in the north of the country) is severe, and the opening of a brewery plant has worsened the situation significantly.

In the Western Sahara, Morocco is allowing endangered-species hunting. In addition, the refugee camps are set up by the United Nations in the Algerian Hamada, which is the most inhospitable part of the desert. In contrast, in the liberated territories that are not under United Nations protection, vegetation is more diverse (indeed, the paintings in the caves of Erqueyez show that thousands of years ago, this was a jungle landscape with freshwater wells). And finally, what really prevents the return of the Saharawis to their land is that the Moroccans laid between seven and ten million mines along the entire length of the wall. Floods along the barrier cause it to move, and so the Moroccan wall, due to its nature (consisting mainly of landmines) and the extreme and changing conditions imposed by desert winds and rains, needs to be constantly rebuilt.

The Palestinian case has historically attracted more attention than the other two.[52] The livelihood of the predominantly rural population has been damaged because the orchards and gardens have been separated from their owners' houses. The Israeli government has looted centenarian olive trees, giving them as presents to other states. Green colonialism planted pine forests over destroyed Palestinian villages in 1948. Yet, the critical point is water. In Gaza, the sanitary emergency due to water contamination is severe.[53] In the West Bank, the wall can be understood as a control device for the aquifers. Several organizations have denounced the unequal distribution of water among Jewish settlers and the Palestinian population, among them the United Nations and Amnesty International.[54] Area C, under Israeli administration, is not granted any permits for maintenance, construction, or revamping of water tanks. In general, the extremely winding nature of this wall, compared by Eyal Weizman to the Scandinavian fjords,[55] can be mainly explained as a water-source deprivation mechanism.

The Jerusalem part of the wall divides Palestinians from Palestinians (at Abu Dis, it is very clear how it lies between houses of the same families). Political theology resonates in the *hollow land* in relation to the dispute of the god of monotheism versus the local cultures' gods. With the rains, sometimes the power of Gaia prevails (in Mexico, we could think of Tláloc). Rains have frequently destroyed parts of the enormous concrete wall near the Shuafat refugee camp.[56] As I have noted before, water respects neither walls nor military engineers who believe they can stand in its way. The settlers should know this from the biblical flood account.[57]

V. In the Face of the Absurdity of Oppression: The Mirror of Irreverence

> More than just a technology overloaded with cultural and political meanings, the fence is an active, networked object that shapes political practice and communication.
>
> —Anna Feigenbaum, "Concrete Needs No Metaphor"

In conclusion, in considering the three cases examined here, I would like to highlight the power of carnivalesque, Bakhtinian humor, which manages to outsmart the authoritarian horizon of discourse, unlike the useless denunciation that is respectful of the discourse hierarchy. Regarding all three walls, an *F* should be added before the word "utility." As mentioned before, the economic "utilities" or benefits produced by the Wall have been rendered as "futilities" by the disobedient on both sides. The *(f)utility* of the Wall is monstrously ridiculous.

Palestinians and Saharawis share a language and the demand for the right of return to their lands. Regarding Mexicans, even though they do not claim this right as such, they (especially the indigenous communities) have always inhabited these southern areas (full of Spanish toponyms), even before the annexation of northern Mexico by the United States in 1848. Just as an example, Geronimo, the Apache, was born in Sonora.

I will state here only a few of the creative forms of *re-existence* of these three peoples,[58] as "an effort to get these fences talking, to make people's stories of struggle echo off the concrete and razor wire."[59]

The band Los Tigres del Norte sings, "Yo no crucé la frontera, la frontera me cruzó: / I did not cross the frontier, the frontier crossed me: América nació libre y el hombre la dividió. / America was born free, Man has divided it."[60] Two architects, Ronald Rael and Virginia San Fratello, built a cross-border children's seesaw as an intervention to the wall, turning it into a communicational political practice.[61] Ronald Rael had previously documented other forms of utilization of this fence by the people, such as binational yoga meetups.[62]

Saharawis in the Tindouf refugee camp practice hospitality as a form of resistance. Respecting the cease-fire, their way to show themselves to the world honors the Bedouin tradition of hospitality. They offer outsiders their experience of an exiled republic, as a call for heteronomous responsibility for the other. The strong commitment by the Spanish people to the stymied decolonization process is remarkable: families from both countries adopt each other, and many people from different regions of Spain collaborate to bring a dignified standard of living to the camps. Cuba has supported the refugees in the areas of health and education, while Venezuela founded the excellent Simón Bolívar preparatory school at the Sahrawi refugee Smara camp. There too, a particularly lovable Bedouin physician, known by the nickname Castro, also founded the first Educational Center for Cognitive Diversity (Centro de Educación para las Personas Con Diversidad Cognitiva).[63]

Lastly, I would like to mention a couple of experiences in Gaza and the West Bank that are relevant here. The Gaza siege involves situations that are not always well known. The fishing area is frequently restricted. Electricity is rationed; for long periods, it has been limited to as little as four hours a day. Food supply is at the threshold of a minimal diet.[64] There is a detailed list of a wide variety of restricted products.[65] In addition to the weekly Friday demonstrations, which are part of the "Great March of Return," started on March 30, 2018, people use their imagination in a promising way, we could say with Günther Anders. For instance, Khaled Bashir, from Deir al Balah, is known as the man who cooks "Chicken and vegetables à la Gaza," using the rays of the sun to circumvent the shortages caused by the siege.[66]

In the West Bank, biologist Mazin Qumsiyeh from Bethlehem University founded the Palestine Institute for Biodiversity and Sustainability.[67] In this fabulous place, the relationship between nature and culture is deeply cultivated, applying permaculture to social and political life.[68]

Finally, thinking about humor in resistance, about using creative forms to assert life in the midst of the architecture of death, I invoke Mahmoud Darwish's poem "The Wall":[69]

A huge metal snake coils around us, swallowing up the little walls that separate our bedroom, kitchen and living room. A snake that does not move in a straight line, to avoid resembling us as we look straight on. It twists and turns, a nightmare of cement segments reinforced with pliant metal, making it easy for it to move into the fragmented bits of land and beds of mint that are left to us. A snake eager to lay its eggs between our inhalations and exhalations so that we say, for once, because we are nearly choking to death, "We are the strangers." When we look in our mirrors all we see is the snake making for the backs of our necks, but with a bit of effort we can see what is above it: a sky yawning with boredom at the architects adorning it with guns and flags. And at night we see it twinkling with stars, which gaze at us with affection. We also see what lies behind the snake wall: the watchmen in the ghetto, frightened of what we're doing behind the little walls we still have left. We see them oiling their weapons to kill the gryphon they think is hiding in our hen coop. And we cannot help laughing.

Notes

1.   Especially in Mexico. This may be checked in the report *El papel de Israel en la militarización de México*, Brigadas para leer en libertad, Mexico City, 2019, https://brigadaparaleerenlibertad.com/libro/el-papel-de-israel-en-la-militarizacion-de-mexico.

2.   Cf. the Trojan horse Mexican artist Rolando de la Rosa placed in front of the wall in 2008. The traveling exhibition "Mexicanos, palestinos y saharauis: Del mismo lado de muros diferentes" (Mexicans, Palestinians, and Saharawis: On the Same Side of Different Walls) Project PAPIIT IN 401119 "Heteronomies of Justice: Nomad Territorialities" will initiate its tour at the Museo Nacional de las Culturas del Mundo INAH as soon as the pandemic situation allows it.

3.   I have discussed the differences between Levinas's and Deleuze's heteronomy in "Vulner(h)abilidades cosmopolíticas: Polinizando a Levinas en América Latina," *MOTRICIDADES: Revista da Sociedade de Pesquisa Qualitativa em Motricidade Humana* 4, no. 1 (2020): 27–35. In other articles, I have discussed political differences with Buber.

4.   We will come back to the water and environmental concerns raised by the existence of certain walls.

5.   See Anabel Hernández, *El traidor: El diario secreto del hijo del Mayo* (Mexico City, Grijalbo, 2019). There are references to land and sea transportation owned by Pemex (pp. 140 and ff.) and also Bachoco's poultry company trucks (161–62).

6.   Évelyne Ritaine, "La barrière et le checkpoint: Mise en politique de l'assymétrie," *Cultures and Conflits* 73 (Spring 2009), http://journals.openedition.org/conflits /17500.

7.   I use the verb "territorialize" as per Gilles Deleuze and Felix Guattari in *Mil mesetas* (Valencia: Pre-Textos, 2015). The difference between asymmetry and dissymmetry specified by Ritaine, quoting Marwan Bishara, is very interesting. In a belligerent context, asymmetry refers to the parties' qualitative difference (as regards means, styles, and values) while dissymmetry refers to a quantitative difference (in power). See Marwan Bishara, "L'ère des conflits asymétriques," *Le Monde Diplomatique*, October 2001, https://www.monde-diplomatique.fr /2001/10/BISHARA/7896.

8.   Dal Lago quoted by Ritaine, "La barrière et le checkpoint," 22.

9.   See Gilberto Conde, "The Physical and Mental Walls of Israel and the United States over Palestine and Mexico," accessed December 17, 2019, https://book .stopthewall.org/the-physical-and-mental-walls-of-israel-and-the-united-states -over-palestine-and-mexico/. It is worth highlighting the author's distinction between a colonial and a neocolonial relationship: "Direct colonialism implies a more violent relationship of subjection than neo-colonialism, as well as more exacerbated reactions by the directly colonized population. In the neocolonial relationship there is an independence that allows the subjects of the dependent State to create their own forms of government and elect their own rulers in a way that is at least formally free."

10.   Damien Simonneau, "Des murs incomparables? Enjeux et élaboration de d'une comparaison des mobilisations pro-barrière en Israël et en Arizona (États-Unis)," *Revue internationale de politique comparée*, 24, no. 4 (2017): 349–72. See https://www.cairn.info/revue-internationale-de-politiquecomparee-2017 -4-page-349.htm.

11.   Bishara, *Checkpoint*, quoted in Ritaine, 29.

12.   See Said Sadikki, *World of Walls: The Structure, Roles and Effectiveness of Separation Barriers* (Cambridge, U.K.: Open Book, 2017).

13.   See "'¡Un muro es un muro!': Donald Trump no quiere usar otro palabra," *La Nación*, January 1, 2019, https://www.nacion.com/el-mundo/politica/un-muro-es-un-muro -donald-trump-no-quiere/XOLRDGWRCNFQZN6GAXQE2VYJ64/story/.

14.   See Natasha Turak, "Trump Officially Recognized Israel's Annexation of the Occupied Golan Heights. Here's What It Means," CNBC, March 27, 2019, https://www .cnbc.com/2019/03/27/trump-officially-recognized-israels-annexation-of-golan -heights.html and Michael Bachner, "Netanyahu Vows Unity Government's 1st Move Will Be Jordan Valley Annexation," *Times of Israel*, November 11, 2019, https://www.timesofisrael.com/netanyahu-vows-unity-governments-1st-move -will-be-jordan-valley-annexation/.

15. "Ces murs se préoccupent 'd'enfermer dehors' les indésirables . . . C'est cette asymétrie fondamentale, révélée par le caractère unilatéral de la décision d'érection et par les effets arbitraires de l'exclusion, qui caractérise la politique du Mur." Ritaine, 19.

16. When I mention "life," I refer to the Andean concept of "good living," which bears resemblance with the way of life of the indigenous communities who are kept outside the walls. The good living describes a modus vivendi and a way of relating to *others* as inseparable from "nature," just like *us*, and unlike our capitalist version, this "good life" is not mediated by the market.

17. Since this is being written in Mexico, I will refer to "this side" of the wall as the side of the excluded (Mexican, Saharawis, or Palestinians) and to "the other side" as the side of the included (those whose governments, like the United States, Morocco, or Israel, are apparently "protecting").

18. See Paul Virilio, *La administración del miedo* (Madrid: Barataria/Pasos perdidos, 2012).

19. See Simonneau, "Des murs incomparables," 352, and idem., "Dans la fabrique politique du mur israëlien," *COREDEM*, "(Dé)passer la frontière," no. 19 (March 2019): 97, https://www.coredem.info/IMG/pdf/_de_passer_la_frontiere-2.pdf.

20. See Roy Wagner, "Fear and Loathing at the Central Bus Station," in *Anarchists Against the Wall: Direct Action and Solidarity with the Palestinian Popular Struggle*, ed. Uri Gordon and Ohal Greitzer (Oakland, Calif.: AK Press, 2013), 61.

21. Orly Noy, "The Israeli Activists Helping Protect the Palestinian Olive Harvest," *+972 Magazine*, October 7, 2018, https://www.972mag.com/the-israeli-activists-helping-protect-the-palestinian-olive-harvest/.

22. The 1993 Oslo Accords temporarily divided the West Bank into three areas; twenty-six years later, this division is still in place. Area A (18 percent of the territory) is under the Palestinian authority as regards administration and police jurisdiction. Area B (22 percent) is under civilian Palestinian and Israeli military control. And Area C, due to the presence of Israeli settlements, is completely under Israeli civilian and military control. See United Nations, official bulletin, May 5, 1997, https://peacemaker.un.org/sites/peacemaker.un.org/files/IL%20PS_950928_InterimAgreementWestBankGazaStrip%28OsloII%29%28esp%29.pdf.

23. See https://machsomwatch.org/en/content/home-page, accessed December 18, 2019.

24. See Active Stills, "About Us," accessed December 18, 2019, https://www.activestills.org/about_us/.

25. Emmanuel Levinas, *De otro modo que ser o más allá de la esencia* (Salamanca: Sígueme, 1995), 266. This book reveals vulnerability as the most inherently human trait, as opposed to the widely spread idea in our culture that it is a fault to be repaired. We could say that its heteronomous ethics—which is not an opposite of autonomy—conceives humans as fragile and codependent on each other and thus responsible for each other.

26. Interactive map by Élisabeth Vallet, Josselyn Guillarmou, and Zoé Barry, published on the website of the *Economist*, January 2016, http://infographics.econ omist.com/2015/fences/?utm_content=bufferd7800&utm_medium=social& utm_source=bufferapp.com&utm_campaign=buffer.

27. See Naomi Klein, *Fences and Windows: Dispatches from the Front Lines of the Globalization Debate* (New York: Picador, 2002). Also, Jean-Jacques Roche, "Walls and Borders in a Globalized World: The Paradoxical Revenge of Territorialization," in *Borders, Fences and Walls: State of Insecurity?*, ed. Élisabeth Vallet (New York: Routledge, 2014), 105–15.

28. I think that the claim that "uncritical proclamations of globalization pretty much died out after the 1990s" does not take into account the Latin American élites discourse, particularly in Mexico. For them, globalization is a signal of progress. This is especially evident in the discourse of the elites who greatly benefited from the treaties with the USA and are currently opposing President Obrador's policies. The political disputes in Mexico currently keep aiming at the pre-'90s globalization horizon. This is not restricted to Mexico. It can be seen in the "soft coup" policies deployed in several subcontinental countries and currently threatening Mexico. As regards Israel, it acts as if it were Europe, ignoring the Middle East map as planned by Zionism's founder, Theodor Herzl in his book *The Jewish State*. Its role is that of a wall to stop the "Barbarian threat" lurking in the East. Regarding Morocco's kingdom, it acts as France's hit man, managing the phosphate mines in Bou Craa and blackmailing Europe by opening and closing the passage of Africans from Ceuta and Melilla at their discretion as a mechanism of political pressure. This policy of colonial smoke and mirrors is implemented in the name of "globalization."

29. See Irasema Coronado, "Towards the Wall between Nogales, Arizona and Nogales Sonora," in Vallet, *Borders, Fences and Walls*, 247 and ff.

30. See Michael D. Shear and Julie Hirschfeld Davis, "Shoot Migrant's Legs, Build Alligator Moat: Behind Trump's Ideas for Border," *New York Times*, October 1, 2019, https://www.nytimes.com/2019/10/01/us/politics/trump-border-wars.html.

31. See Gaici Nah Bachir, *El muro marroquí en el Sáhara Occidental: Historia, estructura y efectos* (Cairo: Ed. Élite de Impresión y Publicación, 2017). This book includes valuable military details about the Moroccan strategy and the countries that support their annexation ambitions.

32. Polisario is the Spanish abbreviation of Frente Popular de Liberación de Saguia al Hambra a Río de Oro, which emerged in 1970, when the United Nations encouraged the decolonization processes.

33. Moroccan writer Said Saddiki considered that his government's offer was the only viable and safe solution. His book, which considers the Moroccan wall is one among many other walls, is supposed to show academic neutrality, but a colonial political stance undoubtedly underlies the argument. See Sadikki, *World of Walls: The Structure, Roles and Effectiveness of Separation Barriers* (Cambridge, U.K.: Open Book, 2017), 118. This work is the antithesis of Bachir's

tome, quoted above, in which the author openly demonstrates his decolonial political stance.

34. Hego (Instituto de Estudios sobre Desarrollo y Cooperación Internacional) has commissioned several reports on the human rights violations and clandestine mass graves in occupied Sahara. For instance, see Carlos Martín Beristain and Francisco Etxeberria Gabilondo, *La esperanza posible,* accessed June 12, 2021, http://publ.hegoa.efaber.net/uploads/pdfs/233/Exhumaciones_Informe_peri _def.pdf?1488539790. Beristain also participated as a member of the Interdisciplinary Group of Independent Experts for the Ayotzinapa case in Mexico. See for instance *Informe Ayotzinapa II,* accessed June 12, 2021, https://www.oas.org /es/cidh/actividades/giei/GIEI-InformeAyotzinapa2.pdf.

35. According to the *Humanitarian Atlas* by OCHA, in 2018, the 365 km² area was populated by 1,912,267 inhabitants, 1,435,616 of which are refugees. While some have been there since 1948, others came from the West Bank in 1967, and others came as double refugees from Lebanon in 1982. See "Gaza Closure Maps," accessed December 18, 2019, https://www.ochaopt.org/atlas2019/gz closure.html.

36. Isabel Kershner, "Israel está construyendo un muro nuevo, diferente de los demás," *New York Times* (Spanish edition), August 15, 2017, https://www.ny times.com/es/2017/08/15/israel-esta-construyendo-un-muro-nuevo-diferente -a-los-demas/.

37. See Martin Buber, "A Majority or Many? A Postscript to a Speech," in *Una tierra para dos pueblos,* ed. Paul Mendes-Flohr (Salamanca: Sígueme-UNAM, 2009), 155–59.

38. Eyal Weizman, *Hollow Land: Israel's Architecture of Occupation* (London: Verso, 2007), 172–73.

39. Walter Benjamin wrote his "On the Concept of History" in 1939, during a "normality" imposed by the Nuremberg laws, precisely, after Hitler and Stalin's Pact. His statement about the suspension of fundamental guarantees as a rule had to do with the daily reality in Nazi Germany. There is an implicit reference to Carl Schmitt's concept of "state of exception," in order to subvert it from a revolutionary perspective, but this goes beyond the scope of this article.

40. Walter Benjamin, "On the Concept of History," Thesis 8, in *Selected Writings,* vol. 4, ed. Howard Eiland and Michael W. Jennings (Cambridge, Mass.: Belknap, 2006), 392.

41. I developed this concept in "Exilio domiciliario: Avatares de un destierro diferente," *Athenea Digital* 15, no. 4 (2015). See https://atheneadigital.net/article /view/v15-n4-rabinovich.

42. I am using this term as per Giorgio Agamben, *El misterio del mal: Benedicto XVI y el fin de los tiempos* (Buenos Aires: Adriana Hidalgo ed., 2013).

43. Weizman, *Hollow Land,* 182. "After fragmenting the surface of the West Bank by walls and other barriers, Israeli planners started attempting to weave it together as two separate but overlapping national geographies—two territo-

rial networks overlapping across the same area in three dimensions, without having to cross or come together. One is an upper-land—the land of the settlements—a scattering of well-tended hilltop neighbourhoods woven together by modern highways for the exclusive use of its inhabitants; the other, Palestine crowded cities, towns, and villages that inhabit the valleys between and underneath the hills, maintaining fragile connections on improvised underpass." Sergio Langer's comic "La paz es posible: Un territorio para dos Estados" comes to mind. In this comic, an Israeli state on the surface and an underground Palestinian state "share the land." See Sergio Langer, *Judíos* (Buenos Aires: Planeta, 2015), 208–9.

44. Weizman, 180. "As the road threads itself through this folded, topographical arrangement of different jurisdictions, Israeli territory finds itself alternately above and below the Palestinian. This physical separation of transport infrastructure also cuts through the territorial labyrinth created by the Oslo Accords. The tunnel and bridge are under full Israeli control (Area C), the valley below the bridge is under Palestinian civilian control (Area B), while the city above the tunnel is under Palestinian civilian and military control (Area A). When the bridge's columns rest on Palestinian ground, the 'border' runs, presumably, through the thermodynamic joint between the column and the beams."

45. See Bruno Latour, *Face à Gaïa: Huit conférences sur le nouveau régime climatique* (Paris: La découverte, 2015), seventh conference.

46. It has to do with an imbalance between human production capabilities and the poor imagination to foresee their consequences. See Günther Anders, *La obsolescencia del hombre*, vol. 1 (Valencia: Pre-Textos 2011).

47. See Élizabeth Vallet and Charles-Philippe David, "Walls of Money: Securitization of Border Discourse and Militarization of Markets," in Vallet, *Borders, Fences and Walls*, 143–56.

48. The NGO Hamushim investigated this matter (https://en.hamushim.com/) and Yotam Feldman's documentary *The Lab* (2013) shows it clearly. Additionally, there is a report in Spanish about Israel's role in the militarization of Mexico: Aracely Cortés, *El papel de Israel en la militarización de México*, Brigadas para leer en libertad, 2019, http://brigadaparaleerenlibertad.com/programas/5777/.

49. See Weizman, 162: "Although the very essence and presence of the Wall is the obvious solid, material embodiment of state ideology and its conception of national security, the route should not be understood as the direct product of top-down government planning at all. Rather, the ongoing fluctuations of the Wall's route . . . registers a multiplicity of technical, legal and political conflicts over issues of territory, demography, water, archaeology and real estate, as well as over political concepts such as sovereignty, security and identity."

50. Comisión Internacional de Límites y Aguas entre México y Los Estados Unidos, "Amplicación de las medidas de cooperación y adopción de un plan binacional de contingencia ante la escazes de agua en la cuenca del Río Colorado," http://www.cila.gob.mx/actas/323.pdf. Also see Imelda García, "El conflicto líquido,"

in *Reporte Índigo*, October 3, 2017, https://www.reporteindigo.com/reporte/el
-conflicto-liquido/.

51.   This explanation was given by Dr. Marco Antonio Samaniego López, author of
      "El control del Río Colorado como factor histórico: La necesidad de estudiar la
      relación tierra/agua," *Frontera Norte*, 20, no. 40 (July–December 2008), 49–78.
      His opinion about Minute 323 can be read here: "Sobre la minuta 323," *Agencia
      Fronteriza de Noticias*, October 6, 2017, http://www.afntijuana.info/editoriales
      /75002_sobre_la_minuta_323.

52.   Jad Isaac et al., *The Segregation Wall Impacts on Palestinian Environment*,
      Applied Research Institute Jerusalem, 2015, https://www.arij.org/files/arijadmin
      /2016/The_Segregation_Wall_impacts_on_Palestinian_Environment.pdf.

53.   See Oxfam, "Patient Gaza: Water Under Siege," YouTube video, 2019, https://
      www.youtube.com/watch?v=YiDthHut5Pg. The documentary shows the alarm-
      ing increase in the need for dialysis treatments required by people of all ages
      due to extreme contamination.

54.   "Water, Sanitation and Hygiene," United Nations Office for the Coordination
      of Humanitarian Affairs–Occupied Palestinian Territories, last visited Decem-
      ber 20, 2019, https://www.ochaopt.org/theme/water%2C-sanitation-and-hygiene.
      Report updated as of November 2019 at https://www.ochaopt.org/content/gaza
      -strip-early-warning-indicators-november-2019.

55.   Weizman, 177.

56.   "Nature Brings Part of Israel's Separation Wall Down as Palestinians Rejoice
      (VIDEO)," *RT*, February 28, 2019, https://www.rt.com/news/452657-israel-wall
      -falls-palestinians/.

57.   Their reading of the Bible is biased by arrogance and an idolatry of accumula-
      tion by dispossession, which is why they go armed to the teeth to visit the graves
      of the Patriarchs and Matriarchs.

58.   I took this term from Enrique Leff, who in turn took it from Brazilian geogra-
      pher Carlos Walter Porto Gonçalves. Leff explains it as follows: "The peoples
      of the Earth are not only resisting, but *re-existing*: they have started an emanci-
      pation process that reclaims their 'good living' modes, they are reentering life's
      immanence and the ecologic metabolism of the biosphere." See Enrique Leff,
      "Rexistencia," January 29, 2018, http://www.biodiversidadla.org/Documentos
      /Rexistencia.

59.   Anna Feigenbaum, "Concrete Needs No Metaphor," *Ephemera* 10, no. 2 (2010):
      132. See http://www.ephemerajournal.org/sites/default/files/10-2feigenbaum
      _0.pdf.

60.   Los Tigres del Norte, "Somos más americanos," YouTube video, accessed Decem-
      ber 20, 2019, https://www.youtube.com/watch?v=LN30bcu0eb0.

61.   Abel Alvarado, "Arquitectos colocan un sube y baja en la frontera entre México y
      Estados Unidos," CNN, July 30, 2019, htts://cnnespanol.com/2019/07/30/alerta
      -arquitectos-colocan-un-sabe-y-baja-en-frontera-entre-mexico-y-estados
      -unidos/.

62. See Ronald Rael, "Border Wall as Architecture," in Vallet and David, *Borders, Fences and Walls*, 276.

63. Marcelo Scotti, "Un día con Castro," documentary, 2014, YouTube video, accessed December 20, 2019, https://www.youtube.com/watch?v=SCaYRl_uoGA.

64. In 2006 the Israeli government advisor Dov Wiesglass said, "The idea is to put the Palestinians on a diet, but not to make them die of hunger." About the survival diet and restrictions on the Gaza strip see "Israel forced to release study on Gaza blockade," BBC, October 17, 2012, https://www.bbc.com/news/world-middle-east-19975211.

65. List of "Dual Use" Items Requiring a Transfer License, accessed December 20, 2019, http://www.cogat.mod.gov.il/en/services/Documents/List%20of%20Dual%20Use%20Items%20Requiring%20a%20Transfer%20License.pdf. Cf. previous note about the inexplicable prohibition of coriander.

66. Cf. "The Man Who Cooks with the Sun," YouTube video, accessed June 12, 2021, https://www.youtube.com/watch?time_continue=38&v=VmMK16eLViU&feature=emb_logo.

67. Palestine Institute for Biodiversity and Sustainability of Bethlehem University, accessed December 20, 2019, https://www.palestinenature.org/.

68. Cf. Mazin B. Qumsiyeh, *Compartir la tierra de Canaán: Derechos humanos y el conflicto israelí-palestino* (Buenos Aires: Editorial Canaán, 2007).

69. Quoted by Elias Sanbar in *Dictionnaire amoureux de la Palestine* (Paris: Plon, 2010), 267. Translated from Arabic into English by Catherine Cobham (from Mahmoud Darwish, *A River Dies of Thirst* [Brooklyn: Archipelago Press, 2009]).

CHAPTER 9

A Purgative Against Despair

Singing with Mexican Immigrants

CARLOS PEREDA

I would like to repeat a familiar question: Can subaltern minorities have a voice?[1] Do the humiliated of the Earth have a language and identity of their own? And if such identities exist(ed), how could they be articulated? Perhaps only in a conflicted way? What attributes would characterize their languages or bits of language? These are ambitious and comprehensive questions, which I cannot fully examine here. As a start, however, let's start by recognizing that the immense crowd of subjugated people in the world has *sung a lot* throughout history. When emigrating or fleeing terrified in the middle of the night, and even as slaves chained in cargo ships or crossing the desert, desperate people have always managed to sing. Indeed, even under the worst conditions of submission, they have continued singing, often very loudly. Why? Why do crowds sing amid terror?

In respect to people who are often forced to move and flee in fear and even panic, it is worth bearing in mind the distinction between the terms "exile" and "immigration" and the cruel opposition between them: we see the evaporation of prestige and even of honor as one moves from "exile" to "immigration."[2] Of course, there are different types of exile and migrations. However, exile, particularly political exile, usually affects groups of people who are singled out. We can think here of exiles imposed by totalitarian states (Nazism, Stalinism, and so forth.). In Latin America, the exile experience of the Spanish Republicans has been frequently praised in twentieth century, as has (though perhaps in a less conspicuous way) banishment from the southern Latin American dictatorships in the seventies. Furthermore, time and again, many of those sent into exile keep their names, and in some cases are even feared by the powers that forced them out of their homeland because they constitute a threat.

In contrast, the protagonists of the great migrations of the twenty-first century are not named: they are literally undocumented. It is no coincidence that members of this more or less anonymous mass are not subjected to "named" political attacks but rather fuel the creation of an atmosphere of panic. Furthermore, while exile is conceptualized as a relatively qualitative phenomenon that responds to explicitly political causes migration is a quantitative phenomenon that is often wrongfully only understood in terms of economic urgency. So, the problem posed is not faced as a political challenge—as in the case of many exiles—but as a criminal issue or a contagious epidemic that must be stopped by any means. This is accomplished by the portrayal of migrants as a promiscuous crowd that, in violation of the laws and despite all threats, seems unstoppable. Thus, we face a general obsession with building medieval walls and establishing quarantines. We have passed then from the phenomenon of exile as a political confrontation to pseudopolicies that deal with massive migrations without political dimensions. (By "pseudopolicies" I mean delegating the maintenance of order on the political borders to the discretion of the army, police, and some kind of administration.) But these strategies are premised on a major mistake. In contrast to the common prejudices, the people taking part in the great migrations of the twenty-first century are clearly not criminal groups but rather are people fleeing from their countries in hopes of a better future.

Having established these generalities, I would like to focus on a specific group of immigrants and one peculiar, even strange way they cope with their difficult situation: singing, dancing, or listening to certain songs. I do so by exploring possible answers to two questions:

I. How do Mexican immigrants experience crossing the U.S. border?

II. How is this experience portrayed in certain songs? And what do these songs reveal about the identity of such immigrants and their yearnings?

I

Let me try to begin to answer the first question: What are the experiences of poor immigrants who face the risk of death to cross the U.S. border? In the case of Mexican immigrants, emigrating is not a matter of just crossing a border: it involves *the* border. Indeed, the expression "the border" has been immediately associated by many people in the twentieth century, and increasingly in the early twenty-first, with a precise border and passageways—legal or illegal, real or imaginary—that cross that turbulent juncture with the United States. Every day and every night, burdens, anxieties, loves, plans, failures, outrages, betrayals, hatreds, sorrows, ambitions, and deaths proliferate along that border. At the same time, great quantities of dangerous and suspicious merchandise are negotiated. As a consequence, lots of bodies, money, drugs, and weapons flow from one side to the other of this long and unforgiving line. (Often with drugs going to the north and weapons going to the south.)[3] On this border, immigrants have experiences of slightly different natures: some are still waiting in Mexico to cross the border and so must earn money in order to rent a room to sleep and feed themselves. Some have just left Mexico or any other place in Latin America and, as the Border Patrol often reports, are picked up wandering in the desert not knowing if they will survive for the next few hours or days.

On the other hand, as I mentioned earlier, it is a well-known fact that people along the border, men and women looking forward to moving to "the other side," are usually prone to sing, dance, or listen to music.[4] They often do so with songs called *corridos*.[5] Characteristically, these are full of conflicts, nostalgia, other distressed emotions and occasional wonderment as to whether it was all worthwhile.

It should come as no surprise that in these or analogous circumstances, one seeks a little self-affirmation. For example, many feelings are invoked when singing over drinks next to a radio in a smoky saloon. Emotions also emerge while remembering all the miseries suffered, even when they have already been left behind after crossing the border without legal authorization, or when saying goodbye to national affiliations. These attempts at reaffirmation mixed with rage and enjoyment are backed up with catchy melodies and simple verses that invite singers or listeners to move forward and come to grips with life on the border.[6]

II

Let us turn now to the second, and in this chapter, more important question (which is also an extension of the first): What are the contents of those
songs? What do the wailing lyrics that migrants from Mexico often hear and
sing or dance to actually say? To answer this, I will reflect in tandem on two
distinctions.

First, I consider how colonialism is implicitly—but no less effectively—
present in these songs. Thus, I distinguish between a colonialism that is the
subject of accusation, or "liable colonialism," and a colonialism that, to some
extent, permeates the person, or "infused colonialism."

Second, I comment on four types of interactions represented in corrido
songs and that tear apart the identities of migrants. If we combine these two
distinctions, we can encounter different types of experience. As a form of
liable colonialism, we find:

1. An angry attitude toward interactions with an external-external Other,
   or how migrants manage to respond to those positioned above them in a
   social hierarchy, typically their current or future employers in the United
   States.
2. An accusatory attitude toward interactions with an external-internal Other,
   or how migrants manage to respond to the governments and the middle
   and upper classes in their own country, who are described as guilty of the
   social injustices that forced the migrants to leave in the first place.

In its turn, as forms of infused colonialism, we find:

3. A demoralizing attitude toward interactions with an external-internal
   Other, or how migrants both dialogue and fight with the memories of the
   loved ones they left behind (families, friends, fellow workers).
4. A destructive attitude toward the interactions with an internal-internal
   Other, or how migrants talk with her- or himself.

This brief sketch emphasizes the relational conception of individuals.
Human animals can only construct their identities in interaction—both in
reality and in the imagination—with other people. Therefore, reconstructing

the types of links I just mentioned (external-external, external-internal, etc.)
highlights the mechanism at work in several forms of alterity that occur in
the construction of the personal-social continuum of the immigrant memory. Of course, each interaction produces a peculiar form of experience, of
suffering, but not only that.

Imagine, then, the songs played in one of the multitudinous—chaotic and
sometimes wild—presentations by a band like Los Tigres del Norte, or any
other popular group of "northern" Mexican music.[7] Let us be careful here: if
we read the verses of their songs without music, we should keep in mind that
what we have are only words stripped of their other half—of their bodies, so
to speak. It is as if, instead of looking at a person in the flesh, we look at her
with X-rays and see only her bones, her skeleton. Don't forget that these are
stories and a type of music that directly seek to move bodies; they're not just
stories to be told but also, as it is sometimes repeated—with a symptomatic
disdain?—stories intended to sing and dance, "to move our asses."

On the other hand, I would like to return, for a moment, to the distinction
I sketched earlier between exiles and the massive migrations of the twenty-
first century. I now want to reaffirm it with a new contrast. The authority of
the "words of exile" came, in part, from the fact that tyrants exiled not only
political figures but also poets and writers whom they feared because of
their opinions. In contrast, the songs that immigrants often sing and dance
to are not usually written by recognized poets. They are either anonymous
or written by poets whose names are either unknown or are only known
(sometimes disdainfully) within the category of "lyricists."[8] In this sense, "lyricists" are as undocumented—to avoid the offensive word "illegal"—as the
undocumented who sing their lyrics. In both cases, we are facing here—as
the euphemism goes—people "without papers."

Let me now elaborate on the bitter encounters and disagreements to
which these songs bear witness, accounting for the distinctions among the
various forms of interactions I have introduced.

A. Interactions with an External-External Other, or First Challenges to Liable Colonialism

These migrant challenges to an external-external Other, real or imaginary,
are the protests of emigrants against "those who rule" and those who are
"employers" in the United States. It is no coincidence that many corridos

object to an external-external Other who is considered a source of heteronomies—an Other whose aggressiveness won't give us respite. Sometimes this presence is right there, just in front of the migrants, aiming at them with a rifle. Other times it shows up as a detonating anticipation—a scary obsession. This is evoked by the following verses in "Mojado at Heart" ("Mojado de corazón," lyrics by Francisco Ramirez and Carlos Peña):[9]

> *The güeros don't like us*
> *Crossing the border.*[10]

Or consider other hints in these verses of something more than a lack of recognition. In this case we hear gloomy words of loss, which soberly cloak powerlessness. They are intended to offer something like a report of the absence of a friendly second person, in "Braceso's Song" ("Canto del bracero," lyrics by Rubén Menéndez):

> *I toured several states of the Union Americana*
> *In Arizona, Texas and Louisiana*
> *And I always felt the lack of esteem.*[11]

To this lack of appreciation, or pervasive and sometimes armed aggression, migrants answer by singing arguments, in *angry corridos* that are a form of self-defense against Anglo-Saxon residents. In "We Are More American" ("Somos más americanos," lyrics by Enrique Valencia), a self-directed use of memory takes place, foregrounding some uses of the past that prove the emigrant right. The first two verses of this corrido emphasize the memory of the combat zone that surrounds the migrants, even those who have already established themselves "on the other side":

> *They shouted at me a thousand times*
> *That I return to my land because I do not fit here*[12]

Faced with a lack of acknowledgment consolidated by contempt, immigrants develop an argument by choosing as a premise a self-directed use of social memory that appeals to a not-so-distant history. By means of an interpretation of the past that supports the corrido's voice, the singer attempts to question the legitimacy of the persecutions that the external-external Other perpetrates. Therefore, the vulnerability to the calamities inherent in the hostile language of the Other does not imply the elimination of a critical response by those who suffer. This corrido—"We Are More American"—alludes to a lost territory, a torn piece of the homeland with a defiant tone. Memory once again becomes a battlefield. Thus, it refers laconically to the many violations that the Mexican territory has suffered in the past:

> *I want to remind the gringo*:
> *I did not cross the border, the border crossed* me.[13]

The corrido does not explain how this happened—how the border "crossed" him or her. It takes that for granted. It's like an open secret that is best not to touch. What matters is the statement about unjust treatment, alluded to by the complaint against those who want "that I return to my land because I don't fit here."[14]—In this way, harassment leads some Mexican immigrants to resort to the old device of denying the calamities wrought by offensive language. A well-known exhortation resounds again: *Be careful with words*.

Indeed, what this corrido demands is basically a sense of responsibility with words and to not misuse the word "invader": to not confront the emigrant with a lying word. Remember, calamities of language are not just ways to ignore people. They can also be used as weapons loaded with arguments. However, there are many risks involved in contesting the appropriation of a word by a powerful Other. In the circumstances that this corrido dramatizes—although not in other ones—retaining the most common meaning of a word in daily life implies an act of courage and justice.[15]

The voice of this corrido clearly returns the word in the form of a thrown stone: "I am not the invader, if there is an invader here, that invader is you." Once again, by transforming the personal-social continuum of memory into a battlefield, the following now makes sense:

> *They painted the line*
> *for me to jump and call me invader.*[16]

But there are other verses of this type that are rather understated, with no traces of hostility—maybe because the battle seems already lost. Here the singing voice shyly reasons that Mexican immigrants do not really have a belligerent attitude and so do not represent a danger to the United States. On the contrary, migrants are looking for an opportunity to achieve their dreams. The conclusion is that migrants bring with them the expectations of moving forward and prospering. They crossed the border to get jobs:

> *I am not here to give you trouble: I am a working man.*[17]

This way of arguing mixes bits of history with prudence (or is it with a despair that disguises itself as prudence?) and is very common in border songs. (Yet, if I'm not mistaken, there is something else at stake in these verses. They sound a little like the classic argument that, through other means, has been developed by a whole tradition of liberal theory to justify the origin of private property and its legitimacy in primitive appropriation.) However, there are also angry corridos of harsh protest, composed and sung by those who already live "on the other side" or were born there, in which sometimes the elements of resistance become strident, even combative. (Surely because in such a situation, migrants feel safer and don't need to be uncomfortably alert.) These are less popular self-affirming proclamations for those who have not yet crossed the border, as in the words of the corrido "I Am Your Brother, I Am Chicano" ("Yo soy tu hermano / yo soy chicano," with lyrics by Rumel Fuentes):

> *They say I'm a troublemaker*
> *because I want to wake up with my race.*[18]

For many immigrants, the external-external Other is a source not only of many hostilities but also of horror. On the one hand, its presence is a very specific threat that must be tackled. But, on the other, that external-external Other is more than a presence; it is a scary intruder in the memory of migrants. Although it is already difficult to interact with other people who want to prevent their entrance to the United States even with guns, sometimes it is also difficult to deal with those intruders who insult, corner, and crush in the minds of the individuals themselves.

The external Other, real or imaginary figures with whom these emigrants get so tangled, are not only the Anglo-Saxons who give them work and orders. As I already noted, the figure of the negative Other does not reduce to an external-external Other.

B. Interactions with an External-Internal Other, or Second Challenges to Liable Colonialism

These are challenges of the first person directed to a despised second external-internal group of people—real or imaginary opposition by Mexican emigrants especially directed at a sector of the middle classes, the upper classes, and the governments of Mexico. Thus, part of the emigrant's self-affirmation is directed against those who were privileged enough to be able to remain in their land: a criticism addressed to the internal-external Other. These *accusation corridos* attack those who were evil or, at least, irresponsible fellow citizens. This criticism expresses the deep roots of injustice as a way of life and its consequences—social inequalities, rampant corruption, and impunity—that have forced the migrant to leave his or her land:

> *When have you heard of a doctor, an engineer*
> *Crossing as a bracero in order to progress?*[19]

It is clear what this combative accuser-corrido is about. It refers to the predicament of poverty—a product of social injustice—that has led these Mexicans to a painful heteronomy. They've been forced to abandon their social inheritance and families. (It does not really matter then that some of the assumptions of these verses are no longer true: doctors and engineers now *do* cross the border "in order to progress.") On the other hand, it is convenient to emphasize that if some corridos express affirmations seeking to articulate themselves as a form of protest against the external-external Other, they do so more strongly against the figures of the internal-external Other who is considered directly guilty of so much misfortune. Thus, the corrido "The Saint of the Mojados" ("El santo de los mojados," with lyrics by Enrique Franco; also a hit by Los Tigres del Norte) sings out loudly against the Mexico of injustice, the country left behind. In this corrido the singer desperately implores Saint Peter. (Why not pray to the Virgin of Guadalupe, as is usual among emigrants? Is it because Saint Peter holds the keys to heaven and, therefore, of justice?)

> *Grant us, sir, I ask you, to reach the United States.*
> *Don't let me go back to the hell the government has turned my country into.*[20]

Having explored a little the forms of liable colonialism in examples of encounters with two different kinds of an external Other, let us now examine the second type of interactions, infused colonialism, which sometimes also seeks a sense of reaffirmation, although in a less bellicose manner and often tangled with grief and guilt.

C. Interactions with an Internal-External Other, or First Challenges to Infused Colonialism

These are challenges to the internal-external Other (real or imaginary), that is, to the family, relatives and friends left behind in Mexico. Regrettably, many migrants encounter the disapproving gaze of their own, of those people they for. The hostile looks of those we love dishearten us the most. Although the rejection of strangers, and even of those who are indifferent to us, sometimes hurts, the perpetrators usually do it, so to speak, "from afar." Those wounds are usually not deep; we might suffer for a while, but our frustration soon fades away. In contrast, if anyone dear and near to us hurts us, we suffer deeply, and the pain tends to linger as a disturbing intruder in our memory. (This might be one reason why many of the great tragic plays from the most diverse traditions build on some calamity that breaks into the life of a family.)

As such, immigrants must also justify and excuse themselves to their dear ones, the internal-external Other left behind in Mexico, even if they don't feel they really have to. In "The Other Mexico" ("El otro México," with lyrics by Enrique Franco), another tune popularized by Los Tigres del Norte, the voice warns us, in a sad tone:

Don't criticize me because I live on the other side,
I am not a rootless, I came here of necessity.[21]

Again, we are exhorted to be responsible with the use of words. In this case, we are asked to be careful with the word "rootless." Leaving the place where you once lived and have family and friends cannot be voluntary or pleasant. It is, rather, a painful agony. (More often than not, the journey to the north carries deadly dangers.) So, no sensible objection can be leveled against those who have migrated. It is an old necessity that makes them abandon the place where they used to live and, in certain respects, prevents them from being who they once were. Therefore, these are *demoralizing corridos*, which are usually a way of vindication of migrant identity against the opinion of relatives and friends. But in this search for justification, immigrants usually take yet another step. Since the 1930s, a positive proposal has been added to the historical explanation of the Mexican immigration to the United States. According to this perspective, the dismaying pain and emotions of loss must be transformed into a new point of departure: anger and sadness must now serve as materials to build a situation of the type I call "being on the threshold." This is an endearing, although surely crazy utopia—the making, as the title of this corrido reads, of another Mexico in the middle of the United States:

The other Mexico that we have built here
In this soil that was once national territory[22]

However, the erection of such a deterritorialized community is no safeguard. The migrant is affected not only by the reality he or she has left behind and the one he or she has encountered along the journey but also by obstinate intruders in his or her memory: the hostile intruders of the external-external Other and the external-internal Other as well as sad, uncomfortable intruders in the form of the internal-external Other—family, relatives, friends. This gives rise to an overwhelming situation of nonbelonging—and perhaps of *absolute non-belonging*.[23] because living "neither here nor there" is like camping in the open air of a nonplace. That third place, that *other* Mexico, does not *really* exist (what a harsh adverb!). Consequently, for many people who migrate, there seems to be no reconciliation with themselves, neither in the past, present, nor future.

One might object: if we break down into parts even the most brazen utopia—like building another Mexico in the middle of the United States—we might find within it desires and emotions that can be rescued in *another way*. Perhaps we should try to erect a communal "third space" from that "other Mexico," one no longer here or there but both from here and there.[24] We can imagine a "third space" or, even better, a multitude of temporary communities for people to meet again. (After all, what place is not provisional? What place does not end up being a little "neither here nor there" and a little "here and there"?)

It is not only those Others—individually and socially—who require us to remember and, thus, suggest and even compel us to certain visions of the past. The self also remembers spontaneously or voluntarily; often, it remembers and examines itself. By withdrawing, the self adopts forms of self-understanding and self-construction—in this case, rather more in a negative than in a positive way.

D. Interactions with an Internal-Internal Other, or a Second Challenges to Infused Colonialism

The fourth and perhaps most forceful defiance that we find in these songs is the challenge of the first person to him- or herself. In this sense, let us consider a few more corridos with self-directed uses of memory, in which the self tries very gently to assert itself by looking for traces of its identity elsewhere. These are *self-destructive corridos*, which revolve around words often expressing the loss of "one's" place. They are songs of indignation against that purely internal Other that is part of oneself.

In "Dear Town" ("Pueblo querido," lyrics by Ismael Armenta), there's a confession of the emotional estrangement in which the immigrant lives. The old house is longed for, and, above all, the loved ones are missed. Thus, the singer loosely blames destiny for all his pains and hardships:

It is very sad to be absent from the land where one was born,
and sadder if friends and loved ones are not present,
Destiny made us leave them . . .[25]

Another self-destructive corrido, sung by the Los Tigres del Norte, is "South of the Bravo River" ("Al sur del Río Bravo," with lyrics by Paulino Vargas). A desolate landscape surrounds the singer, the consequence and/or cause being the social grievances suffered. Unfortunately, integrating a self amid such an ignorant, indifferent, and even hateful environment implies few opportunities to affirm oneself:

I have seen men, very rough men, breaking into tears
Overcome by the sadness of a kind gesture.[26]

This is why it seems so tempting to integrate oneself with the materials of an imaginary past in which many false memories evoke bucolic scenes that cannot soothe. Worse still, keeping these scenes in mind makes the situation in which one lives even more unappealing. And there's no use in evoking a completely idealized country left behind. Those fantasies keep afflicting the immigrant:

> *South of the Bravo River there is a valley where the sun laughs with the*
>   *people;*
> *Maybe that is where you belong, where even the sea is warm*[27]

It is important to bear in mind that the first stanza of this song seems to discard all value in economic success by reasoning—or maybe pseudo-reasoning?—that if a person is far from the place where he or she was born, far from his or her relatives and friends, away from what he or she considers his or her homeland, then disintegration and self-condemnation are only to be expected:

> *No matter how much you're worth or how much you have,*
> *If you are not where you want and the sun is not warm.*[28]

These words of misfortune are only an introduction to more self-denying, soulless verses of the self against the self, in which the first person itself as you would a hideous enemy. One such corrido is "The Golden Gage" ("La jaula de oro," with lyrics by Enrique Franco),[29] a very popular tune of Los Tigres del Norte. The verses mirror the moods that continue to pervade many of those who have immigrated. Far from glimpsing some reconciliation with the days and nights past or present, the singing voice tells us about growing discomforts, of an adversity that persistently hounds the emigrant. It's a cruel portrait in the form of an interior monologue:

> *In the United States, ten years have already passed,*
> *when I crossed as a wetback*
> *I still don't have documents, I am still an illegal.*[30]

There are some nuances. Again, the protagonist reports that, from the financial point of view, he has not fared badly in the United States. However, complaints come immediately to the foreground. Thus, any affirmation, however positive, is described again as a defeat. Every morning you feel broken. Each achievement implies a depersonalization, new losses:

What use is money
if I am a prisoner of this great nation?
When I remember I even cry,
For even a cage of gold
no freedom does hold.[31]

Again, pay attention to the careful choice of words. Although the corrido describes the United States as a "prison," the almighty country is described—surely not just as a commitment to rhyme in the original Spanish—as a "great nation." Thus, we find here the depiction of certain achievements and satisfactions that only frame misfortune. How can this be? The combination of success and the persistence of bitterness can seem frustrating. Worse still, we find no signs of pride in having achieved some of the proposed objectives. But perhaps this is something more common than generally supposed. For instance, note that many of these self-destructive corridos depict situations in which the satisfaction of desire is clouded by frustration, which is sometimes so deep that fulfilled desires lose all their value. Why? Often the satisfaction of wishes implies events that were not considered or discounted. In the case of many emigrants, achieving a better economic situation is sometimes accompanied by unexpected costs—not only because of the pain brought by the distance that separates the emigrant from family and friends but also because of a break with social inheritances. Thus, emigrants end up surviving in a bitter solitude, as suggested in the already mentioned "Golden Cage":

My children don't talk to me,
They've learned another language and forgotten Spanish[32]

It is assumed here that singers' children may be able to integrate in a rather distant future into another tradition with few or no relationships with the past. Furthermore, there is an overwhelming gap of communication, and in spite of the passage years and the achievement of relative economic stability, fear does not go away. It is the old fear we can hear in songs revolving around the pain caused when we are forced to leave somewhere. In consequence, unlike angry, or accuser, or even demoralizing corridos, protest songs about encounters and disagreements with an external or internal Other in real life or in the memory of migrants become self-destructive corridos. Their verses express uses of memory that become a purely denying self-examination or, more precisely, a form of self-condemnation. In consequence, amid the aggressive presence of the Others, the loss of their own cultural inheritances, the many expectations from the past with which they tend to populate their subjectivity, and a present that does not console, migrants sometimes end up embracing helplessness.

III

What can we learn from these corridos that Mexican emigrants hear, sing, or dance to before and after they cross the border? Their contents, just as the contents of any song, usually have unexpected effects. (In an extreme example, tragic plays do not invite to suicide but to live more wisely.) Regarding the lessons of the corridos, I used the expression "purgative against despair." We typically use the word "purgative" to refer to substances that are used to *cleanse* (particularly the digestive system, facilitating bowel movements, and the proper functioning of the whole body). But this word is also generally used to refer to things that remove or help to remove whatever is bad, harmful, and prevents people from seeking the goods they have set out to achieve. Now, to return to the case of immigrants, we might wonder: How can these corridos-as-purgatives operate for them as a therapy against despair and, at the same time, as an aid to help them resume their lives once they overcome their anguish? I suspect the reason they can actually perform this double task—the task of cleansing and of preparing listeners for a new point of departure—is that these songs often contain or suggest different ways of resisting. The word "resist" refers to a continuum. At one end, there are ways of educating people or social groups so they can stand firm in relation to what they are willing to do or not do. But at the opposite end, there are ways of questioning, or open forms of rejection. Once again, I presume that in the corridos we have just analyzed there are asymmetric interactions that in various ways generate forms of resistance. Let us briefly address this suspicion.

In the interactions with an external-external Other, many corridos articulate the social anger of migrants feeling overwhelmed by many of the attitudes of those who not only give them jobs but are also in authority in the country where they have arrived. As is well known, social irritation tends to generate anger and even a desire for revenge, but it also motivates forms of resistance, which in turn promote self-control, the outputs of adaptation efforts. Therefore, we can find here ways of resisting that maintain the appropriate behaviors in order to get along with—though not necessarily to appreciate or even respect—those who provide work, but which at the same time set limits to what people are willing to obey and not to say. Thus, this type of resistance is not only a way of not giving in to the temptations of a furious reaction but also a resource to avoid becoming a mere instrument of those who basically control things in the country of arrival. On the other hand, a noteworthy outcome of the interactions with an external-internal Other are corridos that challenge the unjust moral, legal, political, and economic structures of the society that was left behind. These corridos present evidence that allows the singers to blame governments, the upper classes, and even the middle classes for the great social inequalities that force so many people to emigrate. But the accusation is not judicial in nature; it is obviously not made before any established authority and no precise penalty is requested. It is a social accusation. Of course, these accusations may remain as only a form of censorship, but many of these corridos also offer, or hint at, resistance that investigates the causes of misfortune. In interactions with an internal-external Other, one can find corridos full of dismaying and even intimidating emotions. We hear in them people dear to the emigrants reproaching them for having left. These are often disheartening and sometimes undermine the enthusiasm of emigrants for undertaking their journey. Hence the great mental efforts that are often needed in order to learn how to keep going on and to attain ways of resisting that explain why one should resist and not be depressed; to adopt new ways of thinking and behavior that would justify why families and friends have been left behind. As noted before, there are also corridos in which the interactions with an internal-internal Other are articulated and a nostalgic self feels estranged from itself. Not only friends and property have been left behind, but also the old familiar places and beloved landscapes. The immigrant faces the loneliness of the unknown, and the unfamiliar is anticipated as hostile and frightening. As if this wasn't enough, these self-destructive corridos usually take one step further and depict the new circumstances as a prison. While it may be an economically rewarding and even comfortable prison, it is still a discouraging and intimidating condition for living. However, this process of estrangement from oneself—just like other sorrows expressed in corridos—often forks in different paths. It might lead in the direction of discouragement or self-destruction. Or, once a certain point of discouragement is reached, the process might stop as the migrant finds ways of devising self-reassuring resistance in the midst of collapse—a form of protest of the first person against him- or herself wanting to give up.

However, let us still ask what we can learn *in general* from all these corridos, and also from what is surely a closely related matter, from the poems of exiles.[33] Once again, I think it is worthwhile to emphasize that if we reflect on any concrete situation and abstract from the peculiarities that most distinguish it, chances are we will find lessons of no little value. For example, a first lesson that can be drawn from all these corridos on the theme of emigration and from the many words spoken during forced displacements is that, more often than not, we will all, at some point of our lives, have to interact with a many-faced Other. This Other may be often overtly or secretly aggressive, usually in diverse ways. That is one reason why it is important to learn to respond to Others by accounting for all their peculiarities; and that is why we will have to find many ways of resisting. A second (and perhaps more decisive) lesson is the importance of remembering that even in the worst circumstances—like the ones endured by emigrants—one can discover purgatives against despair, and thus it is possible to gather strength and continue resisting in situations of distressing displacement.

Notes

1. This question is articulated in a different form by Gayatri Chakravorty Spivak in "Can the Subaltern Speak?" *Die Philosophin* 14, no. 27 (2003): 42–58.
2. I have discussed this in some of my previous work, including, for instance, *Lessons in Exile* (Leiden: Brill-Rodopi, 2019) (Translation of *Los aprendizajes del exilio* [Mexico City: Siglo XXI editores, 2008]).
3. See Mario T. García, "La Frontera: The Border as Symbol and Reality in Mexican-American Thought," in *Between Two Worlds: Mexican Immigrants in the United States*, ed. David G. Gutiérrez (Wilmington, Del.: Scholarly Resources, 1996), 89–118. Also see José David Saldívar, *Border Matters: Remapping American Cultural Studies* (Berkeley: University of California Press, 1997).
4. In Mexico, these songs are everywhere and make up important fragments of the space and times of many people's lives. As José Manuel Valenzuela points out in *Chief of Chiefs: Corridos and Narcocultura in Mexico* (Mexico City: Plaza y Janés, 2002), at least in the border areas this music "is an essential framework of daily life that goes beyond the intimate limits marked by the walls of the houses or the mobile space of the car, forming a fundamental part of the bustle that defines the urban physiognomy" (9). As the subtitle indicates, rather

than studying the emigration corridos, Valenzuela's book addresses *narcocorridos*. While explaining their popularity and the popularity of drug traffickers now transformed into heroes, and even tragic heroes, Valenzuela observes, "Violence spreads throughout our societies, addiction gains followers, and the forces that should control it seem incompetent. Faced with this inability, 'town doctors' proliferate, a euphemistic form that alludes to drug traffickers who can provide relief to those suffering from the ills of addiction" (116). Although the stories told by the emigration corridos and the narcocorridos differ, overlaps also abound.

5. Vicente T. Mendoza traces the origins of these songs back to the Spanish ballads, in *El corrido mexicano* (Mexico City: Fondo de Cultura Económica, 1954). Catalina H. de Giménez, in *Así cantaban la Revolución* (Mexico City: CONACULTA-Grijalbo, 1991), disagrees with Mendoza's conclusions, considering his view too "Spanishizing." According to Giménez, corridos come from expressions of the indigenous peoples (for example, from Nahuatl poetry). Sometimes, in a more nuanced way, other authors consider corridos a mestizo product, as yet one more example of hybrid cultures. See also Guillermo E. Hernández, "What Is the Corrido?" *Studies in Latin American Popular Culture* 18 (1999): 69–92. Without taking sides in this discussion, Carlos Monsiváis characterizes corridos as "novels compressed in verse" in *Los mil y un velorios: Crónica de la nota roja en México* (Mexico City: Debate-Mondadori, 2010), 19. Precisely because we are dealing with a genre that may be called "compressed novel," it would be worthwhile looking at a complete corrido in order to give it justice. However, this is not possible if one wants to compare different types of corridos.

6. Francisco Cantú, *The Line Becomes a River: Dispatches from the Border* (New York: Riverhouse Books, 2019). Let us not confuse this music, "norteño music," with "Tejano music." The latter incorporates not only various technological advances but also musical fragments typical of the United States, such as country and western; in its lyrics Mexico, and everything that has to do with Mexico and the legal and illegal crossing of borders, figures as a distant and vague presence, if at all.

7. The story of Los Tigres del Norte—first a famous group in northern Mexico and some regions of the southern United States and, later, known everywhere or at least its legend, is prototypical (almost a fairy tale). It began in the state of Sinaloa in 1968 when Jorge, the eldest of the Hernández Angulo family—who was only fourteen at the time—managed to convince his brothers Raúl and Hernán and his cousin Oscar to form a musical group and thereby help the precarious family economy. Years later, when Jorge was twenty-two years old, they were hired to play in San José, California. That same year they recorded their first album and established their residence in that city. After a career spanning almost fifty years, they have recorded more than sixty albums with more than eight hundred songs and sold more than thirty-five million albums. Part of the popularity of this group is attributed to its having included narcocorridos early

on in their repertoire (beginning with the extraordinary success of the corrido titled "Contrabando y traición"). See Ivan Carrillo, "Tigres del Norte Challenge Censorship: Tigres del Norte on Tour with La Reina del Sur," Univisión Online, accessed December 1, 2019, http://www.univision.com/content. Also see Leila Cabo, "Los Tigres de Norte: Music with a Social Conscience," *Hispanic Magazine*, July–August 2004. Several of those narcocorridos have been banned, which has predictably further increased the group's fame. See Mark Cameron Edberg, *El Narcotraficante: Narcocorridos and the Construction of a Cultural Persona on the U.S. Mexico-Border* (Austin: University of Texas Press, 2004). On the other hand, this band seems to have been very clear about its commitment to bearing witness to the suffering of people who emigrate. As stated by one of its members, Hernán Hernández, "The protagonist of our songs is the people." See Claudia S. Meléndez, "Portraits of the People: *Los Tigres del Norte*," interview with Hernán Hernández in *Nuevo Mundo*, San José, California, August 29, 2003.

8. When I know the names of these lyricists, I quote them. Why add to so much contempt a new contempt—a new ignorance? On behalf of which colonizing device?

9. To examine some corridos I turn here to the compilation in the book by María Luisa de la Garza, *Ni aquí ni allá: El emigrante en los corridos y en otras canciones populares* (Cádiz: Ayuntamiento de Cádiz, 2005), as well as to the back covers of old albums—I mean "old" considering how fast our time runs, or seems to run.

10. "A los güeros no les gusta / Que crucemos la frontera."

11. "Recorrí varios estados de la Unión Americana / En Arizona, Texas y Lousiana / Y siempre sentí la falta de estimación." For a discussion on the truth assumptions of these corridos, see José Pablo Villalobos and Juan Carlos Ramirez Pimienta, "Corridos and la pura verdad: Myths and Realities of the Mexican Ballad," in *South Central Review* 21, no. 3 (Autumn 2004): 129–49.

12. "Ya me gritaron mil veces / Que regrese a mi tierra porque aquí no quepo yo."

13. "Quiero recordarle al gringo: / yo no crucé la frontera, la frontera me cruzó." In relation to some consequences of the experience alluded to in this verse ("I did not cross the border, the border crossed *me*") Gloria Anzaldúa tells us, "My ancestors lived in the border. The border line was part of the state of Tamaulipas, Mexico, then the United States bought it, they bought the half that corresponded to Mexico, in this way the Anzalduas were split in two. The Anzaldúas with an accent, that is, my family, were north of the border. The Anzalduas without an accent stayed on the other side, and as the decades passed we lost contact with each other. So it was that the Anzaldúas and Anzalduas, originally from the same land, the state of Tamaulipas in Mexico, suddenly became strangers in our country, foreigners in our country. We were a colonized people who were not allowed to speak their language, whose way of life was not valued in this country. Public education tried to erase all this. And here I am now, a kind of international citizen whose life and privileges are not equal to the rights and privileges

of the ordinary white Anglo-Euro-American. My narrative always takes into account these other ethnicities, these other races, these other cultures, these other stories. There is always that kind of struggle." Anzaldúa, introduction to *Critical Intellectuals on Writing*, ed. G. A. Olson and L. Worsham (Albany: State University of New York Press, 2003), 16–17. To live in that "kind of struggle," in her poem-manifesto *Borderlands/La Frontera: The New Mestiza* (San Francisco: Aunt Lute Books, 1987), 195, Anzaldúa recommends: "To survive the Borderlands / You must live without borders / Be a crossroads" (195).

14. In *Mexico Unconquered: Chronicles of Power and Revolt* (San Francisco: City Lights Books, 2009), John Gibler offers in chapter 4 ("The Heist") testimonies of those who stay in Mexico and those who migrate. As background information for those testimonies, Gibler states, "Consider these numbers. In 2000: 389,616. In 2001: 392,003. In 2002: 394,120. In 2003: 396,129. In 2004: 397,998. Thousands of people. Each year, around 400,000 leave their homes all around Mexico to look for a work in the United States" (123).

15. There are many situations in which extending the meaning of words, or modifying the evaluation with which one or more words are used, imply acts of courage and justice and even social subversion. This is the phenomenon Judith Butler calls "resignification of words," such as, for example, the resignification that words like "woman," "black," "gay," and "queer" have received in recent times. The phenomenon is general and affects even the most prestigious words. According to Butler, "a term like 'freedom' can end up meaning what it had never meant before, end up involving interests and subjects that had been excluded from its jurisdiction; 'Justice' may also end up implying what was not included in its description. 'Equality' has become a term whose scope would have been difficult, if not impossible to predict according to its ancient meanings." See Butler, *Excitable Speech: A Politcs of the Performative* (New York: Routledge, 1997), 160–61. In "La reconceptualización de la libertad: Críticas al positivismo en las postrimerías del porfiriato" in *Asedios a los centenarios (1910 y 1921)*, ed. Virginia Guedea (Mexico City: Fondo de Cultura Económica, 2009, 226–82), Guillermo Hurtado uses the word "reconceptualize" instead of "resignify" to refer to the same technique. He studies how the concept of peace and of freedom, among others, were reconceptualized in Mexico—in a controversy against the positivist content given to those concepts during the Porfirio Díaz dictatorship—by the Ateneo de la Juventud and by what can loosely be called the "ideology of the 1910 Mexican Revolution."

16. "Ellos pintaron la raya / para que yo la cruzara y me llaman invasor."

17. "No vengo a darles guerra / soy hombre trabajador."

18. This corrido collected by María Luisa de la Garza in *Ni aquí ni allá* (120) is found on the album *Rolas de Aztlán: Songs of the Chicano Movement* (Smithsonian Folkways Recordings, 1999), in the interpretation of Grupo Aztlán. It is the only corrido cited in these pages that—perhaps symptomatically?—is not played by a band as popular as Los Tigres del Norte.

19. "¿Cuándo han sabido que un doctor, un ingeniero / se ha cruzado de braceros porque quieren progresar?"
20. "Concédenos, señor, yo te pido, llegar a los Estados Unidos. / No dejes que regrese al infierno que a mi país convierte el gobierno."
21. "No me critiquen porque vivo al otro lado / no soy un desarraigado, vine por necesidad."
22. "El otro México que aquí hemos construido / En este suelo que ha sido territorio nacional."
23. María Luisa de la Garza highlights this situation: "If Mexicans living and working in the United States are discriminated against by Anglo-Saxons and, at the same time, are viewed with distrust by Mexicans who remained in Mexico, they end up not belonging to any of the two worlds they have as a reference, they end up being neither from here nor from there, since they will have a bit of wetbacks and a bit of gringos forever." *Ni aquí ni allá*, 144.
24. See David G. Gutiérrez, "Migration, Emergent Ethnicity, and the 'Third Space': The Shifting Politics of Nationalism in Greater Mexico," *Journal of American History* 86, no. 2 (September 1999): 481–517.
25. "Es muy triste encontrarse ausente de la tierra donde uno ha nacido / y más triste si no están presentes los amigos y los seres queridos / que el destino no hizo dejarlos . . ."
26. "Yo he visto que hombres muy hombres rompen en llanto / vencidos por la tristeza de un gesto amable."
27. "Al sur del río Bravo hay un valle donde el sol ríe con la gente / tal vez allí está tu sitio, allí hasta el mar es caliente."
28. "No importa ni cuánto valgas ni cuanto tengas / si no estás donde tú quieres ni el sol calienta."
29. For more about this author of the lyrics of so many corridos see Juan Carlos Ramírez Pimienta and Jorge Pimienta, "Is the *Corrido* Still the Voice of Our People? An Interview with Enrique Franco," *Studies in Latin American Popular Culture* 23 (2004): 43–54. On the general and more or less spontaneous self-understanding of those who produce corridos, see Elijah Wald, *Narcocorrido: A Trip to the World of Music of Drugs, Weapons and Guerrillas* (New York: Harper Collins, 2001), in which several corrido composers are interviewed.
30. "En los Estados Unidos diez años pasaron ya / en que crucé de mojado / y papeles no he arreglado, sigo siendo un illegal."
31. "De qué me sirve el dinero si estoy como prisionero dentro de esta gran nación / Cuando me acuerdo hasta lloro, aunque la Jaula sea de oro, no deja de ser prisión."
32. "Mis hijos no hablan conmigo / otro idioma han aprendido y olvidado el español."
33. See Pereda, *Lessons in Exile*.

PART IV

Latin Americans and Latina/o/xs in the United States

CHAPTER 10

The Interpreter's Dilemma

On the Moral Burden of Consensual Heteronomy

LORI GALLEGOS

Imagine the following scenario: Jorge wants to get out of a long-term contract that costs more than he can currently comfortably pay.[1] Although the terms of the contract specify that he cannot terminate the contract early, Jorge believes that if one were to argue long enough and with enough people, eventually someone would be willing to cancel it. Jorge does not speak English. His contract is in Ignacia's name, since Ignacia speaks English and is therefore in a better position to handle things like billing and communication. *She* would have to argue for the cancellation of the contract. However, she does not want to, because she believes that the behavior would be contemptible. At the same time, Ignacia sympathizes with Jorge and knows that he cannot better his own situation without her help.

In this chapter, I want to focus on dilemmas like the one Ignacia faces and on the ethical costs to interpreters in such cases.[2] Many families in the United States have members who do not speak the dominant language, so situations like the one described above are likely far more common than people realize. The U.S. Census Bureau's 2016 American Community Survey finds that over one-fifth of the U.S. population speaks a language other than English at home, with Spanish being the most common language (40.5 million people). The survey also finds that 8.6 percent of people in the United States—about 27.8 million—are classified as LEP, or "limited English proficient," which means that they read, write, speak, and understand English "less than very well," that is, at level that does not allow them to communicate effectively with English speakers in a variety of situations.[3] We might wonder how these millions of non-English speakers manage to get by.

The United States does not have a federally recognized official language, and Title VI of the Civil Rights Act of 1964 requires federal and state government agencies, as well as private companies that receive a certain amount of federal funding, to provide certain services to people in languages other than English.[4] The legislation was designed to prohibit discrimination against people based on language or country of origin. Unfortunately, the ideal of equal opportunity expressed in this legislation is far from the reality for most non-English speakers. While it may be possible to obtain service and official documents in Spanish at the DMV, medical centers, schools, and some social service agencies, the process of doing so is often complicated. A notice published in 2000 by the Office of Civil Rights for the U.S. Department of Health and Human Services (OCR) documents its findings about some of the barriers facing non-English speakers:

> LEP persons are often excluded from programs, experience delays or denials of services, or receive care and services based on inaccurate or incomplete information . . . OCR has found that persons who lack proficiency in English frequently are unable to obtain basic knowledge of how to access various benefits and services for which they are eligible . . . For example, many intake interviewers and other front line employees who interact with LEP individuals are neither bilingual nor trained in how to properly serve an LEP person. As a result, the LEP applicant all too often is either turned away, forced to wait for substantial periods of time, forced to find his/her own interpreter who often is not qualified to interpret, or forced to make repeated visits to the provider's office until an interpreter is available to assist in conducting the interview.[5]

In effect, these health and social services are not available or accessible at the time that non-English speakers need them—and these are services that are required to be available by federal law. Many more services, businesses, and organizations do not make any effort to be accessible. As a result, many non-English speakers rely on family members for translation and interpretation in a range of settings, including the doctor's office, banks, stores, legal situations, and parent-teacher conferences.[6] Without this support, they are effectively excluded from the communities in which they live.

Despite the fact that there is federal legislation prohibiting language-based discrimination, there seems to be a widely held belief that the burden of facilitating communication in the United States should fall on non-English speakers—that *they* should learn English if they hope to participate fully in society. Making English the official language was even part of several Republican presidential candidates' platforms leading up to the 2016 U.S. presidential election.[7] But even those who do not support the United States having an official language often seem to take it for granted that non-English speakers have the responsibility of learning English and should not expect to be accommodated. While this view may be reasonable in some contexts, I aim to show in this chapter that the widespread lack of Spanish-language accessibility services in the United States comes at a *moral cost* for members of the Latinx community.

Specifically, I contend that it is not only non-English speakers who are the target of this oppression. Those who interpret for their non-English-speaking loved ones are also affected, because they suffer from a moral burden as a result of their role as interpreter. As I will show, this moral burden can only be fully appreciated in light of a conception of relational autonomy, which has been a central theme in the moral theoretical work known as care ethics. This body of (primarily feminist) work centers on the moral significance of human relationships and dependencies, such as those relationships where practices of caregiving are involved. In addition, the moral burden is better understood through conceptions of the pragmatics of language and the notion of emotional agency.

I also make the case that this moral burden is an *unjust* moral burden, rather than a *merely circumstantial* burden, which is not a matter of justice. An examination of this burden reveals one way that the marginalization of non-English speakers affects more than just the non-English speakers themselves, rippling throughout the broader Latinx community. Calling upon Marilyn Frye's theory of oppression, I argue that this encumbrance can be seen as a facet of the oppression of the Latinx community.

In the first section of this chapter, I examine several aspects of what I call the *interpreter's dilemma*, which arises when those who interpret for family members face the decision of whether to act in accordance with their own ethical values, principles, and commitments, or to act out of love or loyalty on behalf of their dependent loved one who requests that the interpreter act in a way that is inconsistent with the interpreter's values, principles, and commitments. In the second section, I argue that the interpreter's dilemma harms the interpreter because it demands heteronomy—that is, roughly, that the interpreter's will is subject to another. Furthermore, the interpreter must personally invest in their own instrumentalized role in order to carry out their responsibilities effectively. I also discuss the ways in which racism contributes to this dynamic. Lastly, in section three, I show why this moral burden is unjust and can be seen as a facet of the oppression of the Latinx community.

I. The Interpreter's Dilemma

Much of the research on language and culture brokering, or the day-to-day mediation between parties who speak different languages, focuses on assessing the impacts of the practice on children, and falls broadly into two camps. In developmental psychology, one finds an emphasis on the harms suffered by children who are given the role of interpreter. Authors of one study find that "children . . . often feel overburdened in complicated and serious situations, such as when they are required to translate documentation."[8] Another negative outcome is that it can lead to role reversal, where "parents express dependent behaviors and children, in an attempt to meet their parent's needs, acquire nurturing, supportive, and care-giving behaviors."[9] One study obtained data from 182 first- and second-generation Chinese fifteen-year-olds and found that "the children who more frequently acted as interpreters for their parents had poorer psychological health. Frequency of translation was also associated with parent-child conflict, particularly for those who held strong family values."[10]

Researchers in the field of education, however, have cast language brokering in a more positive light. Marjorie Faulstich Orellana conducted ethnographic fieldwork in three immigrant communities where, she says, most children simply see language brokering as a not-so-burdensome part of everyday life, similar to other ways in which kids are often expected to help their families out.[11] Faulstich Orellana also highlights the skills children who interpret and translate develop as a result of the practice.[12] In particular, she argues that the accumulation of experiences of interpreting leads to the cultivation of "an orientation toward and ability to understand the perspectives of people from backgrounds different from one's own, and to adapt behaviors, communicative practices and epistemological stances flexibly in interactions with others."[13] As an educator of children, Faulstich Orellana has designed curricula to help all students cultivate the skills and versatility that interpreters tend to develop.

Faulstich Orellana also considers the relation between language brokers and society and emphasizes that language and culture brokers are not simply interpreting *for family members*—they are providing a vital service *to society* more broadly. This analysis counters narratives that immigrant children are merely a burden to society, taking from educational and health systems without giving back.[14] Faulstich Orellana makes a case for the value of this largely invisible labor, noting that there is a shocking absence of attention to it in historical accounts of child migrants, memoirs, and fiction about immigrant youth. She also notes that children are often represented as lacking agency in immigration narratives—they are the baggage that is "brought along," "sent for," or "left behind" when parents migrate.[15] In sum, Faulstich Orellana challenges the representation of language brokers in the developmental psychology literature and in society as mere victims of immigrant parents who will not learn the language.

In this chapter, I assess the impacts of language brokering in a way that differs from both these approaches. Like Faulstich Orellana, I am interested in acknowledging the agency of this often-ignored group of people, and I also analyze the labor they carry out in terms of a broader social context. However, contrary to her efforts to emphasize the everydayness and innocuousness of interpreting for family members, I argue that the role of interpreter often comes with a moral burden. I do not deny that language brokers often acquire valuable skills as a result of their role. It is important to recognize, however, that people may cultivate skills under conditions that also generate costs to their well-being. For example, a farmworker might harvest turnips with astonishing speed and precision, but it is precisely because they work for a low piece rate that they develop such speed, and it is because the work is dangerous that they learn to work with great precision. At the same time, my goal is not to place blame on non-English-speaking immigrants who depend heavily on family members; it is, rather, to think about the moral burden that interpreters face in terms of how it fits into broader, structural inequalities that affect Latinx people. Further, my hope is that identifying this moral burden will give us an opportunity to begin thinking about the responsibilities that our society has toward immigrant communities.

My analysis of the moral burden faced by interpreters is rooted in the following moral dilemma: On the one hand, the interpreter has a duty to support a dependent family member who wishes for the interpreter to engage in an action on their behalf; on the other hand, the interpreter does not personally endorse the action that they are being asked to engage in.

I call this particular type of conflict the *interpreter's dilemma*. I am not suggesting that it arises in all acts of interpreting, or that all interpreters experience it. Instead, I mean to identify an experience that occurs frequently enough for those who interpret heavily for family members that it is a widely shared and often distinguishing feature of that role. Let's turn to two illustrative examples. You'll remember the first from the beginning of the chapter:

Example 1—Contract: Jorge wants to get out of a long-term contract that costs more than he currently can comfortably pay. Although the terms specify that he cannot terminate the contract early, Jorge believes that if one were to argue long enough and with enough people, eventually someone would be willing to cancel it. Jorge does not speak English. His contract is in Ignacia's name, since Ignacia speaks English and is therefore in a better position to handle things like billing and communication. *She* would have to argue for the cancellation of the contract. However, she does not want to, because she believes that the behavior would be contemptible. At the same time, Ignacia sympathizes with Jorge and knows that he cannot better his own situation without her help.

Example 2—Loan: Jorge wants to start a business and would like to apply for a small-business loan. The local banks do not offer extensive foreign-language services. Jorge turns to Ignacia for help with the process. Ignacia would like to support Jorge's dream of owning a business, but the process of applying for a small-business loan is frustrating and time consuming. It requires detailed and extensive paperwork, evidence collection, as well as interviews and ongoing phone-call negotiations with a loan officer. Jorge may be rejected at one or more banks, and each has its own procedures and documentation requirements, so the process could be lengthy.

In cases like these, the interpreter's autonomy is challenged when we understand autonomy as involving "a person's capacity to act in a way that reveals her sense of what matters to her."[16] As Serene Khader puts it, a person with autonomy "identifies with her chosen courses of action rather than regarding them as instances of mere subjection . . . She has a sense of what matters to her and attempts to act in a way that reveals this."[17]

In the contract example, Ignacia's belief that arguing to get out of a contract is morally contemptible reflects the moral standards she has for herself. To carry out this act would be to act contrary to her own values. The act undermines Ignacia's autonomy in the sense that she feels pressured to act in a way that is inconsistent with what she would choose for herself. It is possible that Ignacia might yet find some way to autonomously reconcile herself to the cost if, for example, she decided that her commitment to considerations of family support would, upon further reflection, have her choose for herself to render Jorge assistance. My point is that, absent some further reconciliation of this sort, there is a pro tanto cost to autonomy in this sort of case.

Now consider the loan example. In addition to being frustrating and emotionally depleting, going through the loan application process will no doubt compete for time with Ignacia's other commitments. Consider, too, that Jorge may be making requests of Ignacia that may be more or less demanding every week.[18] If Ignacia's own projects, goals, and other commitments make significant demands on her time, it's not difficult to see how acting on Jorge's behalf in this situation could contribute to the long-term undermining of her well-being. Ignacia's desire not to help with the loan application can be understood as a desire to act in ways that are consistent with Ignacia's own flourishing, and this, too, is an important value.

At the same time, interpreters' responsibilities to their family members also have weight. In relationships of dependency, the person depended upon may experience an obligation to facilitate the dependent's expression of their agency. Both dependency and the distribution of labor among several people are features of many family relationships. Even when these expectations require some self-sacrifice, they may be for the most part fair within the context of a particular relationship (or at least not obviously exploitative). For the interpreter to transgress against those responsibilities might both harm the dependent loved one and the relationship that the interpreter shares with the loved one. Furthermore, insofar as the well-being of the interpreter is dependent on the well-being of the family member, the interpreter, too, will be harmed by their decision not to aid their family member. Love, loyalty, self-interest, and expectations that have emerged within particular relationships all generate compelling reasons to comply with the desires of the family member.

What an interpreter personally endorses can have moral weight when it is a reflection of their moral autonomy. The interpreter's dilemma is not merely that the interpreter is being called to do something they do not want to do.

Rather, the dilemma is a potentially weighty *moral* dilemma, because it is a matter of having to choose to act contrary to a significant value or commitment in order to act in accordance with another.

The interpreter's dilemma has similarities to other sorts of dilemmas faced by those in relationships that have a significant element of dependency, such as caregivers and those they care for. People in positions of dependency rely on others for a fuller expression of their agency, but facilitating this agency may come at a significant cost to the person depended upon. The ambiguous moral nature of self-sacrifice has been a central theme in care ethics, a body of theoretical work that centers on the moral significance of human relationships and dependencies. As one philosopher puts it, self-sacrifice in the context of caregiving is "neither mere stupidity nor mere heroism."[19] Self-sacrifice is both a celebrated and essential moral activity, but also one that can harm the caregiver.

In the case of interpreters, the question of self-sacrifice is likewise ambiguous and cannot be disentangled from power dynamics within the relationship. One thing that makes the case of interpreters distinctive is the intersection of the social identities of the people involved in these situations. This intersectionality gives rise to distinctive challenges that merit attention on their own terms, particularly since these challenges can be invisible to mono-dominant-language speakers. For instance, language brokering is typically a gendered activity.[20] Girls and women tend to occupy the role of interpreter within their families and thus bear the moral responsibility—and burdens—of this role. The responsibility for interpreting cannot always be separated from the tendency of many families to exploit women's and girls' labor. These factors often add to the messiness of the situation, making it even more difficult for the interpreter to determine the "right" way to respond to the dilemma. In addition, the job of interpreting often falls to children, and this is significant because of the children's often-total dependence on their parents, their need for their parents' love, their own love and dedication to their parents, and their sense of obligation to meet their parents' demands.

Power dynamics outside of the relationship can also exacerbate the interpreter's dilemma. Interpreters may find themselves combating widespread prejudices in order to support their family members' well-being. Racism and its day-to-day manifestations form an important backdrop here. The dependent loved one is regularly at risk of being marginalized, exploited, ignored, mistreated, and having the worst assumed about them because of their ethnic and racial identity. These barriers to the flourishing and agency of the family member add weight to the interpreter's obligation to facilitate the family member's agency. The interpreter might recognize that their advocacy is a kind of resistance to the effects of racism on their loved one.

Illustrating this situation in her ethnographic work, Faulstich Orellana interviewed a fifteen-year-old boy named Josh, who describes helping his father buy a car and feeling that his father was the target of a salesman's prejudice. Josh explains: "I don't think he really wanted someone to, I don't know, translate or whatever. Maybe like, 'Oh, this person doesn't know English, catch him right here with these different prices,' you know. 'By the end of the day, I'll have a sale,' you know. 'This guy doesn't know what he's doing,' you know. We were there, and then my sister said that she heard that guy talking about how us Mexicans can't buy a car."[21]

The pervasive sense that one's family member is subject to prejudice may generate a desire to represent their agency more robustly. It also explains the frequency with which the interpreter may face the interpreter's dilemma. Interpreters may regularly find themselves in situations in which they function as an intermediary in the context of a family member being mistreated. The family member may have their own way of wanting to respond to this abuse—perhaps they want to return an insult, demand certain treatment, or just stay quiet—and this may differ from the way in which the interpreter would react to the abuse. It is not difficult to imagine why such discrepancies could generate significant tension and discomfort for both parties.

Given these various social dynamics, I hope it is clear why those who interpret for family members may find themselves facing a real dilemma time and time again. On the one hand, the interpreter has a duty to support a dependent family member who wishes for the interpreter to engage in an action on their behalf. On the other, the interpreter does not personally endorse the action that they are being asked to engage in.

Note on an Initial Objection

One might object that the interpreter's dilemma is not a real dilemma because of what seems to be an obvious resolution to it: the dependency of a non-English-speaking family member could be addressed if the family member would simply learn English. One might argue that because the non-English speaker is responsible for making themselves dependent upon the interpreter—and because the interpreter may be enabling their family member by allowing them to remain dependent—the dilemma is resolvable by the interpreter simply refusing to interpret, no longer enabling the dependency of the family member. This argument, however, fails to take several factors into consideration. For one, language acquisition for adults may be difficult for a variety of reasons. At the very least, research on language acquisition indicates that while children preserve the ability to learn new grammars, this ability declines rapidly in late adolescence. Indeed, studies show that even full-immersion language learners experience a sharp drop in the learning rate at around seventeen to eighteen years of age.[22] Another reason the assumption that all immigrants should be able to pick up the English language is flawed is that they may actually not be immersed in the English language because their lives may take places largely within foreign-language communities. They may also have other priorities— such as working or caring for children—that outweigh their ability to focus on their own education. In addition, many towns do not offer classes to help those who are unable to learn on their own, or who have learning challenges. Furthermore, the objection that non-English speakers and their enabling family members are responsible for the dependency fails to account for the urgent quality of the needs of family members. It would be unfair to demand that interpreters refuse to help a family member communicate at the doctor's office, with the police, with the IRS, or with the landlord out of a tough-love attitude that would pressure the family member to learn English or suffer the consequences. And most importantly, even if there is a correct way to resolve the interpreter's dilemma in most cases, it's really the *experience* of the dilemma—the feeling that one is either failing to meet their responsibility to their family member or undermining their own autonomy—that is sufficient to constitute a pervasive sense of the weight of moral responsibilities that one cannot adequately meet.

II. The Moral Burden of Consensual Heteronomy

The interpreter's dilemma adversely affects the interpreter when it becomes a moral burden, that is, a kind of responsibility that weighs so heavily that it threatens to damage the moral self. Nancy Sherman's notion of "moral injuries," which she elucidates in her work on military veterans, conveys what is meant by harm to one's moral self. In *Afterwar*, Sherman explains that moral injuries "arise from (real or apparent) transgressive commissions and omissions perpetuated by oneself or others."[23] Sherman notes that moral injury has to do with "a generalized sense of falling short of normative standards befitting good persons."[24] While on duty, military members often witness or participate in acts that violate their own moral standards. Sherman argues that in order to help veterans heal from their experiences, it is important to understand this harm as a *moral* injury, one that should not be understood merely in terms of mental-health diagnoses such as post-traumatic stress disorder.

Likewise, I contend that the interpreter's dilemma produces a moral burden that cannot be merely understood in terms of the psychology of children's role reversal with their parents, or in terms of the stress of heavy responsibility. Instead, the weight of sorting through frequent moral dilemmas causes harm to the moral self because it involves potential transgressions against one's own autonomy. As a result, interpreters may face anxiety, emotional exhaustion, strained relationships, and self-alienation.

The interpreter's dilemma causes harm to the moral self because it demands that the interpreter engage in *heteronomous* action, that is, one that an agent does not identify with, experiencing it instead as subjection to the will of another person or influence. I argue that a central reason the interpreter's dilemma constitutes a moral burden is that complying with the family member's request to act on their behalf often requires not only that the interpreter act in a way that they do not want to but also that they *invest* themselves in this heteronomous action in a way that alienates the individual from herself. In other words, I claim that part of the burden of the interpreter's dilemma is that it requires a person to consent to that which undermines their own autonomy.

Interpretation requires a high degree of personal investment, in part because one is interpreting for a loved one. Whereas a professional interpreter's responsibility for their client is temporary, the well-being of the person who is interpreting for a family member can depend to a greater or lesser degree on the outcome of a communicative exchange. Imagine, for example, that the non-English-speaking parent or spouse or sibling is desperately looking for work, and the interpreter is the intermediary in an exchange with a potential employer. The interpreter must not only live the joy, hope, shame, disappointment, or financial anxiety of their family member;[25] they may feel that they are to some extent responsible for whether their family member gets the job.[26] We can also imagine the burden of being personally invested during very high-stakes medical encounters, such as when the subject matter is very intimate or potentially devastating. In situations like pandemics, interpreters are especially vulnerable, as they are the public-facing voice of their family members. When non-English speakers are required to risk their health in order to carry out some errand, their interpreters will also be required to take the same risks.

Interpreting is also a complex activity that demands quite a bit of skill. Most obviously, the words in one language need to correspond accurately to the words spoken in another language. In addition to this, the interpreter also interprets culture. They must grasp and navigate the cultural context that forms the background to the communication. An interpreter may be more aware than their family member of the two differing sets of cultural norms and attempt to navigate those norms in their communication. For example, the question of whether a potential employee should be "we" focused or "I" focused, or the degree of formality or deference one should show to an employer, may be culturally specific, as are nonverbal communications such as personal space, eye contact, and appearance.[27]

Beyond exercising this specialized knowledge, the interpreter must, in a crucial sense, also wield their own emotional agency on behalf of others. That is, language brokers cannot merely translate words. They must also operationalize targeted emotional expression to be effective. This is because the expression of emotion is part of the pragmatic context of effective speech acts. As Trip Glazer argues, emotions are only expressed when they are perceptually manifested—through the body, face, tone, pace, and energy of an expression. He explains, "Whether a speech act counts as an expression of emotion or not depends in every case on how the words are spoken . . . To be an expression of emotion, a speech act must be spoken with a tone of voice, facial expression, or gesture that makes an emotion perceptually manifest."[28] For example, consider having to communicate the following idea: "She says this has been an unusually hard month. She promises she will have the rent check for you next week." In such cases, the manner in which this content is conveyed will greatly influence how the message is taken up by the listener— whether the listener is likely to respond with compassion or skepticism or something else. In other words, in order to accurately render emotional meaning, interpreters must perform those meanings.

In this way, emotional expression is not only important to accuracy but also serves various crucial social functions. In particular, "emotions serve as incentives or deterrents for other individuals' social behavior" and "emotional communication evokes complementary and reciprocal emotions in others."[29] In other words, we utilize emotional expression to get other people to feel and do certain things. Therefore, an interpreter hoping to advance the interests of a dependent family member must utilize their emotional agency when navigating social situations on their loved one's behalf.

Sociologist Arlie Hochschild captures this aspect of emotional expression in her discussion of what she calls *emotion work*, which "requires one to induce or suppress feeling in order to sustain the outward countenance that produces the proper state of mind in others."[30] Any high-stakes communicative interaction requires attunement and responsiveness to the subtleties of tone, body language, word choice, mood, and so on. The interpreter is concerned to intervene in a myriad of ways and to an appropriate degree in order to advance the interests of their loved one, given the complexity of a communicative interaction. In managing their own feeling in order to manage others' feeling well, interpreters must emotionally gear up to complain, to negotiate, to plead, to impress, or to defend.

While all people manage feeling in themselves and others, and many jobs require this kind of labor specifically, Hochschild's concern is about the possible cost of the work to those who do it often: "The worker can become estranged or alienated from an aspect of self . . . that is used to do the work."[31] Specifically, Hochschild worries that by engaging in frequent emotional management, one loses touch with the part of the self that feels authentically.

A final point is that in language brokering, the interpreter is often concerned to mitigate racial stereotypes or prejudices that others might have about them and their family member. This aspect of emotion management has some resonance with Amia Srinivasan's notion of *affective injustice*: "the injustice of having to negotiate between one's apt emotional response to the injustice of one's situation and one's desire to better one's situation."[32] Srinivasan is particularly interested in the ways in which targets of racism must decide whether to allow themselves to experience justified rage or whether to bury their apt anger in order to better their situation. Perhaps they are concerned about countering the way in which they are already stereotyped as rageful, violent, or shrill.[33] The wrongness of this injustice, Srinivasan argues, lies "in the fact that it forces people, through no fault of their own, into profoundly difficult normative conflicts."[34] Interpreters must be concerned about the impact of their emotional presentation on the way in which they and their loved ones are being perceived by people whose perception of them may be shaped by racial stereotypes. Managing these perceptions may require setting aside more apt or authentic emotional engagement.

For all these reasons, acting on behalf of a loved one in ways one does not personally endorse can be morally burdensome. One cannot simply translate words and divest themselves from their emotional labor. In several ways, this type of work requires an investment, or commitment, of the self. The embodiment of emotional expression demands that, to some extent, the expression becomes one's own. One cannot merely go through the motions; one must care deeply enough to deliver a successful performance. In order to muster the intellectual and emotional energy to perform interpretation in a difficult situation when one does not want to for reasons of moral significance, one must consent to their heteronomy, to the betrayal of their own autonomy. The problem is not merely that the interpreter is experiencing coercion; rather, the interpreter is acting against their own will and must do so in a wholehearted kind of way.

III. The Interpreter's Moral Burden in Social Context

Up to this point, I've been making the case that the widespread lack of Spanish-language translation services generates a moral burden for members of the Latinx community. In this section, I make the case that this moral burden is also an injustice. That is, it contributes to the oppression of Latinxs. Many people face moral burdens, but not all are unjust. Some people may bear burdens that are greater than those that others have to bear, but they are circumstantial rather than the result of an unjust society. For example, being a parent can be morally burdensome. It typically involves a tremendous amount of emotional labor, the sense that one is never doing enough, that one is always failing a little bit, that one never has enough hours in the day to both provide for and nurture their children. People are parents at the expense of other commitments that they value. But we probably wouldn't want to describe all parents as victims of injustice. We can see, however, that *circumstantial* moral burdens can become *unjust* moral burdens. For instance, one might argue that a lack of affordable childcare in the United States unjustly burdens single parents—usually single mothers—and particularly those who struggle to make ends meet. In this case, the structure of society renders these women as a group more vulnerable to certain moral burdens.

We can distinguish unjust moral burdens from circumstantial ones by asking how much of a remainder would be left if the underlying social structure were to change. If affordable childcare were available, the unjust burden for low-income women would be alleviated to a significant degree. However, many of the moral burdens associated with parenting in general would remain.

In a society where there is race-based oppression, it is plausible that the interpreter's dilemma will be a facet of that oppression precisely because the nature and frequency of the dilemma is likely to be produced by an interlocking set of social practices. Marilyn Frye's classic analogy between oppression and a birdcage is useful for illustrating why. According to Frye, oppression is like the birdcage in that it must be understood as a network of systematically related barriers. Focusing on a single wire of the cage without seeing the other wires and the ways in which they connect will lead to confusion about why the bird doesn't simply fly away. Similarly, oppression is hard to see if one focuses on a single situation. The situation must be looked at in terms of its relation to larger schemes in order to be properly understood. Frye thus demonstrates how situations that are seemingly innocuous may actually be facets of oppression. At the same time, she is concerned that the term "oppression" not be overused or applied inappropriately to any encounter with an unpleasant or frustrating force, lest the concept lose its critical thrust. She gives us a set of questions that we can ask ourselves in order to test whether something should be thought of as oppressive. She writes, "One must look to the barrier or force and answer certain questions about it. Who constructs and maintains it? Whose interests are served by its existence? Is it part of a structure which tends to confine, reduce, and immobilize some group? Is the individual a member of the confined group?"[35] If one believes the United States has structures of race-based oppression, then the interpreter's dilemma will itself likely be a facet of wider oppression for the Latinx community.

Applying the analogy to the Latinx community, we might start by looking at the big picture—the birdcage as a whole. Latinxs fare worse than white Americans across many measures, including income, health, political leadership, incarceration, and education.[36] Nationwide, Latinxs are up to five times more likely to experience four or more factors in what is known as compound poverty—a series of unstable circumstances that build upon each other, making it difficult to create stability or escape intergenerational poverty. These circumstances include things like low income, lack of education, no health insurance, living in a poor area, and living within a jobless family.[37] These economic disparities are built upon a brutal history of anti-Latinx discrimination in the United States—a history that began with white settler colonialism and later included school segregation, nation-wide assimilation programs in schools (which included humiliating, frequently corporal, punishment for speaking Spanish), lynchings, mob violence, mass deportations of people regardless of their immigration status, and other kinds of systematic brutality.[38]

Language has been an important part of this history. It is a wire in the birdcage. Gloria Anzaldúa suggests that language manifests the legacy of colonialism, describing the deep shame that she and other people of the Borderlands come to feel around the way they speak, the various subtle and direct ways in which they are punished for the languages they do and do not speak, and whether they speak in the "right way." Language is one of the sites through which social hierarchies are revealed and reinforced. It is a site where cultures undergo marginalization or erasure. As I have shown in this chapter, it also becomes a site through which interpreters are morally burdened.

One reason that language is so heavily policed is because of its links to ethno-racial identity. Anzaldúa writes, "If you really want to hurt me, talk badly about my language. Ethnic identity is twin skin to linguistic identity—I am my language . . . and as long as I have to accommodate English speakers rather than having them accommodate me, my tongue will be illegitimate."[39] Insofar as language is deeply linked to social identity, it is subject to the same forces that oppress people on the basis of social identity: racism, ethnocentrism, and xenophobia.

My account of the moral burden that interpreters face shows how linguistic marginalization ripples beyond just noncitizens, beyond just the non-English-speaking population and throughout the Latinx community. Interpreters occupy the crossroads between mainstream society and the communities of cultural outsiders that make up the margins of that society. Insofar as immigrant communities suffer, so do these liminal members. They are an unseen part of the collateral damage of a white supremacist society. Their hardships, when isolated, may seem like the unfortunate price to pay for having family members who do not speak English. Interpreters themselves may even place significant blame on their non-English-speaking family members. I suggest that this blame is sometimes misdirected. When we put the hardship that interpreters undergo within the context of the many other ways in which Latinx people face barriers to full moral, legal, and social inclusion and recognition, we can see how the interpreter's moral burden constitutes a wire of the cage that surrounds Latinx communities.

What does this mean with respect to the responsibilities of societies in which this oppression occurs? Providing an adequate response to this question is beyond the scope of this chapter, but I would like to conclude by gesturing at what I believe is one of the implications of my account of the interpreter's dilemma. Some might say that although it is unfortunate that Latinx people face some disadvantages, they still have the biggest responsibility when it comes to learning the language. David Miller, for instance, argues that for the sake of social harmony and trust it is reasonable that societies require people to speak a dominant language in order to attain full membership.[40] He acknowledges that societies that make this demand may have reciprocal responsibilities to facilitate people's ability to meet the requirement, perhaps by offering English as a Second Language classes. But rarely is the argument made in the United States that anything beyond this and basic compliance with federal law is warranted.

It strikes me that this intuition—that it is Spanish-speaking immigrants who must adjust to English-speaking society—highlights the invisible privilege of Anglo-American society that allows the bearers of this privilege to assume that the unequal distribution of comforts, access, resources, and opportunities is morally acceptable. The assumption behind this lack of attention to the situation seems to be as follows: *Of course*, people who don't speak the dominant language must live segregated lives, devoid of access to the services and community resources that the rest of us enjoy!

I argue, to the contrary, that if we are concerned with social trust and social harmony, and if we are concerned to address the structures that marginalize immigrant communities, we should work toward a future in which interpreting services are widely available in public spaces, particularly in cities and towns with large immigrant populations. To meet this responsibility, schools must strengthen their foreign-language offerings and requirements in order to promote multilingualism among U.S. Americans. In addition, technology might play a role in alleviating some of the costs of meeting this responsibility. It is not so difficult to imagine walking into a local bank and having the opportunity to video chat with an associate who speaks your language, or trying a restaurant or coffee shop that you would have otherwise been too embarrassed to patronize because they now have digital menus that allow you to make requests of your server or explore the ingredients of a dish in your language. These social changes wouldn't only help to address the exclusion of immigrant communities. They would also help to alleviate the burden on the family-member interpreters who currently bear the weight of this labor.[41]

Notes

1. I thank Bob Fischer, Manuel Vargas, and Francisco Gallegos for their helpful comments on this project.
2. The term "translation" typically refers to written language, "interpretation" refers to spoken or real-time language communication, and "language brokering" refers more generally to the facilitation of communication between linguistically and/or culturally different parties. The literature emphasizes that "brokers mediate, rather than merely transmit information." See Lucy Tse, "Language Brokering in Linguistic Minority Communities: The Case of Chinese- and Vietnamese-American Students," *Bilingual Research Journal* 20, nos. 3–4 (Summer–Fall 1996): 485. In this chapter, I use the three terms loosely and sometimes interchangeably. I tend to use the terms "interpreting" and "brokering" rather than "translating," because I primarily have spoken exchanges in mind, but the translation of written documents is also a part of the labor that I'm describing here.
3. The LanguageLine Solutions Team, "Census Report: More Than 20 Percent of U.S. Residents Speak a Language Other Than English at Home," *LanguageLine.com*, September 20, 2017. http://blog.languageline.com/limited-english -proficient-census.
4. The United States Department of Justice, "Title VI of the Civil Rights Act of 1964 42 U.S.C. § 2000D ET SEQ," *Justice.gov*, updated January 22, 2016, https:// www.justice.gov/crt/fcs/TitleVI-Overview.
5. Health and Human Services Department, "Title VI of the Civil Rights Act of 1964; Policy Guidance on the Prohibition against National Origin Discrimination as It Affects Persons with Limited English Proficiency," Federal Register, October 30, 2000, https://www.federalregister.gov/documents/2000/08 /30/00-22140/title-vi-of-the-civil-rights-act-of-1964-policy-guidance-on-the -prohibition-against-national-origin.
6. Nigel Hall and Sylvia Sham, "Language Brokering as Young People's Work: Evidence from Chinese Adolescents in England," *Language and Education* 21, no. 1 (2007): 16–30.

7. See, for instance, Rebecca, Kaplan, "Bobby Jindal: 'Immigration without Assim-
    ilation Is Invasion," *CBSNews.com*, August 30, 2015, http://www.cbsnews.com
    /news/bobby-jindal-immigration-without-assimilation-is-invasion/; Shane
    Goldmacher, "Trump's English-Only Campaign," *Politico*, September 23, 2016,
    http://www.politico.com/story/2016/09/donald-trumps-english-only-campaign
    -228559; Nolan Feeny, "Sarah Palin Tells Immigrants 'Speak American' in Inter-
    view," *Time*, September 7, 2015, http://time.com/4024396/sarah-palin-speak
    -american-energy-department/; and "The 2016 Presidential Candidates on
    Official English," ProEnglish, 2017, https://proenglish.org/the-2016-presidential
    -candidates-on-official-english/.

8. Hall and Sham, "Language Brokering."

9. Yael Ponizovsky et al., "The Satisfaction with Life Scale: Measurement Invari-
    ance across Immigrant Groups," *European Journal of Developmental Psychology*
    10, no. 4 (2013): 526–32.

10. Josephine M. Hua and Catherine L. Costigan, "The Familial Context of Ado-
    lescent Language Brokering within Immigrant Chinese Families in Canada,"
    Journal of Youth and Adolescence 41, no. 7 (July 2012): 894–906.

11. Marjorie Faulstich Orellana, *Translating Childhoods: Immigrant Youth, Lan-
    guage, and Culture* (Piscataway, N.J.: Rutgers University Press, 2009).

12. Research has shown that "children who translate for parents acquire enhanced
    cognitive, social, emotional and interpersonal skills" due to being exposed to
    adultlike experiences on a regular basis. See Raymond Burielet al., "The Rela-
    tionship of Language Brokering to Academic Performance, Biculturalism, and
    Self-Efficacy among Latino Adolescents," *Hispanic Journal of Behavioral Sci-
    ences* 20, no. 3 (August 1998): 283–97. A survey based on 280 sixth-grade (aged
    around eleven to twelve) Latino family translators at a Chicago school found
    they performed significantly better on standardized tests of reading and math
    than their non-translating peers. See Marjorie Faulstich Orellana, "Responsi-
    bilities of Children in Latino Immigrant Homes," in "Understanding the Social
    Worlds of Immigrant Youth," special issue of *New Directions for Student Lead-
    ership* 2003, no. 100 (Winter 2003): 25–39. In addition to these enhanced
    skills, interpreting may also contribute to self-esteem. In one study, "researchers
    interviewed 25 Latino children of around 12 years who were translating for
    their parents. These children said their responsibilities made them feel proud,
    helpful and useful." See R. Corona, et al., "A Qualitative Analysis of What Latino
    Parents and Adolescents Think and Feel about Language Brokering," *Journal of
    Child and Family Studies* 21, no. 5 (2012): 788–98.

13. Faulstich Orellana, "Immigrant Youth's Contributions to Families and Society
    as Language and Culture Brokers." Lecture given at Fairhaven College, Western
    Washington University, December 8, 2009, https://vimeo.com/8059479.

14. Indeed, language brokers make it possible for their family members to sustain
    themselves as workers and consumers in a host country—a fact that should be
    considered when we contemplate the ways in which economies in the Global

North rely on immigrant labor. See Faulstich Orellana, *Translating Child-hoods*, 124

15. Faulstich Orellana, *Translating Childhoods*, 15.

16. Serene Khader, *Adaptive Preferences and Women's Empowerment* (New York: Oxford University Press, 2011), 113.

17. Khader, *Adaptive Preferences*, 113.

18. On a Reddit forum about interpreters' experiences, one woman's post captures this frustration:

> Ever since I turned 14, I was always ordered/asked to take care of billing issues, inquiries, etc. At first I didn't mind it as much. After all, it wasn't a frequent thing, and my parents couldn't speak English. What else could they do? As I grew older they lumped more translation responsibilities onto me but this time with verbal abuse. This would happen nearly every week. If I didn't take care of it immediately, I was a worthless daughter . . . Health insurance set-ups, phone bill errors, water bill is too high, mom got her name wrong on the dentist insurance. Would you call to see why [sic] got two cards instead of one? What does this stock letter say? Why can't you understand what this technical bank term means, you grew up in America!

> See u/AsianSecretary, "My parents are becoming too dependent on us. Please advise." Reddit.com, posted June 10, 2014. https://www.reddit.com/r/Asian ParentStories/comments/27t3to/my_parents_are_becoming_too_dependent _on_us/.

19. Inge van Nistelrooij, "Self Sacrifice and Care Ethics," in *Sacrifice in Modernity: Community, Ritual, Identity*, Studies in Theology and Religion 22, ed. Joachim Duyndam, Anna-Marie Korte, and Marcel Poorthuis (Leiden: Brill, 2017), 271.

20. Buriel et al., "Relationship of Language Brokering."

21. Faulstich Orellana, "Language Brokering," *MarjorieFaulstichOrellana.com*, accessed January 16, 2020, http://www.marjoriefaulstichorellana.com/archive /language-brokering/. Edited for clarity.

22. Joshua K. Hartshorne, Joshua B. Tenenbaum, and Steven Pinker, "A Critical Period for Second Language Acquisition: Evidence from 2/3 Million English Speakers," *Cognition* 177 (August 2018): 263–77.

23. Nancy Sherman, *Afterwar: Healing the Moral Wounds of Our Soldiers* (New York: Oxford University Press, 2015).

24. Sherman, *Afterwar*, 8.

25. As the expression "don't kill the messenger" implies, the intermediary often bears the weight of their loved one's response to difficult news.

26. Although a professional translator is not as personally invested as someone who brokers for a family member, research indicates that those working empa-thetically with survivors of trauma—such as therapists, social workers, nurses, and lawyers—can still experience vicarious trauma. See K. M. Palm, M. A.

Polusny, and V. M. Follette, "Vicarious Traumatization: Potential Hazards and Interventions for Disaster and Trauma Workers," *Prehospital and Disaster Medicine* 19, no. 1 (January–March 2004), 74. Vicarious trauma can produce PTSD-like symptoms. Interpreters sometimes act as intermediaries between victims of trauma and these professionals, but not much work has been done on the ways in which they take on this trauma. Some studies indicate that interpreters' shared experiences with those for whom they are interpreting creates heightened sensitivity to others. See Mailee Lor, "Effects of Client Trauma on Interpreters: An Exploratory Study of Vicarious Trauma," St. Catherine University, *Sophia*, Spring 2012, https://sophia.stkate.edu/cgi/viewcontent.cgi?article =1053&context=msw_papers. We might surmise that these effects are even more pronounced for those interpreting for family members.

27. Faulstich Orellana gives us an example of this cultural shifting in her research. She refers to a fifteen-year-old boy named Sammy, who describes his experience language brokering between an English-speaking woman and fieldworkers on a golf course. Sammy remembers that when he was talking to the woman, he would use the word "nice," but when talking to the workers, he would use the word "*chido*," or "cool." Sammy was concerned about adapting his level of formality for the comfort of each of the speakers. See Faulstich Orellana, "Immigrant Youth's Contributions."

28. Trip Glazer, "Looking Angry and Sounding Sad: The Perceptual Analysis of Emotional Expression," *Synthese* 194 (2017): 26.

29. Dacher Keltner and Jonathan Haidt, "Social Functions of Emotions at Four Levels of Analysis," *Cognition and Emotion* 13, no. 5 (1995): 505–21 (511).

30. Arlie Russel Hochschild, *The Managed Heart: Commercialization of Human Feeling* (Berkeley: University of California Press, 2012), 7.

31. Hochschild, *The Managed Heart*, 7.

32. Amia Srinivasan, "The Aptness of Anger," *Journal of Political Philosophy* 26, no. 2 (2018): 135.

33. Srinivasan, "The Aptness of Anger," 136.

34. Srinivasan, 136.

35. Srinivasan, 15.

36. Samuel Stebbins and Evan Comen, "Economic Inequality: The Worst States for Hispanics and Latinos," *USAToday.com*, January 19, 2018, https://www.usa today.com/story/money/economy/2018/01/19/economic-inequality-worst -states-hispanics-and-latinos/1035606001/.

37. Gillian B. White, "Poverty, Compounded," *Atlantic*, April 16, 2016, https://www .theatlantic.com/business/archive/2016/04/how-poverty-compounds/478539/.

38. Erin Blakemore, "The Brutal History of Anti-Latino Discrimination in America," *History.com*, September 27, 2017; updated August 29, 2018, https://www.history .com/news/the-brutal-history-of-anti-latino-discrimination-in-america.

39. Gloria Anzaldúa, *Borderlands/La Frontera: The New Mestiza* (San Francisco: Aunt Lute Books, 1987): 59

40. David Miller, *Strangers in Our Midst: The Political Philosophy of Immigration* (Cambridge, Mass.: Harvard University Press, 2016).
41. An aspect of my claim regarding the responsibility to accommodate non-English speakers is that this responsibility extends to Spanish-language speakers, in particular. There are several reasons for this, including the simple fact that it is the most spoken second language in the United States, so there are more people with the need; Spanish speakers lived in what is now considered the United States prior to the existence of the nation, so that Spanish cannot be called a "foreign" language; and, as I am arguing here, because of the history and ongoing oppression of this particular demographic.

CHAPTER 11

Jus Sanguinis vs. Jus Soli

On the Grounds of Justice

EDUARDO MENDIETA

Introduction

Section 3 of Article III of the Constitution of the United States explicitly defines a special type of crime:

> Treason against the United States shall consist only in levying war against them, or in adhering to their enemies, giving them aid and comfort. No person shall be convicted of treason unless on the testimony of two witnesses to the same overt act, or on confession in open Court. The Congress shall have power to declare the punishment of treason, but no Attainder of Treason shall work Corruption of Blood, or Forfeiture except during the Life of the Person attainted.[1]

Three years after the aforementioned was signed and approved as part of the Constitution of the United States, Congress enacted what has been called the "Crimes Act of 1790" and "Federal Criminal Code of 1790." This Act states that

> If any person or persons, owing allegiance to the United States of America, shall levy war against them, or shall adhere to their enemies, giving them aid and comfort within the United States, or elsewhere, and shall be thereof

convicted on confession in open Court, or on the testimony of two witnesses to the same overt act of the treason whereof he or they shall stand
indicted, such person or persons shall be adjudged guilty of treason against
the United States, and *shall suffer death*; and that if any person or persons,
having knowledge of the commission of any of the treasons aforesaid, shall
conceal, and not, as soon as may be, disclose and make known the same to
the President of the United States, or some one of the Judges thereof, or to
the President or Governor of a particular State, or some one of the Judges
or Justices thereof, such person or persons, on conviction, shall be adjudged
guilty of misprision of treason, and shall be imprisoned not exceeding seven
years, and fined not exceeding one thousand dollars. (emphasis added)[2]

Treason is thus defined as a crime against the United States that is punish-
able by death, although in contrast to European nations, acts of treason are
limited to the perpetrator and not the entire family and descendants of the
person judged a traitor. But what do we call it when the nation commits acts
of war against some of its citizens, and sides with enemies, avowed adver-
saries, and despisers, of some of its citizens? What do we call it when the
nation breaks faith and betrays its citizens by treating them as enemy com-
batants, as resident aliens, in fact, as suspect citizens, as unworthy citizens,
as dispensable and contemptible citizens? These are important questions to
ask, particularly when we consider that in 1791 the constitution would be
amended with the "Bill of Rights," which can be understood as a compen-
dium of "rights against the state," or rights that limit the power of the state.

When we think about the fact that already in the original constitution,
and in one of the first Acts of the first Congress, the question of punishment
by death for "treason" is explicitly addressed, but not that of the betrayal of
the state of its people, we are confronted with a unique prism through which
to see the evolution of U.S. conceptions and practices of citizenship. In fact,
the power to put to death for treason is a very striking feature of the U.S.
constitutional jurisgenetic corpus, which is made more notable by the fact
that the articles of the constitution are then followed by the amendments
from 1791—that is, the Bill of Rights. It is in this Bill of Rights that something
like a counterpart to the punishment for treason could have been articulated
in terms of betrayal and treason by the state. What should strike us is that
citizens can be held criminally liable for "betraying" the state, but the "state"
itself can't be held liable for violating the rights of persons, and after 1868, the

rights of citizens. It is only more recently that citizens have been empowered to "sue" the state for violating their rights or for failing to protect them. The state is now held liable for violating the rights of citizens, and while it cannot be called treason, you can say that when the state abridges, disregards, neglects, or fails to protect the rights of citizens, it is itself engaging in treason, a crime made all the more heinous by the fact that it is committed by the putative protector of the liberty and equality of citizens. After World War II, the legal categories of "crimes against the peace" and "crimes against humanity" were introduced at the Nuremberg Trial of Nazi criminals—in this case, the assumption was that the German state was acting treasonously not only against other states but also against its own citizens, by denationalizing them and denaturalizing them, thus rendering Jews, Gypsies, and others stateless.[3] Perhaps by the same token, we ought to be developing a notion of our own state's crimes against its citizens.

Foremost German legal philosopher and constitutional scholar Ernst-Wolfgang Böckenförde, who was also a German federal court judge, addressed the betrayal and treason by the German state of its citizens in an important essay dating from 1997. The title of the essay says it all: "The Persecution of the German Jews as a Civic Betrayal." Let me elaborate further. Böckenförde writes, beautifully and powerfully,

> What happened to the German Jews between 1933 and 1945, their disenfranchisement and persecution rising to systematic annihilation, was organized by the state towards its own citizens, particularly loyal ones; and to that extent that it became known, it was carried out without any broad opposition or at least revulsion and outrage among the population, the very compatriots of the Jewish citizens. That constitutes the betrayal and breach of trust, the disgrace of the disgrace of the Jewish persecution in Germany, apart from its criminal nature . . . Civic Courage-civic bravery, acting as *citoyen*—is what sustains civic society and creates it in the first place. If everyone withdraws upon himself to live only his own life, if fellow citizens and what happens to them cease to matter, civic society is betrayed from within and dissolves.[4]

We can be outraged that someone would betray our state, but why not be more outraged when the state betrays its citizens? What happened under Jim Crow, and then in the aftermath of the partly successful civil rights movements, was a civic betrayal of black Americans—and we continue to betray them. This is what we are witnessing when so-called "anchor babies" are demonized, vilified, criminalized. So much is failing here: our civic imagination is failing, our sense of civic outrage, our sense of civic loyalty and solidarity. We do not have a sense of civic courage and sense of civic hope. I can't tell you how it makes me shudder with outrage and disgust and disappointment and dread to see what is happening at the border, but also what happens when police profile Latino/as, or when people yell at some of us when we speak Spanish, spitting in our faces, telling us to go back to where we came from. The border has become the ground of our civic betrayal and the failure of our civic imagination and courage. This border has moved to the center of our civic life.

Indeed, the United States has a long history of betraying its citizens: African American, Japanese, Native Americans, Hawaiʻians, Puerto Ricans, Jews, and more recently Mexican Americans, in particular, and Latino/as in general. Donald Trump launched his presidential candidacy with an attack on the character and worthiness of Mexicans to be in the United States, thus denigrating the citizenship of Mexican Americans and other Latinos. To recall, Trump questioned the ability of Judge Gonzalo Curiel to be impartial in a class-action suit by students who charged that they had been defrauded by Trump University; his basis for doing so was that Curiel was "Mexican," although he was born in the United States. Trump's presidency was defined not solely by the relentless challenge of the constitution and the separation of powers but most specifically by his racial animus directed at African Americans and Mexicans and Mexican Americans most consistently and relentlessly. The hysterical chanting of "build the Wall," the longest shutdown in the history of the U.S. government in the winter of 2019 over the funding of the Wall, the assault by ICE (Immigration and Customs Enforcement) on immigrant families, the moves in Congress to repeal or qualify the Fourteenth Amendment to the Constitution to disenfranchise so-called anchor babies—all this, and more, projected the nauseous shadow of deep dislike and has fueled hatred of Mexicans and Mexican Americans. The attempt to revoke DACA, the separation of immigrant children from their parents, and the extradition of all kinds of both legal and irregular immigrants also reflects the treason and betrayal by the government of the United States of one of its largest minorities, Latino/as in general and Mexican Americans in particular.

Trump and Trumpism, however, are the culmination of by now nearly four decades of assault on the worthiness and legitimacy of Latinx citizenship. More emphatically, Trumpism should be read as exemplary of what political philosopher Amy Reed-Sandoval calls the "illegalization" of *socially undocumented* citizens and noncitizens of Mexican and Latinx backgrounds.[5] The process of rendering someone illegal comes on the heels of decades of socially undocumented oppression. Leo R. Chavez, in his brief but powerful *Anchor Babies and the Challenge of Birthright Citizenship*, which expands and updates his earlier *The Latino Threat: Constructing Immigrants, Citizens, and the Nation*, chronicles these four decades of the fabrication of Latinos as a threat, beginning with the discourse of their inability to assimilate in the eighties and culminating with the recent attempt to either revoke or amend the Fourteenth Amendment.[6] As Reed-Sandoval shows, however, the fabrication of the "Latino Threat" extends further back into the middle of the twentieth century, with the infamous "Operation Wetback" of 1954 that deported as many as 1.3 million Mexicans and Mexican Americans, many of whom were U.S. citizens.[7]

Trumpism, as a political phenomenon, however, raises a series of important questions about the nature of citizenship in the United States in the twenty-first century. It puts in relief what I will call "the unfinished work of building citizenship" in the United States, not as an aberration but as the culmination of a political and social dynamic. Trumpism, additionally, is the distillation of a particular type of attempt to roll back the accomplishments in the task of building citizenship in the United States. This attempt has taken the form of frontal attack on the Fourteenth Amendment, the constitutional pillar of equal citizenship, guaranteed by law and under the equal protection of the law, which furthermore and most distinctly is granted on the basis of birthright and not descent. The Fourteenth Amendment enshrined into the constitution, and thus into the law of the land, the principle of "Birthright Citizenship."[8] Birthright citizenship constitutionalizes the principle of citizenship by jus soli and rejects the principle of citizenship by jus sanguinis. In this chapter, I want to consider why the juridification of jus soli into the vault of U.S. citizenship is a revolutionary principle that takes the conception of citizenship to new moral and legal heights. Jus soli, as a foundational principle of equal citizenship under the protection of the law, is the complement, the other face, of the Universal Declaration of Human Rights. Jus soli is the ground of the justice promised by both human rights and the rights of citizens declared by the French in 1789.

In order to arrive at this conclusion, I want to, first, focus on what I call the hysterical ethno-racial animus against Mexicans, Mexican Americans, and Latinos through a brief revisiting of an important moment in the attempt to reconfigure the U.S. political imaginary by Samuel P. Huntington, who singled out of Mexican Americans not only as a problem but also as a threat to the very core "identity" and geographical integrity of the United States. Huntington's thesis, however, is not the most egregious chapter in the history of the "fabrication" of Latino/as as a threat.

Second, I want to visit some key moments in the history of citizenship so as to build up the idea that jus soli as the key principle of U.S. citizenship is a unique and unparalleled expansion and accomplishment of a very important, today perhaps the most important, political institution of political membership. Indeed, what I hope will become explicit is that "citizenship" remains an "unfinished" project. Third, and finally, I conclude that unless we abolish all forms of jus sanguinis, the revolutions begun with the American, French, and Haitian revolutions in the eighteenth century remain also "unfinished."

I. The Fabrication of the Latino Threat

In late fall 2000, Harvard political scientist and public intellectual Samuel P. Huntington published two articles, one on the website of the conservative Center for Immigration Studies[9] and the second in the *American Enterprise* magazine, laying out his analysis that Mexican Americans presented a distinct challenge, nay a "problem," to the United States.[10] The arguments first sketched in these two articles were further elaborated and articulated in a lengthy and pugilist feature article published during the spring of 2004 in *Foreign Policy*. The long polemical essay is titled "The Hispanic Challenge" and begins as following: "The persistent inflow of Hispanic immigrants threatens to divide the United States into two peoples, two cultures, and two languages. Unlike past immigrant groups, Mexicans and Latinos have not assimilated into mainstream U.S. culture, forming instead their own political and linguistic enclaves—from Los Angeles to Miami—and rejecting the Anglo-Protestant values that built the American dream. The United States ignores this challenge at its peril."[11]

This is without question quite an alarmist proclamation. I need not note that this was in 2004, barely three years after 9/11. The United States had just launched the so-called Second Gulf War, and while the occupation of Iraq was just shy of a year old, U.S. soldiers were already coming under attack. The rumblings of Iraqi resistance were loudly audible. In this context, in which U.S. soldiers were already fighting in Afghanistan in the midst of a "global war on terror," the publication of this incendiary article was shocking. Indeed, Huntington published in a very notable and highly respected journal, which he helped found, what in fact was a call to arms, so much so that I want to suggest that this piece was instrumental in giving voice to the "white nativism" that would later elect Donald Trump.

However, before I turn to Huntington's piece, I want to exegete the cover of the issue of *FP* (as the journal *Foreign Policy* is known) in which it appeared. On the cover we see a young adult, mestizo male, perhaps of Mexican, but in general of Latin American background. His hand is over his heart holding, tenuously, with extended fingers, a small U.S. flag. He appears to be at a swearing-in ceremony, perhaps at his naturalization ceremony, when he finally becomes a U.S. citizen. I remember very clearly this cover, for I bought it when it first came out. If you look closely, the man's fingernails are long and dirty. The young adult looks awkward in his tie—and he is not clutching the flag but just barely pressing it down with the tips of his fingers. The title of the cover reads, "José, Can You See?" Now, I doubt that *FP* was literally addressing "José"—and it is noteworthy that the editors used the diacritic on José's name, as if to underscore a point. What is it that José is supposed to see? If José had turned to page thirty, where Huntington begins with his ominous three-sentence paragraph, he would have realized, he would have seen that he was a peril, a threat, someone who is a clear and present danger to the United States. Given that the editors of *FP* undoubtedly know who their readership is, the question really should read, "Can't you see what José is doing to our nation?"

Huntington begins his piece by regurgitating the myths about the origins of the United States: that it was "created" in the seventeenth and eighteenth centuries by settlers who were "overwhelmingly" white, British, and Protestant. In the eighteenth century, after defining the colonies on this continent along racial, ethnic, cultural, and religious lines, they, the founding fathers, began to define it along "ideological lines." These white, Protestant males created a "creed" that would both justify and legitimate their independence from the "Mother" country, England. The creed, however, was "the product of a distinct Anglo-Protestant culture." The basic tenets of this creed were framed by "key elements" of that Anglo-Protestant culture: the English language, Christianity, religious commitment, reverence to the English concept of the "rule of law," and the "dissenting Protestant values of individualism, the work ethic, and the belief that humans have the ability and duty to try to create a heaven on earth, a 'city on a hill.'"[12] The creed, then, has at its core the following: English monolingualism, an unwavering commitment to Christianity, a reverence for the "English" respect for the law, and, of course, individualism, deference to the work ethic, and, above all, a religiously fueled sociopolitical utopianism. All these values, norms, principles, and hopes, according to Huntington, are rooted in, they originate, they emanate, and thus belong to a particular racial, cultural, racial, religious profile: the Anglo-Protestant male. Perhaps we should shake our heads in incredulity and disbelief. Perhaps Huntington had drunk for too long at the well of racist imaginaries.

It is this creed, this Rosetta stone, this set core of political, economic, religious, and racial values and profile that Hispanics threaten. Why and how? Huntington is not an uninformed scholar, as is evidenced by the fact that he taught at Harvard for many years. He had teams of researchers at his disposal (as we learn later), and thus, he has an analytics that demonstrates, or aims to persuade his readers, why Hispanics are an immediate, real, and present danger. Although begrudgingly, for there were waves and waves of immigrants who came to join the project of building the glorious "city on the hill," Huntington must frame his invective against Hispanics in terms of how their pattern of immigration differs from those earlier ones. The linchpin of his argument hinges precisely on a selective and distorting reading of the ways in which the United States was a nation of immigrants, who, however, were assimilated into the creed, who cast off their prior identities by becoming members of the Anglo-Protestant project. In fact, the reason why Hispanics are a threat is because "contemporary Mexican and, more broadly, Latin American immigration is without precedent in U.S. history . . . [Then, an interesting slippage in the narrative takes place, barely a sentence later, when Huntington continues] Mexican [note Mexican and not simply Latin American] differs from past immigration and most other contemporary immigration due to a combination of six factors: contiguity, scale, illegality, regional concentration, persistence, and historical presence."[13] The slippage is not unintentional. It is deliberate, as it aims to conflate Hispanic with Mexican and, at the same time, cover over the intricacies but also glaring facts about the convoluted intimacy of Hispanics with the United States.

Let me briefly gloss these six factors. Contiguity: the United States shares a very long border with Mexico, one that was traced, made, and now militarized and fortified by the United States. This border grew with the Mexican-American War (1846–1848), which resulted in the United States taking half of Mexico's territory. The United States also took possession of Puerto Rico, after the Spanish-American War, and then gave special immigrant status to Cubans, who because of the Cuban Revolution in 1959 became exemplars and geopolitical pawns in the Cold War. It can be argued that the United States has labored to increase that contiguity for over two hundred years. Scale: in absolute numbers—that is, in numbers relative to the actual population of the United States—during the late nineteenth and early twentieth centuries, the United States received more immigrants than it is presently receiving from Mexico and Latin America. The number of undocumented Mexicans has waxed and waned in accordance with the needs of U.S. labor markets, but it is also a legal irregularity that is rooted in centuries of labor, economic, cultural, and familiar relations that reach across generations. It is important to note that the construct "illegal" to refer to Mexican migrants is a relatively recent invention, belonging to the last quarter of the twentieth century. Regional concentration is also a rhetorical mirror, as demographers very well know that not all "Hispanic" regional concentrations are the same. "Hispanics" in Connecticut are very different from those in Miami, from those in San Antonio, from those in Los Angeles. The only thing that needs to be said about persistence is that this persistence was inaugurated with the Monroe Doctrine and continued relentlessly until very recently, when, because of the Gulf Wars, the United States diverted its attention away from Latin America. By historical presence, Huntington means, in an oxymoronic or performative self-contradictory way, that "Mexicans" have actually been present since the birth of the United States, since he has to acknowledge that almost a quarter of the United States was taken from Mexico. It is a performative contradiction because they can't be aliens and yet have been already present. Of course, Huntington does not deal with NAFTA, which in 2004 had been in effect for a decade, having thus further settled that "historical presence."

I am not doing justice to Huntington's piece, surely. The *FP* article was a long but also highly condensed version of an entire book, which was published later in 2004, with the title *Who Are We? The Challenges to America's*

National Identity.[14] In fact, "The Hispanic Challenge" was a salvo, an intellectual Molotov cocktail, hurled at the U.S. public sphere at a moment when we were facing several actual war fronts abroad. I want to enter here an important parenthesis. Huntington was the U.S. political philosopher of the armed forces. His career began in 1957, when he published *The Soldier and the State: The Theory and Politics of Civil-Military Relations*, a book that, along with Michael Walzer's *Just and Unjust Wars*, has become canonical text for the U.S. Armed Forces.[15] In 2004, among the first casualties of the second Gulf War was a Hispanic American soldier. As journalist Gabriel Lerner documents in his *Huffington Post* essay, "The Iraq Conflict: The War That Changed Latinos," Latinos—that is Huntington's Hispanics—made up 11 percent of the total casualties, comparable to their enrollment in the armed forces.[16] This parenthesis is about the many lives of Hispanics that were lost in that war and many others. And it is, above all, about the American dream. Among the first casualties in the second Gulf War was Jose Gutierrez (he was either the first or second fallen, along with Therell Shane Childer), a kid who had come from Guatemala, was undocumented, and joined the army as a way to get his citizenship. He was twenty-two. He had a dream, and he was willing to put his life on the line. He earned his citizenship posthumously. Now, close parenthesis.

Huntington concludes "The Hispanic Challenge" with a gloss on Lionel Sosa's book *The Americano Dream*, an inspirational book for entrepreneurs.[17] Here one must wonder why a Harvard scholar would want to quote from a book that can only be found in bookshops in airports in the business section; was it because of the perversion of American dream by that contaminating "o", that Spanglish version of the "American," as an adjective, dream? In any event, this is how the essay ends on page forty-five, after fifteen pages of a minute font: "There is only the American dream created by an Anglo-Protestant society. Mexican Americans will share [I want to underscore this word 'share'] in that dream and in that society if they dream in English."[18] Those are two breathtaking sentences. America only has one dream, which was created by one race and one religion, and it can only be dreamt in English! I wonder what Jose Gutierrez would have said had he read that sentence.

Samuel P. Huntington has been shaping the lexicon of our public vocabulary, if not since 1957, at the very least since 1996, when he published the also highly polemical and debated *Clash of Civilizations and the Remaking of the World Order*, which many in Washington took to be a prophetic text that presaged 9/11.[19] In fact, this text pitted Islam as the great new enemy of civilization. It is not difficult to see that *Who Are We?* is a rhetorical reply of *The Clash of Civilization*, but now brought home. The next *Clash of Civilizations* is not on the world stage but on the home territory, the heartland. It is beyond the present context to elaborate how these two books work on the same semantics and syntax of the American "social imaginary," but I do want to focus, briefly, on three distinct linkages and continuities, which, however, allows me to deepen my argument about the interdependence between a religious imaginary and a racial imaginary that distorts our democratic imaginary.

First, and as I already noted above, Huntington is preoccupied with the way in which the Anglo-Protestant culture that created "America" is being threatened by Hispanics in general and Mexicans in particular. At the core of his racial-ethnic-monolingual culture is what he calls the distinct Protestant character of U.S. Protestantism, which, quoting Edmund Burke, he identifies as the "dissidence of dissent." Burke, referring to Americans, writes, "[They] are Protestants, and of that kind which is most averse to all implicit submission of mind and opinion. All Protestantism, even the most cold and passive, is a sort of dissent. But the religion most prevalent in our northern colonies is a refinement on the principle of resistance: it is the dissidence of dissent, and the Protestantism of the Protestant religion."[20] Implicit in the so-called Latino threat is the challenge to and potential dissolution of the "dissidence of dissent" of all those Catholics who would bring their submissive and deferential religious attitudes to the United States. It is difficult to square this claim with the long history of social activism, dissent, protest, and radical transformation in the history of the United States that was inspired not just by illiterate slaves, subordinated women, poor farmers from Ireland, Italy, and Mexico, without even mentioning the long history of Jewish and Catholic-inspired dissent.

The second linkage has to do with Huntington's discussion of "white nativism." As in the *FP* piece, where a whole page was devoted to it, in *Who Are We?* there are nearly seven pages on this topic. In the book, Huntington refers to "white nativism" as a "rebellion" in quotes, but according to him, it is "not difficult to see" why white people, whether poor or not, might be motivated to "rebel." Among some of their reasons are the emergence of exclusivist sociopolitical movements to challenge their socioeconomic status; the loss of their jobs to immigrants and foreign countries; and—now I am directly quoting—"the perversion of their culture, the displacement of their language, and the erosion or even evaporation of the historical identity of their country."[21] Huntington closes his apologetics for "white nativism" thusly: "The most powerful stimulus to white nativism, however, is likely to be the threat to their language, culture, and power that whites see coming from the expanding demographic, social, economic, and political role of Hispanics in American society."[22] This is nothing but an apologia for the militaristic and vitriolic racial supremacy that we saw culminate in the Unite the Right rally, turned white supremacy riot, which took place in Charlottesville, on August 11–12, 2017, as well as the riot that led to the storming of the United States Capitol on January 6, 2021, during which Trump supporters carried Confederate flags.[23]

Third, and finally, Huntington closes his book with a section titled "America in the World: Cosmopolitan, Imperial and/or National?" There are three possible paths that the United States can pursue as it faces the *Clash of Civilizations*. It can opt to become cosmopolitan—that is, aim to assimilate all cultures—but in the process give up its core Anglo-Protestant culture and identity. It can opt to become an empire, and thus force everyone to be like it, but in the process, its core Anglo-Protestant culture would be compromised and diluted. Or, thirdly, it can hold on to its core identity, pursue the path of nations that are faithful to their identity, and be neither cosmopolitan nor imperial. This is how Huntington articulates the difference among the options:

> Cosmopolitanism and imperialism attempt to reduce or to eliminate the social, political, and cultural differences between America and other societies. A national approach would recognize and accept what distinguishes America from those societies. America cannot become the world and still be America. Other people cannot become America and still be themselves. America is different and that difference is defined in large part by its Anglo-Protestant culture and religiosity. The alternative to cosmopolitanism and imperialism is nationalism devoted to the preservation and enhancement of those qualities that have defined America since its founding.[24]

This is the rhetoric of "America First" and "Make America Great Again." This is the rhetoric of white nativism that demeans, defaces, criminalizes, and rejects the cultural, sociopolitical, economic contributions of African

Americans, Native Americans, Jews, women, gays, and, of course, Latinos. I concur with what José Casanova claimed at a conference at which we were both speakers, namely that Trump was the first candidate to bring together two great civilizational enemies: Muslims and Mexicans/Latinos. I want to close this section by underscoring two things. First, note the power of religious identities in Huntington's image and imaginary of "America." Here race and religion are one. We thus ought to speak of Huntington's racialization of religion, which can evidently cut many ways: Muslims, for instance, in this racial/religious imaginary are terrorists, while Mexicans are lazy, criminal, and uncouth, and so on. Second, notice the biologistic-organicist reduction of the identity of America. America's identity, vitality, future hinges on the purity and inviolability of its racial-religious body: the Anglo-Protestant body.[25]

II. The Unfinished Project of Citizenship

The concept of citizenship that informs, at the very least, Western culture is one that harkens back to the Greeks. The word "citizen" is rooted in the Latin *civitas*, the latter being a translation of *politeia*, from which we get the terms "politics," "political," "police," but also "polite" and thus "impolite." In Greek, politeia refers to not simply the polis but to the web of relations that being a member of the polis entails. Politeia means "on government," or "on ruling," or on the matters of the polis. When Cicero wrote his own version of Plato's *Politeia*, he titled it *De Republica* (On the Republic), which interestingly is the way now we know Plato's *Politeia*, namely as the *Republic*. In Greek, however, "citizenship" is synonymous with politeia. The polis creates the condition of citizenship, and this in turn defines what it means to be a member of a polis. We could say then that politeia by definition includes its performance in terms of citizenship. No polis without citizen, and no citizenship without politics within the polis.

Following a bit in the tracks left by historian Peter Riesenberg's synoptic *Citizenship in the Western Tradition: Plato to Rousseau*, I would note that the Greek notion of citizenship begins to accrue meaning, and be defined, by Cleisthenes's reforms of Greek democracy in 506 BC.[26] Key in Cleisthenes's reforms was the shift from membership in a *gene* or clan to membership in the polis as the condition for claiming membership and thus rights and privileges within the growing cities in the Greek world. While Greek citizenship did retain an element of descent, Cleisthene's reforms unleashed an important dynamic that saw membership in terms of an office that calls for duties and responsibilities rather than something that was granted only by way of blood descent.[27] Pericles, half a century later, as one of the greatest orators and rulers of Athens, presided over the Athenian Enlightenment, expanded Greek notions about citizenship by expanding the rights and privileges of what in Greek were known as *Metics* (i.e., resident aliens). Among the famous *metics* whom Pericles invited to Athens is Cephalus, of Plato's *Politeia* fame. What is noteworthy is that while Plato's *Republic*, to use the now standardized translation of *Politeia*, is the fountainhead of Western political philosophy, this book is not the source for any significant contributions to our understanding of citizenship. That honor goes to Aristotle, who was not native to Athens, was considered a metics, and in fact had to leave Athens after Plato's death because he was seen as a possible spy from Macedonia.

Aristotle's *Politics*, which incidentally is presented as an explicit critique of Plato's *Republic*, actually takes up the question of who is a citizen, or what makes a citizen, a definition that Plato seems to have failed to provide. In book 3, chapter 2, we find what I take to be a remarkable definition of citizenship. In this book, Aristotle acknowledges that there are many types of citizens depending on the polis and after the rules of the polis have changed, as was the case after a revolution, and Aristotle refers specifically to Cleisthenes's reforms. Thus, we have citizens who are so decreed by political-legal fiat, those who were naturalized, those who are descendants of old members of the polis, and so on. Aristotle specifically highlights that there are many different types of citizens. He is interested in what defines the citizen as such and concludes that, as he writes, "the citizen was defined by the fact of his holding some kind of rule or office—he who holds a certain sort of office fulfills our definition of a citizen" (*Politics*, 1276a 2-5).[28] The citizen is he who governs. As Reisenberg put it, "Not origin but action is what makes a man a citizen, at least in a philosophical, analytical sense."[29] What one does, rather than what one is, is what determines one's citizenship. In Aristotle, citizenship is a way of dwelling within a polis; it is not a biological or ontological condition. It is from this definition that civic republican conceptions of citizenship descend to our day.

As was already noted, our notions of citizen and citizenship revert to Cicero's translation of Plato and Aristotle's usage of *Politeia* into *De Republica* or, alternatively, and perhaps more accurately, *res publica*, on the matters and concerns of the polis or republic. Cicero is surely perhaps one of the most important sources for our contemporary conceptions of citizenship. For him, as it is clear from his numerous works on what today we call political philosophy, citizenship is not simply the institution of entitlements and rights but above all a vocation, the exercise of the moral and political excellence of the human being. Citizenship is the vocation of the social animal, his calling, so to speak. For Cicero, and the stoics in general, citizenship is the exercise of man's cosmopolitan dwelling, and it is thus exemplary of our social existence. Like for Aristotle, citizenship is not a *potentia* but a *dunamis*, not a passive state but a kinetic form of existence, civic existence at its height. In fact, in Cicero there is a linkage between citizenship and what we could call civic poetics. This is clearly evident in one of Cicero's most famous speeches, his *Pro Archia Poeta*, given in defense of Archias the poet, who was threatened with disenfranchisement. Cicero rose to his defense and produced one of the most celebrated panegyrics to a poet as well as to the role poetry plays in the civic life of a people, a republic. Cicero challenged the charges to disenfranchise Archias, demonstrating their falsity. Yet he spends most of the speech arguing why, even if Archias had not already been a Roman citizen, due to all the reasons why non-natives of Rome could and would have been made citizens, he should be made one on the grounds of his contributions to poetry. By bestowing on such an exemplary poet the protection of its citizenship, he would do honor to Rome in the annals of human memory by the tribute it paid to the muse of poetry. Cicero added something to Aristotle's notion of citizenship that remains important to our day, and that is that citizenship is the means for the celebration of the creative aspect of our social existence. Citizenship is both an expression and means for the exaltation of our poetic capacities.

During the Middle Ages, after the collapse of the Holy Roman Empire in the West, there was a hiatus in the philosophical contributions to our conception of citizenship. It can be argued that during this period there occurred a redirection of the aims of civil loyalty away from polis and community toward the spiritual self and the *civitate dei*. In fact, Augustine in his famous and momentous *City of God* juxtaposes the city of man against the city of God—the former with its narcissistic and hedonistic love of the material self, and the latter with its selfless love of God. Christian spiritual citizenship in a city "to come" advocated withdrawal from the mundane, materialistic, and corrupt affairs of the city of man, albeit while postulating that we were de jure, if not de facto, citizens of this divine and saintly city. In fact, Christian political thinking, at least as it is expressed in Augustine, synthesized Ciceronian and Aristotelian notions of citizenship into a universalistic creed: We are all citizens of an invisible city—the city of God. To the active and poetic dimension of citizenship is added a spiritual dimension: citizenship becomes a type of sacrament, a sacramental duty.

Still, as we proceed along the Middle Ages, we see the revival of the cities through commerce, and citizenship becomes decisive for the merchant class, which in the works of Medieval historians such as Henri Pirenne became the pivotal agent of social transformation. Citizenship, after its partial eclipse during the Middle Ages, reemerges with a new impetus and importance. Now, however, citizenship is not simply about the privileges of political participation but perhaps principally, if not exclusively, about the economic privileges and rights that citizenship in a given city entitles and bestows upon the rising merchant class. During the Middle Ages, then, citizenship acquires a material dimension that it did not have before, even if economic rights were implicit in the holding of political office in the polis.

During the late Middle Ages and the early Renaissance, however, a unique convergence between the economic and spiritual dimension of citizenship takes place, giving us the phenomenon of the citizen as a benefactor of both the city and the poor. As Michel Mollat has shown in his *The Poor in the Middle Ages: An Essay in Social History* (from 1978 but translated into English in 1986), toward the end of the Middle Ages, as cities became more populous and wealthier, thus becoming destinations for the itinerant poor of the time, it became both a practice and an expectation that the wealthy would endow houses of the poor and would in fact leave a large portion, if not all, of their wealth to such houses.[30]

The Renaissance period gave us humanism, sometimes called Renaissance humanism, which rejected the bleak and negative image of the human being that had crystallized during the Middle Ages. Renaissance humanism instead celebrated the goodness and, above all, the potentiality of the human being. No one gave better expression of this new vision than Pico della Mirandolla in his *Oratio on the Dignity of the Human Being*, which elaborates a humanistic reading of the Christian doctrine of *imago dei*, the doctrine that humans are created in the image of God.[31] Against Augustine and his Neoplatonic political philosophy, which turns the human away from the city of man toward the heavenly city, civic humanists reaffirm the political and communal character of human beings: humans only become properly human within human communities dedicated to the exaltation of each human being. If Pico della Mirandola claimed that there is no greater example of the fact that we are created in the image of God than that we create ourselves through our own will and acts of innovation and imagination, then, by same token, there is no greater creation than the *civitas*. If we are our greatest creation, then, next to it is the creation of the city as the accompaniment to our creative excellence. Cities as such became exemplars of our creative powers and the exaltation of our civic nature.

When we get to the Revolutionary period, which builds on the insights of the Enlightenment, there are some momentous shifts in the conception of citizenship. I think two figures exemplify these: Diderot and Kant. Let me briefly discuss Diderot, who wrote the entry on "Citizen" for the *Encyclopédie* that he co-edited with d'Alembert. In this entry, in fact, Diderot articulated the spirit of both the French and American Revolutions. There is one passage that is noteworthy and merits citation. Diderot, criticizing Pufendorf's restriction of citizenship to the founders of a city and to their descendants, thus advocating citizenship as lineage or as being based on descent, writes the following:

> The *citizens* in their capacity as *citizens*, that is to say in their societies, are all equally noble; the nobility comes not from ancestry but from the common right that honors the primary principles of the magistrate. The moral, sovereign being is to the *citizen* what the physical despot is to the subject, *and* the most perfect slave does not give all of this being to his sovereign.[32]

Diderot expressed here the idea that citizenship, which is understood as the performance of the "principle of the magistrate"—that is, the performance of the duties of the citizen—is the democratization of the spirit of nobility to all citizens. Citizenship is a noble calling, if you will. Second, Diderot juxtaposes the moral sovereign to the despot: to the former corresponds the citizen, to the latter the subject. And furthermore, only in citizenship is the full moral calling of the human being exercised, which not even the condition of being a slave to a despot can hope to extinguish. In this definition of "citizen," then, Diderot links morality as an imperative to the vocation of the citizen.

Diderot eloquently gives expression to the core ideas that will animate the 1789 "Declaration of the Rights of Man and Citizen," which begins in article 1 with the proclamation of the universal equality and freedom of all human beings. This is followed, in article 2, with the affirmation that the "aim of all political association is the preservation of the natural and *imprescriptible* rights of man."[33]

With these two articles, the Declaration of the Rights of Man and Citizen provided us with two ideas that revolutionized our conception of citizenship. First, that citizenship is subordinate—that is, at the service, of the rights of man, above all which are the rights of equality and liberty; and second, that these rights are imprescriptible—that is to say, inalienable. Citizenship thus is universalized as the means for the promotion of the fundamental rights of humans, while at the same time being given as its supreme goal the preservation of these rights. This revolution in the Western conception of citizenship will be brought to higher revolutionary heights with the Fourteenth Amendment to the U.S. Constitution. What are generally known as the Reconstruction Amendments, or the Civil War Amendments, the Thirteenth, Fourteenth, and Fifteenth Amendments that were ratified between 1865 and 1870 abolished slavery while radically transforming U.S. citizenship. These amendments accomplished a foundation of the republic by, on the one hand, making birthright a constitutional principle, while denying states (specifically Southern states) the power of curtailing or suspending citizens' right to participate in government through the denial of the right to vote on the basis of race, gender, class, or past state of servitude.

Let us recall the language of the Fourteenth Amendment, specifically section 1, which is the one that concerns me crucially. It reads,

All persons born or naturalized in the United States, and subject to the jurisdiction thereof, are citizens of the United States and of the state wherein they reside. No state shall make or enforce any law which shall abridge the privileges or immunities of citizens of the United States; nor shall any state deprive any person of life, liberty, or property, without due process of law; nor deny to any person within its jurisdiction the equal protection of the laws.[34]

I want to call your attention to the "born or naturalized" in the first sentence, for in the same breath those born in the United States, or in territories under the jurisdiction of the United States, and those "naturalized"—that is, those who through some legal procedure have become members of the U.S. nation—are "citizens," and no state shall make or enforce any law that may abridge in any way whatsoever the privileges of said citizenship.

The Fourteenth Amendment was meant to make constitutional what had already been enacted with the Civil Rights Act of 1866, which reads as follows:

> That all persons born in the United States and not subject to any foreign power, excluding Indians not taxed, are hereby declared to be citizens of the United States; and such citizens, of every race and color, without regard to any previous condition of slavery or involuntary servitude, except as a punishment for crime whereof the party shall have been duly convicted, shall have the same right, in every State and Territory in the United States, to make and enforce contracts, to sue, be parties, and give evidence, inherit, purchase, lease, sell, hold, and convey real and personal property, and to full and equal benefit of all laws and proceedings for the security of person and property, as is enjoyed by white citizens, and shall be subject to like punishment, pains, and penalties, and to none other, any law, statute, ordinance, regulation, or custom, to the contrary notwithstanding.[35]

In the summer of 1865, after Abraham Lincoln had been assassinated and succeeded by Andrew Johnson, a political fight between the newly inaugurated president and the Republican-controlled Congress ensued. Johnson announced his plan for reconciliation with the South. Although Johnson was an unwavering defender of the Union, he was an "inveterate" racist and strong defender of state's rights. Johnson's plan was to allow southern states to establish their governments in exchange for "abolishing slavery, repudiating secession, and abrogating the Confederate debt, but otherwise letting southerners retain control over local affairs."[36] These new state governments, expectedly, then proceeded to enact the infamous "Black Codes" that for all intents and purposes reinstated slavery by legal means, rather than through property claims. Meanwhile, violence against black freemen was rampant throughout the South.[37] White southerners were as determined to hold on to their antebellum form of life as they were determined to deny black freemen their freedom and newly acquired political rights. The Thirty-Ninth Congress, elected in November 1864 but assembled for the first time in December 1865, called for the abrogation of the new state governments allowed by President Johnson, and the establishment of new ones based on equality before the law and universal "manhood suffrage." This is why Congress quickly enacted the Civil Rights Act of 1866 and set to work on the Fourteenth Amendment.[38]

The Fourteenth Amendment, however, was also meant to resolve ambiguities and tensions within the constitution. The original U.S. Constitution of 1787 recognized both state and U.S. citizenship, but it did not specify how one became a citizen of either states or the nation. This meant that citizenship was left to the discretion of states. The *Dred Scott* decision of 1857, which denied slaves and their descendants claims to citizenship, was exemplary of this constitutional ambiguity. The Black Codes made it clear that former slave states would move to deny former slaves access to the protection of the law by denying or severely curtailing their claims to citizenship. Thus, as Professor of Jurisprudence George P. Fletcher put it in his book *Our Secret Constitution: How Lincoln Redefined American Democracy* (2001), "The first item of business in the Fourteenth Amendment was to establish who, as a formal matter, belonged to the American Polity. To find a simple definition, the Constitution adapted the English rule that it is not blood but place of birth that matters . . . Applying the traditional rule of Jus soli to everyone born on American soil . . . had the radical effect of eliminating family and racial history from the definition of the bond between citizens and government in the United States."[39] The antebellum United States was a racial polity that allowed states to determine the citizenship status of its members on the basis of race: black people could not be citizens, nor their children, as the Dred Scott decision made it clear. Membership was thus defined as white citizenship. The Fourteenth Amendment de jure if not de facto deracialized membership in the U.S. polity.

The Fourteenth Amendment also transformed the relationship between states and federal government. Constitutional theorist Bruce Ackerman in his monumental three volume *We the People* writes that the Fourteenth Amendment "nationalized" the polity both in substance and procedure.[40] What Ackerman means by this is that by producing a unified conception of citizenship, flowing from the Constitution and not the states, the amendment produced a unified nation; and the way this was enacted, first through the 1866 Civil Rights Act of Congress, and then through the states' ratification of the Fourteenth Amendment, meant that states, in concert, assented and approved the modification of the law of the land that would in essence subordinate states to the federal government's protection of the rights of citizens. With its 1866 Act, as well as with the drafting of all the Reconstruction amendments, Congress acted as a "constitutional convention," not unlike that which drafted the constitution of 1787. Ackerman again: "By a remarkable bootstrapping operation, the Convention/Congress was proposing to redefine We the People of the United *States* as We the People of the *United* States."[41] And, as he put it more pointedly in volume 1 of *We the People*, "The Republican Reconstruction of the Union was an Act of *constitutional creation* no less profound than the Founding itself: Not only did the Republicans introduce new substantive principles into our higher law, but they reworked the very process of higher lawmaking itself."[42] With this second act of "constitutional creation," the Republican congress had redefined not only membership but also the role of the federal government. Now, the latter would not be conceived as an enemy or threat to individual freedom—which Jefferson believed it to be; instead, the federal government had become "the custodian of freedom," as the abolitionist senator Charles Sumner from Massachusetts declared.[43] The rewriting and reestablishing of the Constitution on the basis of nationalized citizenship and equality before and under the law meant that "the rights of individual citizens were intimately connected to federal power."[44]

The Fourteenth Amendment was made up of five sections, three of which no longer have any or little significance (those that barred Confederates from office, those dealing with Confederate debt, and those that reduced a state's representation in Congress if men are denied the right to vote—although this last provision was never enforced even as Southern states continued to blatantly disenfranchise former slaves with disastrous consequences for the re-founded Republic). But as Eric Foner put it succinctly and powerfully, "the Fourteenth Amendment has since become, after the Bill of Rights, the most important constitutional change in the nation's history."[45]

The Unfinished Revolution

Eric Foner's indispensable history of the reconstruction has the subtitle "America's Unfinished Revolution 1863–1877." In a sense, Foner is right to have thought that the period of reconstruction after the Civil War constituted the unleashing of a sociopolitical revolution that would transform the very nature of the polity. But Reconstruction was followed by what was called

Redemption, the reassertion of White Southern power. The rollback of the gains of the Reconstruction period would open the floodgates to decades of violence against black freemen, decades of lynching and white race riots against black people, and the legalization of Jim Crow. We have to be sanguine about what the Reconstruction Amendments did, for they were followed by what can justifiably be called a "white supremacy counter-revolution," the effects of which we are still living through, from Jim Crow to the rise of the ghettos, from Reagan to Trump. As Henry Louis Gates Jr. shows in *Stony the Road: Reconstruction, White Supremacy, and the Rise of Jim Crow* (2019), the dismantling of the many gains made during the Reconstruction period by Southern intransigency and anti-black activism and Northern passivity and acquiescence led to the fracturing of the polity, once again, along racial lines.[46] The *Plessy v. Ferguson* Supreme Court decision of 1896 neutralized both the Civil Rights act of 1866 and the Fourteenth Amendment, sundering racially what had been deracialized in 1868.[47] Just as importantly, the period after Reconstruction gave birth to a new racial imaginary that assaulted the worthiness and desirability of black people to be citizens. This imaginary has continued to evolve, expand, resemanticize, and semiotically metastasize into more sophisticated and subtle racial and ethnic stereotypes, even as some of its basic premises have been challenged on scientific, political, and legal basis.

Political philosopher Michael Walzer has written that "the primary good that we distribute to one another is membership in some human community."[48] After the French and American Revolutions, we have a new credo that affirms that political membership is a fundamental good and right that is distributed to members of a polity through the rights of citizens. The con-stitutionalization of jus soli into national citizenship through the Fourteenth Amendment, however, has elevated those nineteenth century revolutionary ideals to a new level: membership on the basis of descent and racial origin are delegitimated and delegalized—just as equality before the law and the right to membership on the basis of birthright and naturalization are asserted. Birthright citizenship is the utmost form of the rejection of jus sanguinis— the deracialization of both membership and citizenship.[49]

Notes

1. The text of the Constitution can be found at: https://www.archives.gov/founding -docs/constitution-transcript#toc-article-iii-.

2.   This is part of statute 2, chapter 9, sections 1 and 2, which can be found online at http://memory.loc.gov/cgi-bin/ampage?collId=llsl&fileName=001/llsl001.db&recNum=235.

3.   See Paul Roland, *The Nuremberg Trials: The Nazis and Their Crimes Against Humanity* (London: Arcturus, 2012).

4.   Ernst Wolfgang Böckenförde, *Constitutional and Political Theory: Selected Writings*, vol. 1 (Oxford: Oxford University Press, 2017), 312, 313.

5.   See Amy Reed-Sandoval, *Socially Undocumented: Identity and Immigration Justice* (New York: Oxford University Press, 2020).

6.   Leo R. Chavez, *Anchor Babies and the Challenge of Birthright Citizenship* (Stanford, Calif.: Stanford University Press, 2017), and *The Latino Threat: Constructing Immigrants, Citizens and the Nation*, 2nd Edition (Stanford, Calif.: Stanford University Press, 2013).

7.   See Erin Blakemore, "The Largest Deportation in American History," *History*, accessed May 12, 2019, https://www.history.com/news/operation-wetback-eisenhower-1954-deportation. This story is unfinished and has more sordid chapters. See Beth C. Caldwell, *Deported Americans: Life After Deportation to Mexico* (Durham, N.C.: Duke University Press, 2019).

8.   See Martha S. Jones, *Birthright Citizens: A History of Race and Rights in Antebellum America* (Cambridge: Cambridge University Press, 2018) and Eric Foner, *The Second Founding: How the Civil War Remade the Constitution* (New York: W. W. Norton, 2019)

9.   See Samuel P. Huntington, "Reconsidering Immigration: Is Mexico a Special Case?" Center for Immigration Studies, November 1, 2000, https://cis.org/Report/Reconsidering-Immigration-Mexico-Special-Case.

10.   See https://www.questia.com/magazine/1G1-68660166/the-special-case-of-mexican-immigration.

11.   Samuel P. Huntington, "The Hispanic Challenge," *Foreign Policy*, vol. 141 (March–April 2004), 30.

12.   Huntington, "The Hispanic Challenge," 32.

13.   Huntington, "The Hispanic Challenge," 33.

14.   Samuel P. Huntington, *Who Are We? The Challenges to America's National Identity* (New York: Simon and Schuster, 2004)

15.   Samuel P. Huntington, *The Soldier and the State: The Theory and Politics of Civil-Military Relations* (Cambridge, Mass.: Belknap, 1957) and Michael Walzer, *Just and Unjust Wars* (New York: Basic Books, 1977).

16.   Gabriel Lerner, "The Iraq Conflict: The War That Changed Latinos," December 20, 2012, https://www.huffingtonpost.com/2011/12/19/iraq-war-changed-latinos_n_1158488.html.

17.   Lionel Sosa, *The Americano Dream: How Latinos Can Achieve Success in Business and Life* (New York: Dutton, 1997).

18.   Huntington, "The Hispanic Challenge," 45.

19. Samuel P. Huntington, *The Clash of Civilizations and the Remaking of the World Order* (New York: Simon and Schuster, 1996).

20. Huntington, *Who Are We?*, 64. Huntington is quoting from Burke's *Reflections on the Revolution in France*.

21. Huntington, *Who Are We?*, 310.

22. Huntington, *Who Are We?*, 315–16.

23. On this rally, see the informative Wikepedia entry: https://en.wikipedia.org /wiki/Unite_the_Right_rally.

24. Huntington, *Who Are We?*, 365.

25. See Chiara Bottici and Benoît Challand, *The Myth of the Clash of Civilizations* (New York: Routledge, 2010); Jeffrey Haynes, *From Huntington to Trump: Thirty Years of the Clash of Civilizations* (Lanham, Md.: Lexington Books, 2019).

26. Peter Riesenberg, *Citizenship in the Western Tradition: Plato to Rousseau* (Chapel Hill: University of North Carolina, 1992). We should also follow Derek Heater, *Citizenship: The Civic Ideal in World History, Politics and Education*, 3rd edition (Manchester: Manchester University Press, 2004), especially part 1.

27. Riesenberg, *Citizenship in the Western Tradition*, 20.

28. Here I am using the translation found in Aristotle, *The Complete Works of Aristotle. The Revised Oxford Translation*, ed. Jonathan Barnes, volume 2 (Princeton, N.J.: Princeton University Press, 1984), 2024.

29. Riesenberg, *Citizenship in the Western Tradition*, 44.

30. Michel Mollat, *The Poor in the Middle Ages: An Essay in Social History*, trans. Arthur Goldhammer (New Haven: Yale University Press, 1986)

31. Pico della Mirandola, *Oratio on the Dignity of the Human Being*, trans. A. Robert Campogrini (Washington, D.C.: Gateway Editions, 1996).

32. Denis Diderot, "Citizen," in *The Encyclopedia of Diderot and d'Alembert Collaborative Translation Project*, trans. Sujaya Dhanvantari. (Ann Arbor: University of Michigan Press, 2005). The translation can be found at http://hdl.handle.net /2027/spo.did2222.0000.070. This is a translation of "Citoyen," *Encyclopédie ou Dictionnaire raisonné des sciences, des arts et des métiers*, vol. 3 (Paris, 1753).

33. See: "Declaration of the Rights of Man," http://avalon.law.yale.edu/18th_century /rightsof.asp.

34. See: 14th Amendment, https://www.law.cornell.edu/constitution/amendmentxiv.

35. See: "Civil Rights Act of 1866," https://en.wikisource.org/wiki/Civil_Rights_Act _of_1866.

36. Eric Foner, "June 13, 1866: Equality Before the Law," in *Days of Destiny: Cross Roads in American History*, ed. James M. McPherson (London: Dorling Kimberly Publishing, 2001), 178.

37. Eric Foner, *Reconstruction: America's Unfinished Revolution 1863–1877*, updated edition (New York: Harper and Row, 2002 [1988]), 119–23.

38. See Eric Foner, *The Second Founding: How the Civil War and Reconstruction Remade the Constitution* (New York: W. W. Norton Company, 2019), 93 ff.

39.   George P. Fletcher, *Our Secret Constitution: How Lincoln Redefined American Democracy* (New York: Oxford University Press, 2001), 125.

40.   Bruce Ackerman, *We the People*, 3 volumes (Cambridge, Mass: Belknap 1994–2014).

41.   Ackerman, *We the People*, vol. 2, *Transformations*, 199.

42.   Ackerman, *We the People*, vol. 1, *Foundations*, 46. My emphasis.

43.   Foner, "June 13, 1866: Equality Before the Law," 178.

44.   Foner, "June 13, 1866: Equality Before the Law," 178–79. Stanford professor of American history Richard White summarized the accomplishments and goals of the Fourteenth Amendment in the following way: "The broad principles of the Fourteenth Amendment were clear. The Republicans sought to abrogate judicial interpretations of the Constitution that, in the name of federalism, had limited the extension of a uniform set of rights applicable to all citizens everywhere in the Union. Congress intended the new amendment to extend the guarantees of the Bill of Rights so that they protected citizens against actions by the states as well as by the federal government. The equal protection clause was supposed to ensure that no state discriminated among its own citizens or against the citizens of another state. The amendment would protect both new black citizens and white Unionists in the South. The Republicans desired a national citizenship with uniform rights. Ultimately the amendment was Lincolnian: it sought, as had Lincoln, to make the sentiments of the Declaration of Independence the guiding light of the republic. It enshrined in the Constitution broad principles of equality, the rights of citizens, and principles of natural rights prominent in the Declaration of Independence and in Republican ideals of free labor and contract freedom." Richard White, *The Republic for Which It Stands: The United States During Reconstruction and the Gilded Age, 1865–1896* (New York: Oxford University Press, 2017), 74.

45.   Foner, "June 13, 1866: Equality Before the Law," 176.

46.   Henry Louis Gates, Jr. *Stony the Road: Reconstruction, White Supremacy, and the Rise of Jim Crow* (New York: Penguin Press, 2019).

47.   See Steve Luxenberg, *Separate: The Story of* Plessy vs. Ferguson *and America's Journey from Slavery to Segregation* (New York: W. W. Norton, 2019).

48.   Michael Walzer, *Spheres of Justice: A Defense of Pluralism and Equality* (New York: Basic Books, 1983), 31.

49.   There are many questions that the abolition of jus sanguinis raises, many of which I cannot take up in the present context. However, making jus soli the primary form of granting and securing citizenship solves more problems than jus sanguinis is able to solve or even begin to address. For instance, what of children born out of wedlock to a parent of one nationality and another of a different one. This child would not live in limbo, as they would be granted citizenship in the country where they were born under jus soli. My argument for the moment is that the jus soli is the culmination of the project of deracialized citizenship that began with the Universal Declaration of the Rights of Man and

the Citizens, and which was advanced by the Civil War amendments to the U.S. Constitution. Another interesting example is that of German Jews who were stripped of their citizenship, because they were not Aryans, who most likely no longer have descendants in Germany or blood descendants that could advocate for their jus sanguinis German citizenship. Under the primacy of jus solis, in my estimation, they could. At the very least, I can see a combination of both developing over the next decades as increasing numbers of constitutional democracies aim to "deracialize" their citizenship laws.

CONTRIBUTORS

Luis Rubén Díaz Cepeda is a philosopher and a sociologist. He is an assistant professor in the Humanities Department at the Universidad Autónoma de Ciudad Juárez in Mexico. His research focuses on ethics, borders, social movements, critical theory, and philosophy of liberation. His works have been published in Mexico, Argentina, Colombia, and the United States, most recently *Latin American Philosophy and Social Movements: From Ciudad Juárez to Ayotzinapa* (Lexington Books, 2020). He is co-editor of *Posglobalización, descolonización y transmodernidad: Filosofía de la liberación y pensamiento latinoamericano* (forthcoming, UACJ).

Lori Gallegos is an assistant professor of philosophy at Texas State University and is the current editor of the *APA Newsletter on Hispanic/Latino Issues in Philosophy*. She researches and teaches in the areas of Latinx philosophy, moral psychology, and the philosophy of emotion.

Margaret Griesse is an associate teaching professor of ethnic, gender, and labor studies in the School of Interdisciplinary Arts and Sciences at the University of Washington, Tacoma. She studied in the United States, Argentina, Brazil, and Germany, receiving her PhD in education and international development at the University of Frankfurt. Her teaching and research interests focus on transnational feminisms, human rights, women's movements, and social responsibility based on Latin American studies and critical (race) theory. She edited (with Frederick Bird) *Responsabilidades sociais: Práticas de empresas internacionais na América Latina*. (Piracicaba: UNIMEP University Press) and has published various articles on social responsibility, feminism, and ethnic studies in books and journals in the United States and Brazil.

Eduardo Mendieta is a professor of philosophy and affiliated faculty at the School of International Affairs, Bioethics, and Latino/a Studies Programs at Penn State University. In spring 2020 he was a visiting fellow at the Forschungskolleg Humanwissenschaften in Bad Homburg, Germany. He is the author of *The Adventures of Transcendental Philosophy* (Rowman & Littlefield, 2002) and *Global Fragments: Globalizations, Latinamericanisms, and Critical Theory* (SUNY Press, 2007). He is also co-editor with Jonathan VanAntwerpen of *The Power of Religion in the Public Sphere* (Columbia University Press, 2011), and with Craig Calhoun and Jonathan VanAntwerpen of *Habermas and Religion* (Polity, 2013), and with Amy Allen, *From Alienation to Forms of Life: The Critical Theory of Rahel Jaeggi* (Penn State University Press, 2018), *The Cambridge Habermas Lexicon* (Cambridge University Press, 2019), and *Justification and Emancipation: The Critical Theory of Rainer Forst* (Penn State University Press, 2019), and *Decolonizing Ethics: Enrique Dussel's Critical Theory* (Penn State University Press, 2021). He is working on a monograph titled *Latinx Philosophy: A Manifesto*. He is the 2017 recipient of the Frantz Fanon Outstanding Achievements Award.

José Jorge Mendoza is an assistant professor of philosophy at the University of Washington and is co-editor of *Radical Philosophy Review*. He is also the author of *The Moral and Political Philosophy of Immigration: Liberty, Security, and Equality* (Lexington Books 2017) and his articles have appeared in venues such as the *Journal of Speculative Philosophy, Public Affairs Quarterly, Critical Philosophy of Race*, and *Philosophy in the Contemporary World*.

Amos Nascimento is a professor of philosophy at the University of Washington, Tacoma and Seattle, affiliated with Interdisciplinary Arts and Sciences, International Studies, and Germanics programs. He studied music, social sciences, and philosophy in Argentina, Brazil, the United States, and Germany.

His areas of teaching and research currently concentrate on cosmopolitanism and human rights. His most recent publications include *Building Cosmopolitan Communities: A Critical and Multidimensional Approach* (Palgrave McMillan, 2014) and two edited books with Matthias Lutz-Bachmann, *Human Rights, Human Dignity, and Cosmopolitan Ideals* (Routledge, 2014) and *Human Dignity: Perspectives from a Critical Theory of Human Rights* (Routledge, 2018). He has also published various articles and book chapters on Latin American philosophy.

Carlos Pereda is an emeritus researcher and professor at the National Autonomous University of Mexico (UNAM). He has published several books and more than fifty papers in philosophical journals.

Silvana Rabinovich holds a PhD in philosophy from the Universidad Nacional Autónoma de México. She is a permanent researcher in the Hermeneutics Seminar at the Philological Research Institute (UNAM), member of the National Research System (Level II), and director of the Project PAPIIT IN 401119 "Heteronomy of Justice: Nomad Territorialities." She is the author of numerous books and journal articles, including *La Biblia y el dron: Sobre usos y abusos de figuras bíblicas en el discurso político de Israel* (Casagrande/Último recurso/Heredad, Rosario: CDMX, 2020) and *Interpretaciones de la heteronomía* (IIFL – UNAM: CDMX, 2019).

Amy Reed-Sandoval is an assistant professor of philosophy at the University of Nevada, Las Vegas. She is the author of *Socially Undocumented: Identity and Immigration Justice* (OUP, 2020) and a number of articles on the ethics of immigration that have appeared in publications such as the *Journal of Social Philosophy, Public Affairs Quarterly, Critical Review of International Social and Political Philosophy*, and the *Journal of Applied Philosophy*.

Raúl Villarroel holds a PhD in philosophy from the Universidad de Chile and an MA in bioethics from the Universidad de Chile and the Universidad Compuletense de Madrid. He is a professor of philosophy at the Universidad de Chile and a researcher in the Department of Philosophy and the Centro de Estudios de Ética Aplicada de la Facultad de Filosofía y Humanidades. He is the author of numerous books, articles, and book chapters and currently coordinates Red Humaniora, a collaborative group of scholars and students working across various academic fields at twelve Chilean universities.

Allison B. Wolf is an associate professor of philosophy and affiliated faculty in the Center for Migration Studies at Universidad de los Andes in Bogotá, Colombia, where she teaches political philosophy, philosophy of immigration, and feminist philosophy. She is the author of *Just Immigration in the Americas: A Feminist Account* (Rowman and Littlefield, 2020) and co-editor of *Incarnating Feelings, Constructing Communities: Experiencing Emotions in the Americas Through Education, Violence, and Public Policy* with Ana María Forero Angel and Catalina González Quintero (Palgrave Macmillan, 2020). Her work has been published in various journals and collections, including *Hypatia, Comparative Studies in Asian and Latin American Philosophies, Hispanic/Latino Issues in Philosophy Newsletter of the American Philosophical Association, International Journal of Feminist Approaches to Bioethics, International Journal of Applied Philosophy, Journal of Medical Humanities* (with Sonya Charles), *Philosophical Inquiry into Pregnancy, Childbirth, and Mothering: Maternal Subjects* (with Jennifer Benson), *Queer Philosophy: Presentations of the Society of Lesbian and Gay Philosophy, 1998–2008*, and the *Journal of Global Ethics*. Currently, Dr. Wolf is working on philosophical issues arising in the content of Venezuelan migration to Colombia, issues in feminist epistemology (especially related to epistemic oppression and feminism and skepticism), and obstetric violence in the context of immigration in the Americas.

INDEX